WINNING

WITH THE

DOW'S LOSERS

Also by Charles B. Carlson:

Buying Stocks Without a Broker
Free Lunch on Wall Street
No-Load Stocks
Chuck Carlson's 60-Second Investor
The Individual Investor Revolution
Eight Steps to Seven Figures
The Smart Investor's Survival Guide

WINNING

WITH THE

DOW'S LOSERS

BEAT THE MARKET WITH UNDERDOG STOCKS

Charles B. Carlson, CFA

HarperBusiness
An Imprint of HarperCollinsPublishers

This book is not designed to be a definitive investment guide or to take the place of advice from a qualified financial planner or other professional. Given the risk involved in investing of almost any kind, there is no guarantee that the investment methods suggested in this book will be profitable. The publisher and the author disclaim liability for any losses that may be sustained as a result of applying the methods suggested in this book.

HarperCollins books may be purchased for educational, business, or sales promotional use. For information please write: Special Markets Department, HarperCollins Publishers Inc., 10 East 53rd Street, New York, NY 10022.

First HarperBusiness paperback edition published 2005

Designed by Nancy Singer Olaguera

The Library of Congress has catalogued the hardcover edition as follows:
Carlson, Charles B.
 Winning with the Dow's losers: beat the market with underdog stocks / Charles B. Carlson—1st ed.
 p. cm.
 Includes index.
 ISBN 0-06-057657-X
 1. Stocks—United States. 2. Dow Jones industrial average.
 3. Investments—United States. 4. Stock exchanges—United States.
 I. Title.
 HG4963.C368   2004
 332.63'22—dc22   2003057092

ISBN 0-06-057658-8 (pbk.)

05 06 07 08 09 DIX/RRD 10 9 8 7 6 5 4 3 2 1

To Denise,

My best pick, by far

Contents

Preface

I've always had a special fondness for the Dow Jones Industrial Average.

I know that sounds a little weird. After all, the Dow is just a market index. The Dow has no feelings, no emotions. It can't return my affection. (Actually, I guess it could by being nice to my portfolio, but you know what I mean.) And I've never worked at any of the 30 companies that comprise the Dow or Dow Jones & Co., the company that owns the Dow index.

Yet, when I retrace my professional career, the Dow has always seemed to be right next to me, day in and day out, a key player in some of the most important moments of my professional life. For example, my first day in this business was Monday, August 16, 1982. I was fresh out of Northwestern University, equipped with a journalism degree and an interest in the stock market. That date may mean something to a few of you. Coincidently, August 16, 1982, is often credited as the birth date of the great bull market of the 1980s (and, for all intents and purposes, the bull market of the 1990s).

On my second day on the job, the Dow rose a whopping *38.81 points*. I know some of you are probably laughing at that statement. A *whopping 38.81 points*. Keep in mind, however, that the Dow Jones Industrial Average started that Tuesday in August *below 800*. That 38.81-point move on my second day was the largest single-day point advance in the Dow's history. In fact, to put that move into today's terms, the Dow Jones Industrial Average would have to rise more than 400 points, or nearly 5 percent, to equal that move on August 17, 1982.

For whatever reason, the Dow decided to launch my professional

career with a bang, and I've never forgotten that. But my kinship to the
Dow doesn't end there. On that Tuesday in August, I was starting my
second day at a company called Dow Theory Forecasts (there's that
Dow again). Dow Theory Forecasts publishes an investment newsletter
by the same name. The company and newsletter, which has been published weekly since 1946, derive the name from a market-timing tool,
the Dow Theory, which was developed by Charles Dow, the first publisher of *The Wall Street Journal*. In a nutshell, the Dow Theory looks at
just two items—the Dow Jones Industrial Average and the Dow Jones
Transportation Average—to discern the market's trend. Little did I
know at the time that my first employer more than 21 years ago would
be my current employer. Although the company name has changed
(our newsletter-publishing arm is now called Horizon Publishing), we
still publish *Dow Theory Forecasts* (for a free trial subscription to the
newsletter, see the information at the back of this book), along with
two other newsletters, *DRIP Investor* and *Upside*.

The next leg of my journey with the Dow came in 1997. In that
year, I had an idea for a mutual fund based on the stocks in the Dow.
However, this would not be your garden-variety index fund that merely
mimics the index. My fund would overweight the best Dow stocks and
underweight the worst Dow stocks in hopes of outperforming the
index. The idea became reality in 1998, when my firm teamed with the
Strong fund family to launch the Strong Dow 30 Value fund. The original managers of the Strong Dow 30 Value fund were myself and Rich
Moroney (the current editor of *Dow Theory Forecasts*). We managed
the fund from 1998 to December 2000. In addition to its investment
approach, it is particularly noteworthy that this was among the first
mutual funds ever to have *Dow* in its name.

The bottom line is that not a workday has gone by in the last 21
years that I haven't followed closely the movement of the Dow Jones
Industrial Average. I grew up with it professionally. I've invested my
and other people's money in it. I've dissected it, analyzed it, cursed it,
and second-guessed it.

That's why I'm especially excited about this book. It provides a
forum for me to discuss everything I've ever learned about the Dow,
including my most recent Dow discovery: Dow "worst-to-first" investment strategies that allow any investor to make big money in the market by betting on the "Dow Underdogs." (These underdogs are the

Dow stocks showing the biggest percentage price declines in a given year.)

I know I'm not the first person who has created a Dow-based system to beat the market. Michael O'Higgins helped to revolutionize Dow-based investing with his 1990 book, *Beating the Dow* (Harper-Collins). While I have great admiration for the simplicity of the O'Higgins Dow dividend-based investment strategy, his is not the only way to beat the market. Nor is it the best way. Indeed (as I show in Chapter 8), my Dow worst-to-first strategies have produced far superior results to Dow dividend-based systems over the last 5- and 10-year periods. Those time periods encompass not only one of the greatest bull markets in history but also the worst bear market since the Depression.

Stock investing has taken on a black eye over the last 3 years. Investors who made lots of money in the 1990s gave back most, if not all, during the bear market that began in 2000. However, it is that bear market that provided special impetus for me to do this book at this time. Burned by the market's collapse, too many investors have simply left the market. They feel betrayed by Wall Street institutions. They believe they have been sold a false story about stocks being the best place to build wealth. They have seen what they thought were investment truisms be turned on their head by the bear market. The pity is that now is exactly the wrong time to give up on an investment program. Indeed, there are more opportunities today in stocks, including those stocks in the Dow, than in the last decade. The trick is developing an investment game plan that is easy to implement and easy to follow, as well as one that forces you to buy depressed stocks—but to do so sensibly.

This playbook is an attack plan for implementing what I think you'll find is perhaps the most logical, sensible, and user-friendly investment strategy in the market today. The rest is up to you.

Acknowledgments

I've done enough of these things to know that lots of people are responsible for getting these ideas from my head into your hands. First, I'd like to thank Avis Beitz, my crack proofreader, as well as my entire staff at Horizon Publishing, especially Ken Pogach and Tanya Habzansky-Yzaguirre, for assistance on this project.

Special thanks go to Dow Jones & Co. and the Center for Research in Security Prices (CRSP) at the University of Chicago for providing data for this project.

I would be remiss if I didn't give special acknowledgment to David Wright, my chief number-cruncher and a great sounding board throughout this project.

I'd also like to thank my agent, Wes Neff, for his guidance and support.

Finally, I'd like to give special thanks to my editor, David Conti. This book represents a sort of homecoming for David and me. David was the editor who pulled my first book proposal from the slush pile over 12 years ago. Fortunately for both of us, David's instincts were correct. We hit a home run with that first book (the best-selling *Buying Stocks Without a Broker*). Over the years, our publishing careers took different paths, but I think both of us always had the feeling that we'd hook up again to see if we could hit another one out of the park. Well, David, batter up!

Author's Notes

The investment strategies in this book are Patent Pending. A patent application has been filed with the United States Patent and Trademark Office regarding the investment strategies discussed in this book. Parties interested in creating commercial financial products based on these strategies should call Charles Carlson at Horizon Investment Services, (800) 711-7969.

The annual price change, ratio of stock price to 200-day moving average, and total return data for all Dow companies in this book were provided by CRSP, Center for Research in Security Prices, The University of Chicago, Graduate School of Business. Used with permission. All rights reserved.

Annual total return data for the Dow Jones Industrial Average were provided by Dow Jones & Co. Used with permission.

Introduction

Sometimes the best ideas stare us in the face for years before we see them. I've been a watcher of the Dow Jones Industrial Average for more than 21 years, as an investment newsletter writer as well as a private investor and professional money manager. I can tell you what 30 stocks comprise the Dow, their stock symbols, and what changes have been made to the index over the years. I can give you thumbnail sketches of the investment fundamentals of all the Dow stocks.

I can tell you how the Dow is computed, why Procter & Gamble matters a lot more to the Dow's performance than Microsoft, and why a stock split in a Dow stock is a big deal for the index. I can explain to you the Dow's divisor, show you why the divisor is actually a multiplier, and exhibit why a 1-point move in each of the 30 Dow stocks translates to a 213-point move in the index.

In short, I *know* the Dow, which is why I'm one of the media's "go-to" guys when it comes to opinions and insights on the Dow and its components. That's what makes this all the more, well, embarrassing. It was so simple, so obvious, that I should have seen it long before I did.

A few years ago while researching the Dow, I made a simple yet (little did I know at the time) profound observation. I was struck by how the worst-performing Dow stock in one year (that is, the Dow stock showing the greatest percentage price decline for the year) turned out to be one of the better-performing stocks in the Dow the following year.

The catalyst for this discovery was the performance of Philip Morris (now called Altria) in 2000. Now, 2000 was a tough year for the

market and most stocks. Indeed, the Dow lost 5 percent. But that
decline was peanuts compared to the 39 percent decline in the Nasdaq Composite in 2000.

But while 2000 was extremely harsh to most stocks, it was
extremely kind to Philip Morris. Indeed, the stock provided a return
of 105 percent for the year. In effect, Philip Morris shareholders saw
the value of their shares more than double in 2000. And remember—
that was during a time when the Dow's total return for the year was a
negative 5 percent.

What struck me most about Philip Morris's 2000 performance
was that it was a huge reversal from the tobacco giant's horrible performance in 1999. In fact, Philip Morris was the *worst-performing* Dow
stock in 1999, with the stock price dropping around 57 percent.
Here's a stock that goes from being the worst performer in one year to
the best performer in the next.

Initially, I didn't do much with this observation. Quite honestly, I
figured it was just a coincidence that Philip Morris did poorly one year
and stellar the next. Surely you couldn't make money simply by betting on the Dow's losers in one year, could you?

What caused me to look a bit deeper into the strategy was what
happened in 2001. In that year, two of the three best-performing Dow
stocks were Microsoft (up 53 percent) and AT&T (up 37 percent).
What was especially impressive about those returns was that the Dow
Industrials (along with nearly every other major market index)
declined during the year. In the Dow's case, the index declined 5 percent.

Interestingly, although AT&T and Microsoft soared in 2001, they
had tanked in the previous year. Indeed, AT&T and Microsoft were
the two *worst-performing* stocks in the Dow in 2000, falling 65 percent
and 63 percent, respectively. Do you see a pattern here?

These observations fueled my curiosity about a worst-to-first
investment strategy with the Dow, leading me to do a bit more
research to see how this phenomenon held up over a longer period of
time. Thus, I conducted a study to see how much a $1,000 invest-
ment, beginning in 1983, would have returned by the end of 2002
simply by investing in the worst-performing Dow stock each year.
Amazingly, this simple strategy of buying the Dow's worst-performing
stock each year would have turned $1,000 into *more than* $68,000 in

just 20 years. That's a return of more than 6,700 percent. During the same time period, $1,000 invested in the Dow Jones Industrial Average grew to approximately $14,000.

In short, what I found was that by simply buying the worst-performing Dow stock each year and holding the stock for the following year, you would have done nearly five times better than the Dow Industrial Average did over that 20-year period. But questions remained:

- Was this simply "data mining" on my part, playing with historical performance numbers to contrive a strategy that worked in theory but would not work in the real world?
- Was a 20-year period long enough to validate the strategy?
- If these amazing returns from such a simple strategy weren't simply random—and I doubted that they were—what was the driving force behind these incredible results?
- Was there a way to improve upon these exceptional results by looking at criteria other than simply the annual price change to determine the Dow's top underdog each year?

Another question that needed to be addressed—and this was a big one for me—was the following: *Is this strategy compatible with my long-time thinking and preaching on investing?* Indeed, I have taken roughly two decades to establish a reputation in the investment world for providing solid, time-tested advice. Would being a proponent of a worst-to-first strategy endanger that reputation? Would it be so inconsistent with my previous writings as to not only discredit this strategy but also the strategies I have espoused in the past?

This book aims to answer those questions by showing how any investor, regardless of the size of his or her pocketbook or level of investment knowledge, can employ a simple, sound, and time-tested strategy to generate impressive wealth over the long term. In addition, *Winning with the Dow's Losers* shows how this strategy fits nicely with many of the concepts and advice that I have preached for years in my books and newsletters.

Methodology

The foundation of the book is my research of the Dow Jones Industrial Average components going back to 1930—a period covering more than 70 years. With data obtained from the University of Chicago's Center for Research in Security Prices (CRSP), I examined annual price changes and total return data for each of the 30 Dow stocks, paying special attention to how the Dow's worst-performing stocks in one year performed the following year. I maintain that this is among the most comprehensive studies of Dow component performance ever attempted. (For comparison, the first edition of Michael O'Higgins's best-seller, *Beating the Dow*, covered a period of less than 20 years.)

Findings

As you'll soon see, the results of this study were rather impressive. Indeed, a variety of Dow worst-to-first investment strategies handily beat the Dow index over short, medium, and long time frames. Also impressive was the strategies' ability to do well regardless of market conditions. For example, from 2000 through 2002—arguably the worst bear market since the Depression—an investor who followed the simple strategy of buying the Dow's worst-performing stock at the beginning of each year would have seen his or her portfolio increase more than 140 percent. And a less risky portfolio containing the five worst-performing Dow stocks posted a more subdued but still impressive 19 percent return during the bear market of 2000 through 2002. Incidentally, over the same 3-year time period, the Dow Industrials *declined* more than 23 percent. A full rundown on the historical performance numbers for various worst-to-first strategies, going all the way back to 1930, is provided in Chapter 5.

The Strategy's Foundation

The underlying principle driving the worst-to-first strategy, which you'll learn more about in Chapter 1, is called reversion to the mean. Basically, reversion to the mean states that things—human emotions, weather patterns, and, yes, stock prices—cannot exist forever at their extremes. At some point, all things migrate to their long-run average, their equilibrium state.

Stock prices are vulnerable to mean reversion simply because they are driven ultimately by the laws of supply and demand. And those laws can get out of whack over the short run based on buyer emotions, fads, herd mentality, and so on. Reversion to the mean is really the basis for contrarian investing. Contrarians say that the best opportunities in stocks are created when values have run to extreme levels and are ready to swing back to their long-run equilibrium points. The worst-to-first strategy is a form of contrarian investing in that it forces investors to buy out-of-favor stocks.

To be sure, just because a stock declines sharply in one year doesn't make it an automatic candidate for success the following year. That point has been driven home with many technology stocks that have been murdered in recent years. Thus, the trick is to find those stocks where reversion to the mean is most likely to occur, stocks that have a long history of weathering economic ups and downs, stocks with an ample long-run trading history. What stocks fit these criteria? Dow stocks.

What I also like about this strategy is that it is compatible with a lot of the investment ideas and approaches I have espoused in my newsletters and previous books, such as

- *Leave your emotions at the door.* I am a big proponent of any investment approach that strips the investment process of emotion. Why? Because emotions make you do things that your intellect says you should not do. For example, emotions (fear, greed, etc.) generally cause us to sell stocks at the bottom or to buy stocks at the top. If you can eliminate being a reactive investor by taking emotion out of the mix, you will make logical, reasoned decisions. My worst-to-first strategies take the guesswork out of the investment process. They eliminate emotional decision making.

- *Keep it simple.* The best investment approaches are usually the simplest investment approaches. Why? Because complexity in anything—investments, businesses, relationships—creates a lot of "moving parts" that have to be monitored, evaluated, managed, and so on. Unfortunately, too many moving parts usually lead to too many opportunities for mistakes and failures. Simple investment strategies are easy to implement, easy to monitor, and easy to adjust. And they don't get much easier than my worst-to-first strategies.

- *Buy low, sell high.* The name of the game in investing is truly buy low, sell high. Few strategies, unfortunately, cause you to do either particularly well. And while I acknowledge that I am not a proponent of frequent selling in an investment program, I also acknowledge that *sell* does not have to be a dirty word when it comes to investing. This point has been driven home in the last 3 years, when taking at least some money off the table after the big market run in the late 1990s would have been a prudent thing to do. The beauty of my worst-to-first strategies is that they force you to buy stocks that are down. True, you may buy a stock that goes from cheap to cheaper. Still, successful investing oftentimes is all about running against the herd, about buying stocks that scare off most investors, about buying stocks that have been trampled. The worst-to-first strategies accomplish this by forcing you to buy losers. And the strategies take care of the second part of the formula (sell high) by forcing you to sell stocks (presumably after they have risen) after the 1-year holding period. Thus, the strategies put on "autopilot" the two most important decisions an investor makes: when to buy and when to sell.

- *The importance of "micro" portfolios to a "macro" investment strategy.* Perhaps the biggest lesson of the last 3 years is that investors need to have a diversified, balanced, and varied approach to investing. This is accomplished in a variety of ways: diversifying across asset classes (stocks, bonds, real estate, etc.), diversifying within asset classes (large-cap stocks, small-cap stocks, U.S. stocks, foreign stocks, high-yield bonds, investment-grade bonds), time diversification (dollar-cost averaging), and diversifying across investment styles (growth, value). In short, a diversified macro investment program is a compilation of micro portfolios, each with its own risk and return objectives and correlation coefficients. My vision of the worst-to-first strategies is not so much as the only investment approach for an investor but as a micro strategy that complements an investor's macro investment program. When framed in this way, worst-to-first strategies become yet another tool to improve portfolio diversification. Obviously, the book will show investors how to incorporate the strategies into a well-rounded investment program. That discussion will include the best vehicles for conducting the strategy (taxable versus nontaxable investment accounts), the percentage of portfolio dollars that should be devoted to the strategy, the types of investors best suited for the strategy (young versus old, traders versus long-term investors), and the melding of this strategy with other popular investment approaches (such as buy and hold).

Of course, with any book that introduces a new investment strategy, the author must address the following issues:

- The book must provide a clear, step-by-step blueprint for implementing the strategy.
- The book must provide a logical, sound, reasoned basis for why the strategy works.
- The book must show how this strategy has worked in the past, in both up and down markets.
- The book must show why the strategy will work going forward.
- The book must show why this strategy is superior to other strategies, especially similar investment approaches.
- The book must show why the Dow is an important benchmark, a worthy index to beat, and why Dow stocks are the best vehicles for putting this strategy into practice.
- The book must address the inevitable criticisms that unbelievers will use to discredit the strategy.
- The book must show how to incorporate this strategy into a well-rounded investment program.
- The book must provide more advanced approaches that enhance the performance of the strategy.

Thus, each chapter of the book addresses these issues. For example:

- THE CONCEPT—MEAN REVERSION AND
  CONTRARIAN INVESTING
  Chapter 1 introduces the concepts (mean reversion, contrarian
  investing) that support the worst-to-first concept.

- THE TOOLS—THE DOW JONES INDUSTRIAL AVERAGE
  Chapters 2 and 3 take a look at the primary tool used to implement my worst-to-first strategies—the Dow Jones Industrial Average. Chapter 2 dissects the Dow—how it's computed, why it's a
  relevant benchmark, why it's appropriate for mean-reversion
  investment strategies. Chapter 3 looks at the current components
  of the Dow.

- THE STRATEGY—BASIC AND ADVANCED
  WORST-TO-FIRST STRATEGIES
  Chapters 4, 5, and 6 look at a variety of worst-to-first strategies,
  from the basic strategy (buying the worst-performing Dow stocks)
  to more sophisticated strategies (long/short strategies, enhanced
  index strategies) that play off the worst-to-first phenomenon.
  Each strategy is spelled out in step-by-step instructions so that any
  investor will know exactly how to put these strategies into action.
  The historical performance records of the various worst-to-first
  strategies are also provided.

- THE PORTFOLIO—PUTTING THE PIECES TOGETHER
  Chapter 7 discusses ways to use the worst-to-first strategy both as a
  stand-alone portfolio as well as within a diversified investment
  program.

- THE COMPETITION—"DOGS" VERSUS "UNDERDOGS"
  Chapter 8 examines similar investment strategies—most notably
  the Dogs of the Dow strategy, which invests in the 10 highest-
  yielding Dow stocks—and shows why the worst-to-first strategy is
  superior.

- THE NAYSAYERS—POINT/COUNTERPOINT
  Chapter 9 plays devil's advocate and tries to poke holes in the strategies using likely arguments from critics. This chapter also addresses the strategies' shortcomings and vulnerabilities.

- CONCLUSION
  Chapter 10 concludes the book with a look at the future and how likely changes to the Dow will impact my worst-to-first strategies.

- THE HISTORY—TRACKING THE DOW
  COMPONENT PERFORMANCE
  For you data junkies, the book includes an appendix showing a year-by-year listing of the 30 Dow components (beginning in 1930) and their price performance and total return numbers for each component during the year.

True, the market has been a tough place to make a buck in the last 3 years. But that doesn't mean it couldn't be done. With the right game plan and approach, investors can make money even in the face of crooked corporate accounting, shaky CEO ethics, biased Wall Street research, and cascading market indexes.

Can I guarantee that the impressive results of my worst-to-first strategies will continue? Of course not; no investment system can guarantee investment success.

Am I confident that the strategies discussed in this book are built on sound principles that should, over time, produce superior results? You bet.

So, for you people who are looking for a new, simple, easy, and—best of all—profitable way to invest, I think you'll like what you're about to read.

Part I

The Concept—Mean Reversion and Contrarian Investing

1

Worst to First—Why It Works

. . . And the last shall be first.

I'm about to reveal to you an investment strategy that is so powerful yet so simple and logical that it will change the way you invest. Bold statement? You bet. But it's also true.

Indeed, by following this simple strategy since the end of 1930, an investor would have turned a $1,000 investment into more than $2 *million.* That's roughly double the return of the Dow Jones Industrial Average over that same time frame. Of course, few of us have 74 years to invest. So let's look at how the strategy performed over shorter time frames:

- Over the last 50 years, this investment strategy (which, by the way, requires you to look at just 30 blue-chip stocks, once a year) turned $1,000 into nearly $258,000, outperforming the Dow Jones Industrial Average over the same time period.

- Over the last 30 years, this investment strategy (which makes all the investment decisions for you, including the always-difficult sell decision) turned $1,000 into more than $56,000—a gain of 5,500 percent on your investment and a profit that was 56 percent greater than the return of the Dow over the same time period.

- Over the last 20 years, this investment strategy (which is so easy that you don't even need a calculator) turned $1,000 into nearly

$17,000—a gain of 1,600 percent, handily beating the Dow over the same time frame.

- Over the last 10 years, the strategy (which is so inexpensive that your total "research" cost is the price of one *Wall Street Journal*) once again trumped the Dow, more than tripling your money over that time frame.

- Over the last 5 years, the strategy (which will take you less than an hour to research and can be implemented anytime during the year) produced a 101 percent return on your investment versus a 25 percent return in the Dow. And remember—that 101 percent profit occurred during one of the worst bear markets in history, when most investor portfolios and major market indexes were deep in the red.

- And for 2003, this investment strategy (which requires less than $1,000 of investment capital) returned 42 percent on your investment, beating the 28 percent return of the Dow.

To summarize, this investment strategy has handily beaten the Dow Jones Industrial Average

- Over the last 74-year period
- Over the last 50-year period
- Over the last 30-year period
- Over the last 20-year period
- Over the last 10-year period
- Over the last 5-year period
- Over the last 4-year period
- Over the last 3-year period
- Over the last 2-year period
- Over the last 1-year period

And if you don't think the Dow Jones Industrial Average is a worthy benchmark to beat, consider this: The Dow Jones Industrial Average has whipped the S&P 500 Index, Wilshire 5000, Nasdaq

Composite, and most other major market indexes over the last 5 years, as the following chart shows:

Major Indexes—5-Year Performance

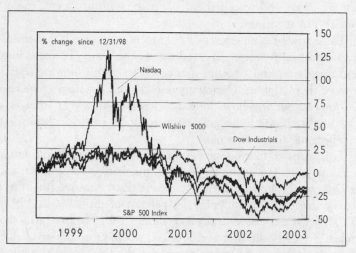

So what is this too-good-to-be-true investment strategy? Read on.

THE WORST-TO-FIRST PHENOMENON

Everyone's favorite investment mantra is "buy low, sell high." The problem is that *nobody* actually buys low and sells high. Rather, we buy high and (we hope) sell even higher.

The stock market is the only market on earth where the merchandise becomes more popular as it becomes more expensive. Why? Because investors feel comfortable staying with the herd when it comes to buying stock. After all, if everyone loves a stock and its price is rising, it must be worth buying, right?

The problem is that investing with the herd is a surefire way to lose money. Look at all the technology stocks that soared in the late '90s only to come crashing down in the last 3 years. Everyone wanted to buy those technology stocks when they were skyrocketing and trading at extreme prices; nobody wanted to buy them when they crashed.

Successful investing is all about forcing you to do the smart thing even when your emotions are telling you otherwise. And the smart thing to do as an investor *is* to buy low and sell high. Fortunately, strategies exist that force investors to buy high-quality stocks when they are down and to sell them when they are up. I call them my worst-to-first strategies.

These strategies emerged as a product of my research into the Dow Jones Industrial Average. As an editor of *Dow Theory Forecasts* investment newsletter and a money manager, I've been following the Dow for more than 20 years. During my research of Dow stocks, one theme that jumped out was how the Dow's losers in one year (that is, the Dow stocks showing the greatest percentage price decline for the year) became winners the next.

This worst-to-first phenomenon has been especially pronounced in recent years. For example, in 1999, the worst-performing stock in the Dow was Philip Morris (now called Altria). An investment in the tobacco giant lost a whopping 54 percent of its value in 1999. In 2000, however, the story was much different for Philip Morris shareholders. To say Philip Morris rebounded would be an understatement; the stock was the best-performing issue in the Dow in 2000, returning 105 percent. In fact, Philip Morris's triple-digit return in 2000 was nearly twice the return of the runner-up that year, aerospace giant Boeing. Even more impressive was that while investors were more than doubling their investment in Philip Morris in 2000, the Dow actually *lost* money (nearly 5 percent) during the year.

In 2000, same story, different players. The two worst-performing stocks in the Dow in 2000 were AT&T (down 65 percent) and software behemoth Microsoft (down 63 percent). In 2001, Microsoft and AT&T went from worst to first. Microsoft was the Dow's best performer in 2001, rising 53 percent. And AT&T was the third-best performer in the Dow that year, returning 37 percent. (For the record, IBM, which rose 43 percent in 2001, was the meat of the Microsoft/ AT&T performance sandwich. Interestingly, IBM's big gain in 2001 came on the heels of a 21 percent decline in 2000.) And those big gains in Microsoft and AT&T (and IBM) came during a year when an investment in the Dow *lost* money (about 5 percent).

Although the worst-to-first story for 2001–2002 is not as compelling, it still makes for interesting reading. The worst-performing Dow stock in 2001 was Boeing, losing 40 percent of its value. And while Boeing still showed a loss in 2002 (a decline of 13 percent), that performance still outpaced the 15 percent loss in the Dow.

The worst-to-first phenomenon returned to prime form in 2002–2003. The Dow's worst performer in 2002 was Home Depot. Shares of the do-it-yourself retailer, hurt by a slowdown in same-store sales and increased competition from Lowe's, lost 53 percent for the year, or roughly $60 *billion* in market value. Fortunately, Home Depot's terrible performance in 2002 was followed by a stellar rebound in 2003. Indeed, Home Depot rose 49 percent in 2003 versus a 28 percent increase in the Dow.

Of course, 4 years is too short a time frame to evaluate any investment strategy. Thus, I decided to undertake one of the most comprehensive studies of Dow returns ever attempted. I gathered data on the Dow and its components going back to 1930 to test a variety of worst-to-first strategies. (The basic worst-to-first strategy, which entails buying equal amounts of the five worst-performing Dow stocks each year, is discussed in great detail in Chapter 4. Variations of the strategy, including more sophisticated investment techniques that play off the worst-to-first phenomenon in the Dow, are introduced and explained in Chapter 6.)

I discovered that buying a basket of the Dow's worst-performing stocks (I call these underachieving stocks "Dow Underdogs") and holding them for a year outperformed the Dow by a wide margin going back to 1930. What's more, the strategy has been even more profitable over more recent time periods, including the last 10-year period and especially during the volatile markets since 2000.

VALIDATING AN INVESTMENT APPROACH

My guess is that you are probably skeptical about my claims. You've seen too many ads on late-night television or in financial publications touting investment schemes that promise—no, they usually *guarantee*—huge investment results. And you know it's all hype.

Well, the fact is you *should* be skeptical about any investment strategy—including my worst-to-first strategies—that claims to produce superior results. Beating the market consistently over time is tough stuff. In any given year, about 7 out of 10 professional investors fail to beat the market. Over longer periods, hardly anyone beats the market.

Another reason you should be skeptical is that anyone with a decent computer and lots of data can contrive an investment strategy that works phenomenally on paper. It's called "data mining," and it is a favorite pastime of Wall Street money-chasers. Data mining is the practice of picking through reams of market and stock data to find patterns that can be melded into an investment strategy.

My favorite example of data mining is the "Super Bowl Theory" of investing. The theory says that if a team from the National Football Conference (or an American Football Conference team that was a member of the premerger National Football League) wins the Super Bowl (which is played every January), the stock market will show a gain that year. If the AFC team wins, the market will decline. How well has this strategy worked? The Super Bowl Theory has "called" the market about 80 percent of the time.

Now, if I tried to sell you on the Super Bowl Theory as a valid investment strategy, you would probably think I was nuts. And you're right. Sure, a "correlation" exists between the winner of the Super Bowl and the market's direction. But is there truly a cause and effect relationship? In other words, does the winner of the Super Bowl actually have some impact, some direct influence, on the stock market's performance? I think not.

And that is the danger of so many investment strategies. Mining historical data can always produce correlations between market returns and various investment data. But is there an underlying logic, a fundamental reason, that links cause and effect?

When evaluating any investment strategy, the following factors need to be present to validate its usefulness:

- *Consistency of performance over various time frames.* Be dubious about any investment strategy that shows big results—but only over a relatively short period of time. Any investment strategy can get lucky in the short run. What you want from an investment strategy is consistent performance over a variety of time frames— short run (1 to 5 years), intermediate term (5 to 15 years), and long term (15 to 30 years, and even longer). You also need to see performance over a variety of market cycles. Given the run-up in stocks during the 1990s, you would have been hard-pressed to come up with an investment approach that *didn't* make a lot of money. Everything was going up in the 1990s. However, many of those supposedly winning investment strategies blew up during the ensuing bear market. A good investment strategy stands the test of time. It may not put up market-beating numbers every year, but it will hold its own—regardless of market conditions—over most time frames.

- *Simplicity*. The best investment strategies are often the simplest. Simple strategies are easy to understand, easy to implement, and easy to monitor. Complex investment strategies tend to be confusing and are often ambiguous, potentially frustrating, and certainly difficult to monitor. I always get nervous when someone pitches an investment approach that has lots of variables requiring lots of decisions. Lots of variables mean lots of moving parts that can go wrong. And lots of decisions increase the likelihood of making a wrong one that can be lethal to your investment results.

- *Affordability*. An investment strategy that requires hundreds of thousands of dollars to put into practice has no real value to most individual investors. These people want strategies that can be started with $5,000 or less. In addition to being affordable to fund, an investment strategy has to be affordable to implement and operate. Most individual investors don't have thousands of dollars to devote to investment research tools.

- *Tax-friendly*. Most "winning" investment strategies that are sold to investors exist in a world free of taxes. The problem is that such a world doesn't exist. True, recent tax reform has reduced the burden of taxes on investments (both capital gains and dividends). Still, taxes have to be factored into any investment strategy. A successful investment strategy must maximize investment tax breaks (such as the favorable tax break on long-term capital gains) and/or can be implemented easily within a tax-preferenced account, such as a Roth Individual Retirement Account.

- *Transaction-friendly*. We live in an age of rock-bottom transaction costs for investors. Commission rates have plummeted over the last decade to a point where you can actually buy 100 shares of stock for just $1 through some brokers and for free through some company dividend reinvestment plans. (I'll show you how to buy stocks for little or no fees in Chapter 4.) Having said that, transaction costs still matter to a portfolio, especially portfolios with minimal assets. For example, let's say you buy into an investment approach that requires you to make just 5 trades per month. That translates to 60 trades per year. Now, let's say you use Charles Schwab, the popular discount broker, to make those trades. Schwab's minimum online commission charge is $19.95 per trade. Making those 60 trades at Schwab would cost you $1,197. Now, if your investment portfolio is $1 million, that $1,197 represents just 0.12 percent of the value of the portfolio. However, if your investment portfolio is $10,000, that $1,197 in commissions trims your investment stake by nearly 12 percent. Obviously, no investor can afford to lose 12 percent of his or her portfolio to commissions each year. Bottom line: fees matter, especially to smaller investors, and you need to take transaction fees into account when considering any investment strategy.

- *Discipline*. Effective investment strategies strip emotion from the investment process. Effective investment strategies take the decision process out of your hands and put your portfolio on autopilot, where you can't tinker or make decisions based on your mood or feeling. Because the investment decisions that usually make you the most money oftentimes are the hardest to make—buying stocks that have been beaten up, staying in the market during bear markets, and so forth—any investment strategy worth its salt doesn't leave those tough decisions up to you and your emotions. A good strategy hardwires the decision-making process so that you have no choice but to follow the strategy.

- *Risk-friendly*. What if I told you that I had a great investment strategy, but it would require you to invest all of your money in a single penny stock. You probably wouldn't do it, right? Too risky. Effective investment strategies provide a palatable trade-off between risk and return. Effective strategies don't require all-or-nothing investment approaches. Effective investment strategies are complementary to other strategies that you may be employing in a well-rounded investment program. Effective investment strategies don't force you to play in the riskiest areas of the market.

• *Easy to keep score.* "How am I doing?" is a frequent question investors ask themselves or their advisors. It would seem that knowing how your investments are doing should be an easy task. However, assessing a strategy's performance requires more than raw performance numbers. For example, a portfolio consisting of large-company stocks that rose 15 percent in 1999 would have seemed like a good performance. After all, 15 percent is better than the market's long-run average annual return of around 10 percent. Actually, a 15 percent gain in 1999 was rather paltry considering the Dow Industrials were up more than 27 percent for the year. It is important to not only be able to determine your portfolio's return—and that can be rather complicated if your investment strategy requires frequent buying and selling as well as additional investment capital throughout the course of a year—but also how that return compares to a valid benchmark. Investors generally fall short on this latter point. If you own a portfolio exclusively of small companies, comparing your return to an index of large companies, such as the Dow or the S&P 500 index, is inappropriate. Your benchmark should be an index that focuses on small companies (such as the Russell 2000 or the S&P 600). Likewise, if you have a diversified portfolio consisting of bonds, large-company stocks, small-company stocks, and foreign stocks, the appropriate benchmark is a blended one that takes into account benchmark performance for each of these individual sectors. A valid investment strategy leaves no confusion when answering the question, "How am I doing?"

• *Flexibility.* A good investment strategy can be implemented *anytime*, not just during a full moon or a solar eclipse or the third Friday of the month.

• *Sell discipline.* Knowing when to sell is the hardest part of any investment program. To know when to sell, you have to know why you bought. And, surprisingly, many investors buy stocks for no legitimate reason or with no definitive strategy in mind. Oh sure, we *think* we have good reasons: "My brother-in-law told me it was a good stock." "I heard a guy on CNBC say it was a good stock." "The stock was going up—it must be a good stock." The problem with buying stocks based on such flimsy analysis is that you'll never have a good sense when it's time to head for the exits. Any worthwhile investment strategy has an exit plan—some mechanism for helping you decide to take money off the table. And, preferably, this sell mechanism kicks in automatically without you having to make the call.

- *Stock-centric*. Good investment strategies focus on stocks. True, asset allocation—that is, how your investment dollars are allocated across stocks, bonds, and cash—will have a huge impact on your portfolio. Nevertheless, if you expect to *build* wealth via investing, you cannot do so without focusing on stocks. Despite the market's performance in recent years, stocks remain the best game in town for creating real wealth.

But perhaps the most important characteristic of any investment strategy is that it has to be based on some fundamental truth, some logical premise that passes the "smell test." The Super Bowl Theory, despite its track record, doesn't pass the smell test. The Super Bowl Theory draws no connection between cause and effect. It has no logical premise, no basis in some fundamental market truth or law of nature.

So how do my worst-to-first strategies stack up to this checklist? You be the judge:

- *Consistency of performance over various time frames*. My basic worst-to-first strategy of buying the five worst-performing Dow stocks each year has outperformed the Dow over 1-, 2-, 3-, 4-, 5-, 10-, 20-, 30-, 50-, and 74-year holding periods. Those time frames encompass lots of bull and bear markets.

- *Simplicity*. You tell me if this is too difficult for you: (1) Make a list of 30 stocks in Dow Industrials. (2) Compute the 12-month price change. This will take you about 30 minutes—I show you how in Chapter 4. (3) Buy five Dow stocks that have performed the worst over the last 12 months. (4) Hold said five Dow stocks for 12 months and 1 day. (5) Sell stocks. (6) Repeat.

- *Affordability*. Do you have $5,000? You can implement my strategy. Do you have $1,000? You can implement my strategy. Do you have $1? That's the total cost of the research tools you'll need to pick your Dow Underdogs.

- *Tax-friendly*. My worst-to-first strategies can be employed in a tax-exempt account, such as an Individual Retirement Account. And because I minimize capital gains taxes by holding worst-to-first investments for 12 months and 1 day, the strategy is friendly in taxable accounts as well.

- *Transaction-friendly*. The largest number of trades you will make in a year employing the basic worst-to-first strategy is 10.

- *Discipline*. Once you buy into the strategy, you have no decisions to make. There is no ambiguity, no confusion. The strategy goes on autopilot. You buy the stocks, go away, and come back in 12 months and 1 day.

- *Risk-friendly*. The worst-to-first strategy fits well as a stand-alone investment strategy or within an investment program incorporating a variety of investment strategies. (Chapter 7 shows how worst-to-first strategies can be incorporated into a diversified investment program.) And even though the basic strategy involves owning a portfolio of just five stocks, the strategy has been only marginally riskier than the Dow over the long run and less risky over the short run. Furthermore, ways exist to limit your risk with such a small portfolio if you so desire. (I show you how in Chapter 4.)

- *Easy to keep score*. Since there is no frequent trading and because you are not providing cash infusions during the year, tallying up your performance is rather easy with any of my worst-to-first strategies. And benchmarking those results is easy, too. Since you have only Dow stocks from which to choose, the Dow Jones Industrial Average provides a clear-cut benchmark by which to judge the strategy's performance.

- *Flexibility*. While the historical performance numbers provided in this book are based on implementing a worst-to-first strategy at the beginning of the year, the underlying basis for the strategy suggests that investors can implement the strategy anytime during the year, provided they hold the investments for 12 months and 1 day.

- *Sell discipline.* My worst-to-first strategies provide clear-cut guidelines for selling investments. In fact, the sell decision is made for you, every year.

- *Stock-centric.* You are only buying stocks with the basic worst-to-first strategy. Furthermore, the stock investments are focused on perhaps the bluest of all blue-chip stocks—the 30 issues that compose the Dow Jones Industrial Average.

Finally, and most importantly, the premise and concepts underlying the worst-to-first investment strategy combine time-tested investment truths with a fundamental law of science and nature.

MEAN REVERSION AND CONTRARIAN INVESTING

The stock market is no different from any other market. The laws of supply and demand ultimately determine the price of the merchandise. If there are more buyers than sellers for a particular stock, the price of that stock will rise. If there are more sellers than buyers, the stock price will fall.

The conventional market wisdom for many years driven by research coming out of the University of Chicago was that the stock market, as a result of the interplay between these vast numbers of buyers and sellers, was truly "efficient." Proponents of the efficient market theory believe that since all market participants have access to the same information about a stock, the price of a stock should reflect the knowledge and expectations of all investors. Thus, an investor should not be able to beat the market since there is no way for him or her to know something about a stock that isn't already reflected in the stock's price. For that reason, stock prices move in a random fashion as new information comes into the market and is quickly reflected in the stock price.

As a graduate of the University of Chicago's Graduate School of Business, I do believe that markets are efficient, *to a point*. However, market efficiency assumes all market participants behave in a rational fashion all of the time. Unfortunately, the human condition (and, remember, humans ultimately decide stock prices) does not lend itself to full-time rational thinking.

Was it rational, for example, to buy Internet stocks in the late 1990s when it was clear to everyone—including the people who were doing the buying—that these companies (many of which had no profits, barely a revenue stream, and no history of weathering difficult markets or economies) were extremely overvalued?

A proponent of market efficiency might argue that investors, given the best information at the time (information that included pretty crazy growth projections), were acting rationally. However, I think we all know better. The simple truth was that all of us got caught up in a mania concerning the latest and greatest thing. Our actions were driven by greed more than logic. And greed can make you do some pretty irrational things.

That humans behave irrationally when it comes to things financial has gained momentum in the academic world in recent years. In fact, the Nobel prize in economic sciences in 2002 went to Daniel Kahneman, who isn't even an economist. Kahneman is a psychologist who still teaches Psychology 101 at Princeton. Kahneman, along with his longtime collaborator Amos Tversky (who passed away in 1996), published a paper in 1979, "Prospect Theory: An Analysis of Decision Under Risk." That paper formed the basis for the concept of loss aversion—that is, people generally derive more pain from a loss than they do pleasure from a gain.

Although the purpose of their work was a psychological study, the applications were far-reaching, especially in the areas of finance. For example, loss aversion explains why investors tend to stick with losing stocks in order to avoid locking up a loss by selling.

Kahneman and Tversky also found that individuals tend to overweight recent data in making forecasts and judgments. Think about how most decisions are made. All of us have a tendency to focus on recent information, to extrapolate the near term into the long term. This tendency helps to explain the herd mentality on Wall Street. People buy winning stocks because they expect near-term winners to be long-term winners. Or, people sell stocks that everyone else is selling simply because recent data (i.e., the stock is falling in price) influence their decisions.

A student of Kahneman, University of Chicago professor Richard Thaler, has been one of the leaders in applying behavioral psychology to the world of economics and finance. For example, Thaler has used behavioral psychology to research contrarian investing. Contrarian investors buy investments that are out of favor with the general investing public. Contrarians believe that if the essence of successful investing is buying stocks at cheap prices, then stocks that are being shunned by investors should represent the stocks offering the best value.

Contrarian investment strategies are successful because they take advantage of investor overreaction. This overreaction, so say behavioral psychologists, is partly a result of investors making bad projections about stock prices as a result of overweighting recent events.

Of course, buying a stock that has fallen sharply won't make you any money if it stays down forever. That's where the second important piece of the puzzle comes into play. Contrarian investors also depend on the concept of mean reversion.

Think for a moment about the world around you. Things—weather patterns, people's emotions, even societal behavior—tend to track some equilibrium range, a steady state, if you will. Occasionally, this steady state gets disrupted. In the case of weather, you have tornadoes and hurricanes and floods. In the case of societal behavior, riots and revolutions and looting. In the case of human emotions, the peaks and valleys caused by big events (marriage, children, death). Thus, in the short run, things have the ability to run to extremes. Over time, however, things tend to revert to the equilibrium state, the long-run average. Indeed, it requires too much energy for things to stay at the extremes. As the energy that created the extremes (think wind for hurricanes) dissipates, things tend to revert to their steady state.

A good analogy for mean reversion is a rubber band. A rubber band can stretch and contort when pressure is applied. Once the pressure ceases, however, the rubber band returns to its steady state. Mean reversion has important implications for investing, especially contrarian investing. Contrarians believe that if you buy stocks that have run to extremes on the downside (or sell stocks that have run to extremes on the upside), you will eventually be rewarded when mean reversion returns the stocks to their long-run equilibrium price level.

To be sure, mean reversion/contrarian investing is not as simple as going out and buying any beaten-down stock. For example, the last thing a contrarian wants to do is buy a cheap stock that gets cheaper and cheaper and cheaper . . . and then becomes extinct. Bankruptcy is the bane of any contrarian investing strategy. Bankruptcy steals the time a stock needs to revert to its mean.

For that reason, stocks that seem best situated for a mean-reversion strategy are large, seasoned, time-tested companies with sound finances and the ability to weather down cycles in the economy and stock market. When these stocks show extreme price declines, especially relative to some appropriate benchmark, smart investors buy.

A 2001 research paper by Jonathan Lewellen at the MIT Sloan School of Management supports this logic. Lewellen's study looked at all stocks on the New York Stock Exchange, American Stock Exchange, and Nasdaq over a very time long period (1926 through 1998) and a shorter period (1946 through 1998). He found that mean reversion in stock prices is "stronger than commonly believed." Lewellen found that price reversals—that is, returns in one period being negatively correlated to returns in the preceding period—were most reliable when looking at 1-year time periods, and these reversals were economically significant. Lewellen also found that mean reversion appears strongest in larger stocks, although mean reversion appears to drop off for both the very smallest and very largest stocks.

BRINGING IT ALL TOGETHER

Lewellen's work, when coupled with the work of other researchers, seems to give support to the idea that certain stocks do show characteristics of mean reversion over certain periods of time. This mean reversion occurs primarily as a result of investor behavior that cannot be readily explained by the efficient market theory. In fact, it is becoming more apparent and, indeed, accepted that investors do not always act rationally, that certain decisions, at least in the short run, are driven by psychology and emotion rather than logic. And opportunities arise in these instances for the contrarian investor to take advantage of these short-term inefficiencies.

How do my worst-to-first investment strategies fit into this more contemporary view of the investment world? Rather well.

- My worst-to-first strategies focus exclusively on buying beaten-up, blue-chip issues in the Dow. These are the type of companies that have demonstrated over many decades the sort of financial firepower and staying power that makes them well suited for a mean-reversion investment strategy.

- My worst-to-first strategies focus on 1-year periods. This time period is consistent with Lewellen's work showing that 1-year returns have predictive power.

Another reason my worst-to-first strategies make sense in today's investment environment is that the strategies' investment methodology relies solely on one data point: a stock's 12-month price change. This data point cannot be fudged, obfuscated, or manipulated. A stock's price change is an absolute. The same can't be said for revenue, net income, debt, or any other investment metric found on the balance sheet or income statement. As we've seen in recent years, corporate America is not above employing fuzzy accounting or even downright fraud to distort or puff these numbers.

INTERMEDIATE POTENTIAL RISK INDICATOR—
A MEAN-REVERSION TOOL FOR THE MARKET

Throughout this chapter I've discussed mean reversion as it applies to individual stocks. The concept works pretty well for markets, too. Look at the historical total returns of the Dow Jones Industrial Average going back to 1931:

Year	%	Year	%
1931	−47.6	1938	32.2
1932	−17.1	1939	1.0
1933	72.4	1940	−8.0
1934	7.8	1941	−9.6
1935	42.9	1942	13.4
1936	29.7	1943	19.1
1937	−27.9	1944	16.9

Year	%	Year	%
1945	31.0	1975	44.4
1946	−4.3	1976	22.7
1947	7.4	1977	−12.7
1948	4.2	1978	2.7
1949	20.1	1979	10.5
1950	25.7	1980	21.4
1951	21.3	1981	−3.4
1952	14.2	1982	25.8
1953	1.8	1983	25.7
1954	50.2	1984	1.1
1955	26.1	1985	32.8
1956	7.0	1986	26.9
1957	−8.4	1987	6.0
1958	38.6	1988	14.9
1959	20.0	1989	31.7
1960	−6.2	1990	−0.6
1961	22.4	1991	23.9
1962	−7.6	1992	7.4
1963	20.6	1993	16.7
1964	18.7	1994	5.0
1965	14.2	1995	36.5
1966	−15.6	1996	28.6
1967	19.0	1997	24.8
1968	7.7	1998	18.0
1969	−11.6	1999	27.1
1970	8.8	2000	−4.7
1971	9.8	2001	−5.4
1972	18.2	2002	−14.9
1973	−13.1	2003	28.3
1974	−23.1		

Notice that large 1-year returns are often reversed the following year. This is especially the case when the Dow suffers a big decline in a particular year. Indeed, since 1931, the Dow has lost 15 percent or more of its value five times: 1931 (−47 percent), 1932 (−17 percent), 1937

(–28 percent), 1966 (–16 percent), and 1974 (–23 percent). In 4 of those 5 years, the Dow showed a rebound the following year of at least 19 percent. (The only exception was 1932, when the Dow followed a –47 percent drubbing in 1931 with a –17 percent return in 1932.) The average gain in those 4 rebound years was a hefty 42 percent.

Reversion to the mean following good years in the Dow is also present but a bit less pronounced. For example, since 1931, the Dow has posted a 30 percent or higher return 10 times: 1933 (+72 percent), 1935 (+43 percent), 1938 (+32 percent), 1945 (+31 percent), 1954 (+50 percent), 1958 (+39 percent), 1975 (+44 percent), 1985 (+33 percent), 1989 (+32 percent), and 1995 (+37 percent). Interestingly, three of these years—1933, 1938, and 1975—followed big down years in the Dow. Several instances existed when the Dow followed one good year with a decent second year. These back-to-back positive performances usually occurred, however, after the Dow was coming off one or more clunker years. The upshot is that it appears reversion of the mean does work reasonably well for the Dow following big gains, but the reversion process seems to take a bit longer to occur (roughly 2 years versus 1 year for mean reversion after a major down year in the Dow).

One tool that I have found especially useful for assessing the likelihood of mean reversion for the broad market is the *Intermediate Potential Risk Indicator*. In fact, it is the best tool I have ever seen for providing a quick snapshot of market risk on a 3- to 6-month basis.

The Intermediate Potential Risk Indicator looks at the percentage of stocks on the New York Stock Exchange trading above their 200-day moving average. This information is provided every day in *Investor's Business Daily* newspaper. It is found on page B2 of the newspaper, in the chart of the S&P 500 on that page.

A stock's 200-day moving average line is determined by taking the average of a stock's closing price over the last 200 trading days and plotting that point. You then drop a day and add a day, compute a new average, and plot that point, . . . and so on. Thus, a 200-day moving average line, because it encompasses a rather sizable number of trading days, represents a reasonable proxy for a stock's long-run equilibrium range. (One of my advanced worst-to-first strategies, discussed in Chapter 6, uses the 200-day moving average rather than a stock's 1-year price change to select the Dow Underdogs.)

The premise behind the Intermediate Potential Risk Indicator is that if lots of stocks on the New York Stock Exchange trade above their 200-day moving averages, reversion to the mean says that at some point you would expect those stocks to decline to their long-run average price. Conversely, when lots of stocks on the New York Stock Exchange trade below their 200-day moving average, at some point you would expect those stocks to migrate up to their 200-day moving average.

To quantify things, when fewer than 40 percent of the stocks on the New York Stock Exchange trade above their 200-day moving average, I consider that lower risk. Between 40 and 70 percent is classified as neutral risk. Above 70 percent is higher risk.

One reason I like the Intermediate Potential Risk Indicator is that it does not depend on absolute market levels. It is a *relative* tool for that specific market period. As the chart indicates, the reading around midyear 2003 was 85 percent. That is, more than 8 out of 10 stocks on the New York Stock Exchange (NYSE) traded above their 200-day moving average.

Such a high percentage indicates that stocks had become quite popular. For comparison, the percentage of stocks on the New York Stock Exchange trading above their 200-day moving average had

Intermediate Potential Risk

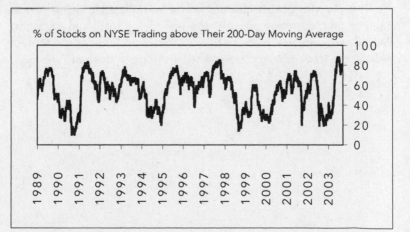

fallen to around 20 percent during the bear-market low of October 2002.

Clearly, when 85 percent of the stocks on the NYSE trade above their 200-day moving average, stocks are extremely popular and have built up quite a bit of froth—froth that will likely have to be purged. Be aware that markets can remain in higher or lower risk for extended periods. Eventually, however, reversion to the mean occurs.

CONCLUSION

The stock market can be a punishing place to do business. In the last few years, many investors have seen their portfolios decline by 50 percent or more. Individuals who were thinking early retirement now wonder if they'll ever afford retirement.

And, unfortunately, it is unlikely that the go-go markets of the 1980s and 1990s will return anytime soon. After all, if you believe in reversion to the mean, the fact that the Dow had only 2 down years from 1978 through 1999 probably means that we still have some mean reversion to go before this market embarks on a multiyear advance.

In such a volatile and potentially difficult market environment, having at least part of your investment funds in a strategy that has a history of producing decent and, in some years, even spectacular results during up and down markets would be a major weapon with which to go to battle. My worst-to-first strategies provide such a weapon.

The purpose of this chapter was to introduce the worst-to-first concept and, more importantly, the underlying logic and reasoning behind the strategies. Now it's time to discuss and dissect the tool for putting the strategy into action—the Dow Jones Industrial Average.

PART II

THE TOOLS—
THE DOW JONES
INDUSTRIAL AVERAGE

2

Worst to First— Dissecting the Dow Jones Industrial Average

I always find it ironic that perhaps the most significant figure in the history of Wall Street—a man whose name is literally synonymous with "the market"—was not an investor. He was not a financier. He was not a captain of industry. He was a journalist. His name was Charles Dow.

Dow was born in 1851. A New England farm boy with an analytical bent, Dow didn't possess an MBA degree, a chartered financial analyst designation, or other accreditations commonly found today on Wall Street. In fact, Dow didn't finish high school let alone attend college.

But the lack of academic credentials didn't hold Dow back from pursuing a career as a journalist. At age 18, Dow became a reporter for *The Springfield Daily Republican*. Other reporting stops included *The Providence Journal* and the *Kiernan News Agency*, where he met Edward D. Jones and Charles M. Bergstresser. The three men left Kiernan to form Dow Jones & Company in November 1882.

Dow Jones & Company published daily financial news bulletins, including the *Customer's Afternoon Letter*, which eventually evolved into *The Wall Street Journal* in 1889. Interestingly, the moneyman behind the venture was the one whose name was probably too long to include in the company moniker—Charles Bergstresser. According to Dow historian Richard Stillman, Bergstresser was the "driving financial force behind the company during its formative years." And it was Bergstresser who came up with the name *The Wall Street Journal*.

Almost immediately after forming Dow Jones & Company, Charles Dow began playing with the idea of creating an index composed of stocks that would help investors make sense of the seemingly random movements of stock prices. On the day before Independence Day 1884, Dow published the first index of American stocks in *Customer's Afternoon Letter*. The index consisted of the following 11 companies:

Chicago & North Western	Union Pacific
Delaware, Lackawanna & Western	Missouri Pacific
Lake Shore	Louisville & Nashville
New York Central	Pacific Mail
St. Paul	Western Union
Northern Pacific preferred	

The bulk of the stocks in the first index were railroads. This should come as no surprise to historians. The railroad industry was a dominant force in the United States in the late 19th century.

According to John Prestbo, the current keeper of the Dow at Dow Jones, Charles Dow compared his average to "placing sticks in the beach sand to determine, wave after successive wave, whether the tide was coming in or going out." In a nutshell, if the average's peaks and troughs rose progressively higher, then a bull market would be in force. Conversely, if the peaks and troughs mapped out a downward direction, stocks would be in a bear market.

If that sounds familiar to you, it should. Charles Dow's work on interpreting market movements provides the foundation for much of what today is called technical analysis. Technical analysts examine, among other things, chart movements in order to predict future stock trends. In fact, Dow's Theory of price movements—which looks at the movement of both the Dow Jones Industrial and Transportation averages—is the main tool my firm uses for determining whether the market's primary trend is bullish or bearish.

From 1884 through 1896, Dow made several changes to his index. Most of the changes involved dumping railroad stocks and adding industrial stocks. These changes led to the introduction on May 26, 1896, of Dow's first average composed entirely of industrial stocks:

American Cotton Oil   Laclede Gas
American Sugar   National Lead
American Tobacco   North American
Chicago Gas   Tenn. Coal & Iron
Distilling & Cattle Feeding   U.S. Leather preferred
General Electric   U.S. Rubber

When examining the 12 stocks that comprised the first Dow Jones Industrial Average, two things are worth mentioning:

1. The only charter member of the Dow that is still in the average today is General Electric. But GE has not been a continuous member in the Dow since 1896. Indeed, GE was booted from the Dow in September 1898 only to be reinstated in April of the next year. GE also was dumped from the Dow on April 1, 1901. More than 6 years later, it returned to the Dow to stay on November 7, 1907.
2. The first Dow Industrial Average included a preferred stock (U.S. Leather). Today, no preferred stocks are members of the Dow.

In October 1896, Dow introduced what would become the Dow Jones Railroad Index. Somewhat surprisingly, this index maintained its *Railroads* moniker all the way up until 1970, when it was changed to the *Transportation* average. Whereas the first Dow Jones Industrial Average had only 12 stocks, the first Dow Jones Railroad Index had 20 stocks.

The first major expansion of the Dow Industrials occurred on October 4, 1916, when the number of components increased to 20 industrial companies (and all common shares). Sadly, Dow was not around to see the evolution of his brainchild. He died in 1902 at age 51.

How many names do you recognize from the 20-member Dow Industrial Average of 1916?

American Beet Sugar   General Electric
American Can   Goodrich
American Car & Foundry   Republic Iron & Steel
American Locomotive   Studebaker
American Smelting   Texas Company
American Sugar   U.S. Rubber
American Telephone & Telegraph   U.S. Steel
Anaconda Copper   Utah Copper
Baldwin Locomotive   Western Union
Central Leather   Westinghouse

On October 1, 1928, the average expanded to its current 30-company limit:

American Can   Nash Motors
Allied Chemical   North American
American Smelting   Paramount Publix
American Sugar   Postum
American Tobacco B   Radio Corporation
Atlantic Refining   Sears Roebuck
Bethlehem Steel   Standard Oil (N.J.)
Chrysler   Texas Corp.
General Electric   Texas Gulf Sulphur
General Motors   U.S. Steel
General Railway Signal   Union Carbide
Goodrich   Victor Talking Machine
International Harvester   Westinghouse Electric
International Nickel   Woolworth
Mack Truck   Wright Aeronautical

And what about the last remaining Dow average—the Dow Utilities? This average was introduced at the beginning of 1929.

Over the years, the Dow Industrial Average has had its share of changes. The catalyst for many of the changes has been a corporate action, such as a takeover or massive restructuring. The keepers of the Dow have generally opted on the side of consistency and stability when it comes to making changes. The Dow has never been quick to make changes based on investor fad and fashion. There is no Internet

Dow Jones Industrial Average

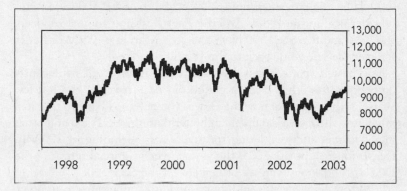

stock in the Dow, for example, even though plenty of investors were calling for Internet and other new technology stocks to be included during the tech boom of the late 1990s. And it took until November 1, 1999, for the first Nasdaq-traded stocks—Intel and Microsoft—to join the Dow Industrials.

That the Dow has been slow to make changes over the years is one of the major criticisms of the index. This criticism is unwarranted, in my opinion. Charles Dow's aim in creating the index had as much to do with creating a barometer for the *economy* as creating a window into market movements. For that reason, the keepers of the Dow make it a priority to include not just companies important to the stock market but companies important to the overall economy. That's why you see such cyclical companies as Caterpillar and General Motors in the Dow. Some would argue that such companies are irrelevant to today's stock market. These companies represent the past, not the future, of corporate America. The keepers of the Dow, however, believe that such companies serve a vital purpose in the Dow. They provide windows into important segments of the economy—segments crucial to millions of Americans who work in these sectors or buy their goods and services.

What makes criticism of the Dow as an antiquated index even more ludicrous is that virtually every other index that focuses on large-company stocks—the S&P 500 being the major favorite of Wall Street pros—exhibits price movements that compare very closely to the Dow. In the 1980s, for example, the correlation between the Dow

Industrials and the S&P 500 was 0.997842. (Perfect correlation is 1.0.) Thus, the movements of the Dow and the S&P 500 were virtually identical in the 1980s. And this decade was no anomaly. Indeed, the Dow and the S&P 500 have had a correlation of 0.922 or better for every decade going back to the 1920s.

To be sure, periods will exist when one average will significantly outperform the other. Such a period has occurred over the last few years. Partly because of how the Dow is computed—I'll get to that in a moment—the Dow held up much better than the S&P 500 and other major market indexes during the meltdown beginning in 2000. In fact, through June 30, 2003, the 3-year average annual return of the Dow was –3 percent versus –11 percent for the S&P 500.

Bottom line: It's silly and, quite honestly, unproductive to argue whether the Dow is or isn't a valid market index. More than 100 years of the Dow being synonymous with "the market" answers that debate. What is important, from an investor standpoint, is taking advantage of the Dow's strengths and weaknesses to make money off the index. That's the aim of this book.

PRICE-WEIGHTED INDEX

An investor who wants to make money off the Dow needs to understand how the index is computed. Interestingly, the Dow is computed simply by adding up the per-share prices of all 30 components and dividing that sum by the divisor. (I'll explain the purpose of the divisor in a moment.)

For example, below were the stock prices of the 30 stocks in the Dow at the close of June 30, 2003:

AT&T $19.25

Alcoa $25.50

Altria Group $45.44

American Express $41.81

Boeing $34.32

Caterpillar $55.66

Citigroup $42.80

Coca-Cola $46.41

Disney $19.75

DuPont $41.64

Eastman Kodak $27.35

Exxon Mobil $35.91

General Electric $28.68

General Motors $36.00

Hewlett-Packard $21.30

Home Depot $33.12

Honeywell International $26.85

IBM $82.50

Intel $20.81   Microsoft $25.64
International Paper $35.73   Procter & Gamble $89.18
Johnson & Johnson $51.70   SBC Communications $25.55
J.P. Morgan Chase $34.18   3M $128.98
McDonald's $22.06   United Technologies $70.83
Merck $60.55   Wal-Mart Stores $53.67

To compute the index for June 30, 2003, you first add up all of the stock prices. On this particular day, that sum was $1,283.17. You then need to take that sum and divide by the divisor, which was 0.142799. The result? On June 30, 2003, the Dow closed at 8985. From this simple example, a sharp reader should glean two critical points about the Dow:

1. The Dow is a price-weighted index—that is, the highest-priced Dow stocks carry the most weight in the index.
2. The divisor, because it is less than 1, is really a multiplier. The fact that the divisor is really a multiplier has implications for the volatility of the index.

How the Dow is computed is a significant departure from most market indexes, including the S&P 500 and the Nasdaq Composite. Unlike the Dow, which is price weighted, these market indexes are market-cap weighted. A stock's market capitalization is the product of the stock's per-share price and the number of outstanding shares. For example, a company with a stock price of $100 with one million common shares outstanding has a market cap of $100 million. Thus, in market-cap–weighted indexes, the biggest companies (in terms of market capitalization) have the greatest influence. In the Dow, however, market cap is irrelevant. Stock price is what matters.

This may seem a bit, well, goofy. After all, companies can manipulate their per-share price in a variety of ways. A company can reduce its per-share price by implementing a stock split. For example, a stock that trades for $100 per share can become a $50 stock simply by splitting its shares 2-for-1. Conversely, a firm that wants a higher per-share price can implement a reverse stock split. That is, a $2 stock can become a $20 stock simply by implementing a 1-for-10 reverse stock split.

Under each split scenario, no real value is created. A company's worth (as well as a shareholder's investment) is not changed by the split. Thus, it would seem that market cap is a better measure of a company's market value. And that's true. However, remember when the Dow was developed back in the late 1800s, there were no Pentium processors. Michael Dell was still a long way from selling computers out of his college dorm room. The best tools Charles Dow had to compute his index were a pencil (or pen) and his brain. It is not surprising then that the methodology for computing the Dow was basically adding up the components' stock prices.

When you understand that the Dow is a price-weighted index, it makes sense that the index would hold up better during the technology meltdown at the beginning of this decade. The stocks that got creamed the most were the big market-cap giants. Those were the sort of stocks that carried the greatest weight in the S&P 500 and Nasdaq Composite. However, the tech meltdown did not impact the Dow nearly as much since the tech influence in the Dow was tempered as a result of the Dow being a price-weighted index.

The table below shows the divergence in performance between the price-weighted Dow Industrials and the market-cap–weighted S&P 500 and Nasdaq Composite from 2000 through 2002:

2000	Dow (–5 percent), S&P 500 (–9 percent), Nasdaq Composite (–39 percent)
2001	Dow (–5 percent), S&P 500 (–12 percent), Nasdaq Composite (–20 percent)
2002	Dow (–15 percent), S&P 500 (–22 percent), Nasdaq Composite (–31 percent)

As you can see, the tech implosion was especially brutal on the Nasdaq Composite. Indeed, a $1,000 investment at the end of 1999 became $336 by the end of 2002—a decline of 66 percent. But the Dow, partly because its tech components were price weighted rather than market-cap weighted, held up extremely well. Even today, Intel and Microsoft—two technology giants whose combined market caps total well over $400 billion—account for less than 4 percent of the Dow.

On the next page is a table showing the current 30 Dow stocks, along with their market caps. I also show the stock's weighting in the

Dow (price weighted) as well as the stock's weighting if the Dow were a market-cap–weighted index.

	Price (4/12/04)	Outstanding Shares (mil.)	Market Cap	Price Weight (%)	Market Cap Weight (%)
Alcoa	34.26	868.49	29,754.50	2.31	0.80
Altria Group	55.61	2,037.26	113,292.19	3.75	3.05
American Express	52.26	1,284.00	67,101.84	3.53	1.81
American International Group	76.77	2,608.45	200,250.48	5.18	5.39
Boeing	42.15	800.28	33,731.93	2.84	0.91
Caterpillar	83.75	343.76	28,790.06	5.65	0.78
Citigroup	52.06	5,156.95	268,470.78	3.51	7.23
Coca-Cola	50.85	2,441.53	124,151.90	3.43	3.34
Disney	25.70	2,013.30	51,741.81	1.73	1.39
DuPont	44.06	997.28	43,940.33	2.97	1.18
Exxon Mobil	43.11	6,568.00	283,146.48	2.91	7.63
General Electric	31.62	10,063.12	318,195.85	2.13	8.57
General Motors	46.77	562.00	26,284.64	3.16	0.71
Hewlett-Packard	22.63	3,052.00	69,066.76	1.53	1.86
Home Depot	36.46	2,273.00	82,873.58	2.46	2.23
Honeywell International	35.01	862.33	30,190.17	2.36	0.81
Intel	27.60	6,487.00	179,041.20	1.86	4.82
IBM	93.74	1,694.51	158,843.28	6.33	4.28
J.P. Morgan Chase	41.56	2,042.62	84,891.32	2.80	2.29
Johnson & Johnson	51.20	2,967.97	151,960.21	3.46	4.09
McDonald's	29.02	1,261.90	36,620.34	1.96	0.99
Merck	44.89	2,221.76	99,734.98	3.03	2.69
Microsoft	25.61	10,789.00	276,306.29	1.73	7.44
Pfizer	35.67	7,629.00	272,126.43	2.41	7.33

(continued on next page)

	Price (4/12/04)	Outstanding Shares (mil.)	Market Cap	Price Weight (%)	Market Cap Weight (%)
(continued from previous page)					
Procter & Gamble	107.12	1,292.40	138,441.88	7.23	3.73
SBC Communications	24.47	3,305.24	80,879.13	1.65	2.18
3M	83.62	784.12	65,567.86	5.64	1.77
United Technologies	89.19	514.06	45,849.19	6.02	1.23
Verizon Communications	37.57	2,767.76	103,984.74	2.54	2.80
Wal-Mart Stores	57.34	4,327.78	248,154.75	3.87	6.68

As you can see, some of the largest stocks, in terms of market capitalization, carry little weight in the Dow as a result of their modest stock prices. Conversely, Procter & Gamble, the highest-priced stock in the Dow as of April 12, 2004, and the one that accounts for the greatest weighting in the Dow (7 percent), would represent less than 4 percent of the Dow if the Dow were a market-cap–weighted index.

DOW AND STOCK SPLITS

Because the Dow is price weighted, stock splits in Dow components truly matter to the index's makeup. Indeed, a $100 Dow stock that splits 2-for-1 becomes a $50 Dow stock, reducing its weighting in the index by half.

While some market pros see this quirk in the Dow as a negative, you could argue that stock splits in Dow components tend to limit one or two stocks from becoming an overly large factor. In effect, stock splits provide a rebalancing mechanism for the Dow. Market-cap–weighted indexes don't have a mechanism for reducing a stock's weighting. With market-cap indexes, for example, a large-cap stock that continues to rise becomes an increasingly bigger and bigger factor in the index. Even if the stock splits, it doesn't affect the market cap. In contrast, the Dow has this self-correcting mechanism in the form of splits that helps reduce a component's weighting when it becomes particularly outsized.

When a stock splits in the Dow, the divisor adjusts to keep consistency in the average. This divisor also adjusts to reflect corporate actions, such as restructurings and spin-offs. It is important to know that with every stock split and corporate restructuring in the Dow, the divisor shrinks. Because of how the math works, a shrinking divisor leads to greater movement in the index in terms of absolute points.

For example, let's say every stock in the Dow on a certain day rises by 1 point. What does that mean for the index? Simple. A 1-point move in all 30 Dow stocks translates to a 221-point move in the index. (You come up with this number by taking the 30 points and dividing by the divisor, which at the time of this writing is 0.13561241.)

Now, let's say a few Dow stocks split, dropping the divisor to 0.11258. How does that impact the Dow? Let's return to our previous example. If all 30 stocks in the Dow increase by 1 point, adjusting for the new divisor, the gain in the Dow average on that day would be 266 points. Same advance in the stocks; bigger gain in the Dow average. Once you see the impact of the divisor on the Dow's computation, it should not be a surprise that the number of 100-point days in the Dow has surged in recent years.

BEATING THE DOW

Why am I spending so much time discussing the price-weighted nature of the Dow? Any investment strategy that uses Dow stocks to beat the index needs to take component prices into account. Let's say you've researched all of the Dow stocks and have selected the following 10 Dow stocks for a portfolio that you hope outperforms the index. (I've included the stock's price and weighting in the Dow as of April 12, 2004.):

IBM ($93.74; 6.3 percent weighting in the Dow)

3M ($83.62; 5.6 percent)

Procter & Gamble ($107.12; 7.2 percent)

Disney ($25.70; 1.7 percent)

Intel ($27.60; 1.9 percent)

United Technologies ($89.19; 6.0 percent)

Home Depot ($36.46; 2.5 percent)

Microsoft ($25.61; 1.7 percent)

Hewlett-Packard ($22.63; 1.5 percent)

SBC Communications ($24.47; 1.7 percent)

Now, as part of your strategy, you invest equal dollar amounts so that each stock in your 10-stock portfolio represents 10 percent of your portfolio. If you have $10,000 to invest in this portfolio, you would invest $1,000 in each of the 10 stocks.

Remember that what you are trying to do with this portfolio is outperform the Dow. Thus, the stocks that will have the greatest bearing on your ability to outperform the Dow are those stocks where the weightings in your portfolio (remember—each of your stocks carries a 10 percent weighting) differ dramatically from the stocks' weightings in the Dow.

You should see immediately that the stocks that will make or break your performance, relative to the Dow, are the lowest-priced stocks. Indeed, whether Procter & Gamble rises or declines 10 percent is fairly irrelevant to your portfolio's performance versus the Dow. Why? Because your portfolio's weighting in P&G of 10 percent is just slightly higher than P&G's weighting in the Dow. Thus, P&G's performance will have roughly the same impact on your portfolio as it will on the Dow.

What will matter big time to your portfolio performance is how Disney, Hewlett-Packard, and the other low-priced stocks perform. For example, if Disney rises 30 percent, its impact on the Dow (because of its meager 1.7 percent weighting in the Dow) will be rather trivial. It won't be trivial in your portfolio, however, given Disney's 10 percent weighting there.

Bottom line: Any investment strategy that purports to beat the Dow by investing in Dow stocks should have a consistent methodology for pinpointing opportunities among the Dow's lowest-priced stocks. Indeed, if you can make successful bets on the Dow's lowest-priced stocks (and, conversely, determine what high-priced Dow stocks are pricey and avoid or short them), you should consistently generate index-beating returns. That's because the impact of a low-priced stock in an equal-weighted portfolio will be much greater than a low-priced stock's impact on the Dow. That's how you can achieve a positive spread between the performance of your portfolio and the performance of the Dow.

Fortunately, my worst-to-first strategies, which call for investing in the worst-performing Dow stocks, usually isolate low-priced Dow stocks ready to rebound. And when these stocks rebound in equal-weighted portfolios, the results can be impressive. A good example was 2002. The five worst-performing Dow stocks that year were

Home Depot (–53 percent)

Intel (–50 percent)

McDonald's (–39 percent)

General Electric (–39 percent)

IBM (–36 percent)

Interestingly, four of these stocks—Home Depot (stock price at the end of 2002: $24.02), Intel ($15.57), McDonald's ($16.08), and GE ($24.35)—were trading at prices at the end of the year that were well below the average price of all Dow stocks (around $40). In fact, Intel and McDonald's were the two lowest-priced stocks in the Dow at the end of 2002. So how did these low-priced Dow Underdogs perform in 2003? Exceptionally well. Indeed, in 2003, Home Depot (+49 percent), Intel (+106 percent), McDonald's (+57 percent), and General Electric (+31 percent) all outpaced the 28 percent return in the Dow.

DOW—FERTILE HUNTING GROUND FOR MEAN-REVERSION STOCKS

As explained in Chapter 1, an important concept underlying my worst-to-first strategies is reversion to the mean. Over time, stock prices that have moved to extremes tend to revert to some equilibrium price range, a steady state.

To be sure, some stocks are more likely to exhibit mean reversion than others. This should come as no surprise. A stock that has been publicly traded for a few months does not have enough of a trading history to determine its long-run average price level, its equilibrium range. Also, a young company at the onset of a massive growth phase in revenue and earnings may have the ability to continually establish higher and higher "equilibrium" price ranges. Thus, the stocks that have the greatest tendency to exhibit mean-reversion characteristics have the following features:

- *Maturity.* What generally creates a new equilibrium range for a stock is some major shift in the growth curve for the company: either an acceleration of growth (creating a higher equilibrium price range) or a massive deceleration of growth (creating a lower equilibrium range). Mature companies have narrower swings in their growth rates over time. True, mature cyclical companies may experience big swings in revenue and earnings growth from year to year. But over time, the cycle highs and lows tend to be relatively consistent. In fact, most mature companies have a tendency to grow more or less at the rate of the general growth in the economy. Thus, when a mature company's stock swings to extreme levels (perhaps driven by a cyclical peak or trough in earnings and revenue), it is unlikely that the firm has entered a new growth era and it is not likely to sustain the extreme price for long. The stock price will tend to revert to its mean.

- *Financial strength.* In order to play the mean-reversion game with stocks, you want companies that have the ability to rebound, so you want companies that have been battle-tested through a variety of economic cycles. You also want companies with decent financial strength. I cannot stress this point enough. Bankruptcy is the bane of a mean-reversion strategy.

When it comes to these characteristics, it doesn't get any better than Dow stocks.

- *Maturity.* Dow stocks, on average, have been around for a long time. In fact, approximately two-thirds of the 30 companies currently in the Dow have roots that go back more than 100 years. The youngest company in the Dow—Home Depot—has been around for a quarter century. Clearly, Dow stocks are seasoned companies that have stood the test of time. And although recent additions to the Dow Index, such as Microsoft, Home Depot, Intel, Wal-Mart, and Johnson & Johnson, have punched up the Dow's growth potential, no investor is ever going to confuse the Dow with the Nasdaq when it comes to being the home of growth stocks. Even the companies that are perceived as growth stocks—

like Intel, Johnson & Johnson, Hewlett-Packard, and Microsoft—are probably past their primary growth years. Thus, with rare exceptions, it is extremely unlikely that Dow companies—especially the old-line, cyclical Dow stocks like GM, Boeing, and Caterpillar—will ever be able to jump their sustainable growth rates to the higher levels needed to support a dramatically higher equilibrium price range. Therefore, whenever Wall Street gets especially bullish or bearish on a Dow stock in a given year, chances are pretty good that the stock price will revert as the extreme optimism/pessimism that drove the stock out of its equilibrium range subsides.

- *Financial strength.* Dow stocks don't go bankrupt. Okay, maybe that statement needs to be toned down a bit. After all, Bethlehem Steel was once a Dow stock. Still, it is a rare occurrence when a Dow stock goes belly up. Because Dow stocks have good finances, they can buy the time needed for their stock prices to revert following declines.

BEATING THE DOW IS GOOD STUFF

The aim of this book is to show you how to beat the Dow. Some of you may wonder if the Dow is an index worth beating. After all, isn't the Dow filled with stodgy companies well past their prime? How hard is that index to beat?

The following table shows the Dow's performance over the last five years (ending June 30, 2003) versus other indexes and popular mutual funds. Note that the Dow has beaten all of them.

5-Year Annualized Return (Through June 30, 2003 [%])	
Dow	+1.9
S&P 500	−1.6
Russell 2000	+1.0
Fidelity Magellan	−1.0
Janus 20	−3.0

Bottom line: If you can consistently beat the Dow over an extended period of time, you will make a lot of money in the stock market and, in the process, outperform probably 7 out of 10 professional investors.

Now that you have been properly introduced to the Dow and understand why it is a great hunting ground for mean-reversion stocks, the next step is to get up close and personal with each of the 30 stocks currently in the Dow Jones Industrial Average.

3

WORST TO FIRST—
THE 30 DOW COMPONENTS

Perhaps the most exclusive club on Wall Street is the Dow Jones Industrial Average. Indeed, since 1931, only 68 different companies have gained membership.

Dow stocks at the end of 1931:

American Can, Allied Chemical, American Smelting, Bethlehem Steel, Borden, Chrysler, Eastman Kodak, General Electric, General Foods, General Motors, Goodyear, Hudson Motor, International Harvester, International Nickel, Johns-Manville, Liggett & Myers, Mack Trucks, National Cash Register, Paramount Publix, Radio, Sears, Standard Oil (N.J.), Standard Oil of California, Texas Corp., Texas Gulf Sulphur, U.S. Steel, Union Carbide, United Air Transport, Westinghouse Electric, Woolworth.

Additions (Note that a few stocks were in and out of the Dow during this time period—1931–1999):

1932—American Tobacco, Drug Inc., Procter & Gamble, Loew's, Nash Motors, International Shoe, IBM, Coca-Cola

1933—Corn Products Refining, United Aircraft

1934—National Distillers

1935—DuPont, National Steel

1939—American Telephone & Telegraph, United Aircraft

1956—International Paper

1959—Anaconda Copper, Swift & Company, Aluminum Company of America, Owens-Illinois Glass

1976—Minnesota Mining & Manufacturing

1979—IBM, Merck & Co.

1982—American Express

1985—Philip Morris, McDonald's

1987—Boeing, Coca-Cola

1991—Caterpillar, Disney, J.P. Morgan

1997—Travelers Group (now Citigroup), Hewlett-Packard, Johnson & Johnson, Wal-Mart Stores

1999—Microsoft, Intel, SBC Communications, Home Depot

2004—American International Group, Pfizer, Verizon

One reason for the exclusivity is that the keepers of the Dow make changes rather sparingly. For example, from 1940 through 1955, no changes were made to the index. And from 1956 through 1982, only nine changes were made, or an average of one every 3 years.

Changes in the Dow were a bit more common in the '90s. Indeed, in 1991, three changes were made to the Dow, followed by four in 1997 and four more in 1999.

The flurry of changes in the '90s—11 changes in all—represented a 37 percent turnover in the index. And this Dow makeover over the last 12 years has important implications for my worst-to-first strategies as well as other Dow-based investing strategies (most notably the "Dogs of the Dow" dividend-driven strategies, discussed in Chapter 8).

What has changed with the Dow? For starters, the index's performance has become less dependent on industrial stocks. If you look at the stocks that have been added since 1991—Caterpillar, Disney, and J.P. Morgan (1991); Travelers (later to become Citigroup), Hewlett-Packard, Johnson & Johnson, and Wal-Mart Stores (1997); Microsoft,

Intel, SBC Communications, and Home Depot (1999); and American International Group, Pfizer, and Verizon (2004)—only Caterpillar is a bona fide industrial, cyclical stock. The other companies are situated in more traditional growth sectors (health care, telecom, financial services, retailing, technology). This growth bent is one reason the Dow held its own during the go-go growth years in the late 1990s.

Still, I'm not trying to sell the Dow as a growth stock index. The Dow is and always will be represented by industry-leading companies that are probably past their best growth years but nevertheless have plenty to offer quality-seeking investors.

The following are reviews of the current 30 members of the Dow Jones Industrial Average. Each of the listings provides

- Stock symbol and exchange (NYSE—New York Stock Exchange; NASDAQ—Nasdaq market) on which the stock trades
- Corporate address
- Telephone number
- Web address
- Year of the company's origins
- Year the company first joined the Dow
- Current weighting in the Dow
- Value of $10,000 invested 5 years ago
- Business profile

I also provide my current take on the company as well as what I see in the firm's future. A stock chart is included for each company. Stock charts were created using MetaStock® software. MetaStock is a registered trademark of Equis International.

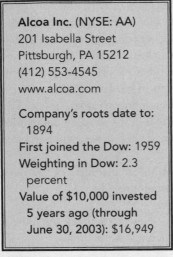

Alcoa Inc. (NYSE: AA)
201 Isabella Street
Pittsburgh, PA 15212
(412) 553-4545
www.alcoa.com

Company's roots date to:
1894
First joined the Dow: 1959
Weighting in Dow: 2.3
percent
**Value of $10,000 invested
5 years ago (through
June 30, 2003): $16,949**

BUSINESS PROFILE: Alcoa (formerly Aluminum Company of America) is the world's largest aluminum producer. Alcoa's roots date to 1894, when the firm was known as the Pittsburgh Reduction Company. In 1907, the company was renamed Aluminum Company of America.

Alcoa is a good company in a lousy industry. The aluminum industry over the years has been the classic feast-or-famine sector. Strong economic periods create strong earnings for Alcoa. And when that happens, Alcoa stock can perform quite well. Indeed, in 1999—the height of the technology and Internet boom—Alcoa was the best-performing stock in the Dow, posting an Internet-like stock return of 126 percent for the year. Not surprisingly, Alcoa gave back a lot of that gain in subsequent years as the economic slowdown took its toll on profits and the stock price.

Actually, if you look at the price history of Alcoa, the stock's cyclical nature comes through very clearly. The stock generally peaks in the $40s during boom times and bottoms in the mid- to upper teens.

It is not likely that Alcoa will extricate itself from the cycle of ups and downs that characterize the stock. True, aluminum demand is growing as a substitute for steel in some markets, notably the automotive and aerospace sectors. Still, the increased demand is not expected to be enough to bring a growth stock label back to Alcoa.

BOTTOM LINE: In portfolios in which I plan to buy and hold investments, I favor growth stocks. Alcoa is not a stock that I would be inclined to include in those portfolios. However, Alcoa is the type of stock that fits well with our worst-to-first strategy simply because it is the sort of stock, as is the case with many cyclical issues, that runs to extremes both on the upside and downside, creating excellent mean-reversion opportunities.

Alcoa (NYSE: AA)

Altria Group Inc.
(NYSE: MO)
120 Park Avenue
New York, NY 10017
(917) 663-5000
www.altria.com

Company's roots date to:
  1854
First joined the Dow: 1985
Weighting in Dow: 3.8
  percent
Value of $10,000 invested
  5 years ago: $15,220

BUSINESS PROFILE: Altria, formerly Philip Morris, is the world's largest cigarette producer and the nation's largest food company (Kraft Foods). Altria's roots date to 1854, when Philip Morris opened a single shop on London's Bond Street. The shop sold tobacco and "ready-made" cigarettes. In 1919, the firm was acquired by a U.S. company and incorporated in Virginia under the name Philip Morris & Co. The company introduced its popular Marlboro brand in 1924. Today, Philip Morris is a dominant player in the cigarette industry, shipping nearly one trillion cigarettes worldwide in 2002. The company's Kraft unit is the home of such popular brand names as Kraft, Nabisco, Oscar Mayer, Maxwell House, and Post. The company changed its name to Altria on January 27, 2003.

Few stocks have generated as much attention from Wall Street as Altria. Legal wranglings continually put the stock in the spotlight. In many respects, Altria makes a fascinating case study. This company sells a product the government says is harmful, yet the government cannot afford to eliminate the product or the company. Altria, via its tobacco settlement with the states, provides billions of dollars to the coffers of state governments. In fact, the agreement calls for the major cigarette manufacturers to pay the states a total of $246 billion over 25 years to settle lawsuits. That money is even more important now that many state budgets are under water.

Because state governments are now addicted to tobacco money, the firm has some interesting friends rushing to its defense every time a legal loss threatens to kill the goose laying those golden eggs. A court case in Illinois in 2003 is a classic example of how tobacco money and politics have joined to create interesting bedfellows.

Altria lost a class-action case heard in Illinois. The court awarded around $10 billion to the class. In order to appeal the case, the judge initially ruled that Altria would have to post a $12 billion bond. Altria said that posting such a huge bond could force the firm to file bankruptcy.

If you're a state treasurer, the last thing you want to hear coming from Altria is the word *bankruptcy*. Bankruptcy would likely put an end, at least temporarily and perhaps permanently, to the billions in payments to the states. Not surprisingly, many states were ready to intervene and argue for a much lower bond for the company. The judge agreed to reduce the size of the bond that Altria would have to post in order to appeal the case.

The Illinois case helps to bring into view what the future holds for Altria and shareholders. On the one hand, the firm will continue to be under siege from various legal corners. On the other hand, it is very clear that Altria has friends in high places with a vested interest in keeping the cash cow alive.

In such an environment, trying to value a company like Altria is very difficult. Sure, Altria is a cheap stock if you use traditional valuation metrics, such as price/earnings ratios and dividend yields. The 83.9 percent Kraft ownership alone accounts for a major chunk of Altria's stock price. When you put all of the pieces of Altria together, you get a company with a lot of earning power for a very low price tag.

Still, the stock is perennially cheap for a reason: The company is facing billions of dollars in litigation risk. Furthermore, Altria's business is growing increasingly competitive. The inelasticity of demand for Altria's products appears to have reached its breaking point. Discount tobacco competitors are gaining market share, and Altria will have to spend to defend its share. And while Kraft remains a major moneymaker, it, too, has had some rough sledding in growing its business.

To me, the most interesting aspect of Altria is its yield but not for reasons you might expect. Sure, the hefty yield (which was over 5 percent at the time of this writing) appears huge in today's low-interest-rate environment. But what strikes me about that yield is that it is the type of yield you see on public utility stocks. And that brings me to my point: Valuing Altria within a framework of a regulated utility might be a more valid way to view the stock. After all, the company is clearly in existence now as much to benefit state governments as it is to benefit Altria shareholders. And the Illinois case shows how quickly states will run to the aid of the company to keep it afloat.

If you view Altria as a sort of public utility, with shareholders allowed some "reasonable" rate of return, you can come to some interesting valuations. For example, valuing Altria may be more an exercise of determining what is a reasonable yield on the stock relative to other utility stocks, such as electric or natural gas utilities. If the typical electric utility stock is yielding around 6 percent, a similar 6 percent yield for Altria may not be all that out of the question. And once you determine what the proper yield should be for Altria, it is easy to back into the expected stock price (just take the annual dividend and divide by the projected yield, and that is the projected stock price).

BOTTOM LINE: I like Altria for its total return potential. True, the company is always one court case away from filing for bankruptcy. But a lot of constituencies have a vested interest in keeping the company in business. Thus, I would feel very comfortable buying these shares on bankruptcy fears. Interestingly, the growing litigation issue for the company might give the keepers of the Dow some pause as to whether these shares belong in the index. A switch to Anheuser-Busch, for example, would not be surprising at some point if the litigation heat gets turned up.

Altria Group (NYSE: MO)

American Express Co.
(NYSE: AXP)
200 Vesey Street
New York, NY 10285
(212) 640-2000
www.americanexpress.com

Company's roots date to:
 1850
First joined the Dow: 1982
Weighting in Dow: 3.5
 percent
Value of $10,000 invested
 5 years ago: $11,457

BUSINESS PROFILE: American Express provides travel-related and financial services. Travel-related services (charge cards, traveler's checks) account for roughly 75 percent of total revenue.

American Express is toughening out two major headwinds in recent years: slowing financial and travel-related markets. The company, best known for its charge-card business, has a big stake in financial markets via its financial services business. This segment has traditionally been a strong profit center for the company. However, the decline in the stock market impacted demand for financial services as well as profits coming from this sector.

American Express is also suffering from a slowdown in global travel as a result of soft worldwide economies, September 11, and, more recently, the SARS scare. Considering the major problem areas in its business lines, American Express has turned in strong results.

The bottom line, benefiting from cost controls, has managed to rise in the face of sluggish markets. That kind of resiliency should pay off handsomely once its businesses return to full strength.

Because of the company's reasonably strong track record over the years, American Express has generally avoided being among the worst-performing stocks in the Dow. Since it joined the Dow in 1982, the stock has been among the 10 worst-performing Dow stocks five times. And in four of those five times, the stock handily outperformed the Dow the following year.

BOTTOM LINE: I like American Express. I like the company's exposure to the financial services and travel industries. I like its focus on profits. I like the stock's long-term potential. I would feel comfortable owning the stock in a buy-and-hold portfolio and would welcome the chance to buy the stock in a worst-to-first portfolio.

American Express (NYSE: AXP)

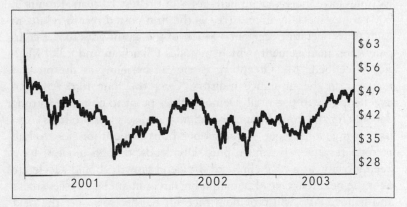

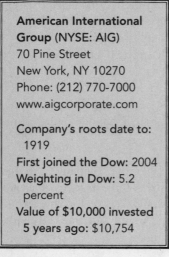

American International Group (NYSE: AIG)
70 Pine Street
New York, NY 10270
Phone: (212) 770-7000
www.aigcorporate.com

Company's roots date to:
1919
First joined the Dow: 2004
Weighting in Dow: 5.2 percent
Value of $10,000 invested 5 years ago: $10,754

BUSINESS PROFILE: American International Group (AIG) is a leading player in a variety of insurance and financial services markets.

American International, along with Pfizer and Verizon, are the newest members of the Dow, having been added to the index in April 2004. The company is a world leader in the insurance market. The company sells property and casualty insurance, along with individual and group life and health insurance. The firm also provides risk-management services and retirement and asset-management services.

AIG has a solid record of earnings growth. Indeed, per-share earnings have increased annually for 9 of the last 10 years. Results in 2003 were especially impressive, as the firm posted record results in each of its operating segments. Much of the credit goes to the company's top management, which includes Chairman and CEO Maurice Greenberg. Mr. Greenberg is viewed by many as the premier manager in the insurance industry. Over the long run, AIG has excellent growth potential. Demographics point to continued strong demand for the firm's insurance and financial-services products. And its growing global clout—foreign operations account for close to half of total revenue—is a huge plus. Dividends, though modest, have been growing at a nice clip, and dividend growth should accelerate over the next few years. I remain a big fan of financial services stocks and believe AIG will provide a nice lift to the Dow over the next several years. I would have no problem owning AIG in a long-term portfolio.

BOTTOM LINE: AIG traded for more than $103 per share in 2000. I would expect these shares to return to that level over the next year or two. I view the stock as a solid long-term pick.

American International Group (NYSE: AIG)

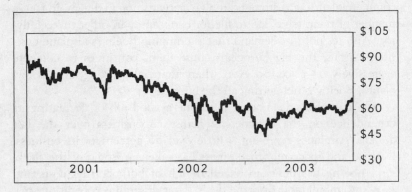

Boeing Co. (NYSE: BA)
100 North Riverside Plaza
Chicago, IL 60606
(312) 544-2000
www.boeing.com

Company's roots date to:
1916
First joined the Dow: 1987
Weighting in Dow: 2.8
percent
Value of $10,000 invested
5 years ago: $8,309

BUSINESS PROFILE: Boeing is the world's largest commercial airplane maker. The company also has sizable defense-related and satellite operations.

William Boeing made his first fortune not in airplane building but in trading forest lands around Grays Harbor, Washington. Boeing moved to Seattle in 1908 and, 2 years later, went to Los Angeles for the first American air meet. He became intrigued with the science of aviation. Boeing began building seaplanes in his boathouse in 1915 and incorporated his new airplane company, Pacific Aero Products Company, in 1916. World War I was the opportunity Boeing's company needed. The company's seaplanes enjoyed demand from the Navy, launching the fledgling company on its way.

When the company first started, there weren't a lot of buyers of airplanes. Ironically, that situation kind of exists today. Your customers can't buy if they don't have any money, and Boeing's primary commercial airline customers aren't exactly rolling in dough. In fact, a number of them have had to file for bankruptcy in order to keep flying. And it's not just demand that is crimping Boeing's airplane business. Airbus, the big European consortium, continues to compete aggressively on price. So even when financially strong airlines buy planes, Boeing is not getting all the business.

On the plus side, Boeing has done a good job of decreasing its dependence on the commercial aerospace business over the last decade. Airplanes represent a little over 50 percent of its business. Defense and space-related business has taken up some of the slack. And Boeing has done an excellent job of both cutting costs and avoiding unprofitable airplane deals. That disciplined operating style should serve it well when demand improves in the airline sector.

That, of course, is the big question for Boeing: When will demand improve? A pretty convincing argument could be made that the near-term future of commercial aviation is all about shrinking rather than growing, making do with what planes you have and avoiding the huge costs of buying new aircraft. In that world, Boeing may find its airline business under continuing pressure.

Now, Boeing's stock reflects a lot of the bad news surrounding the airline sector. These shares, which peaked at nearly $70 in 2000, declined 40 percent in 2001 and 13 percent in 2002 before rebounding in 2003.

BOTTOM LINE: Big price swings are nothing new to these shares. The low 20s have historically been a good place to buy the stock. I wouldn't be surprised if Boeing, following a few soft years, posts decent price gains in 2004.

Boeing (NYSE: BA)

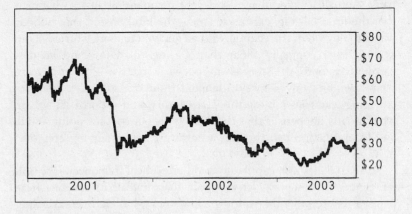

Caterpillar Inc.
(NYSE: CAT)
100 NE Adams Street
Peoria, IL 61629
(309) 675-1000
www.cat.com

Company's roots date to:
  1890
First joined the Dow: 1991
Weighting in Dow: 5.6
  percent
Value of $10,000 invested
  5 years ago: $12,151

BUSINESS PROFILE: Caterpillar is the world's largest producer of earth-moving equipment. Caterpillar was formed from the 1925 merger of Holt Manufacturing Company and C.L. Best Tractor Company. Holt's "Caterpillar" track-type tractors were used in 1915 by the Allies in World War I. Caterpillar produced its first diesel tractor in 1931.

Whenever I think of Caterpillar, I go back to when I was comanager of the Strong Dow 30 Value fund in the late '90s. Caterpillar would disappoint Wall Street with its quarterly earnings number but reaffirm its earnings estimate for the year. In essence, what the firm was saying was that despite this crappy quarter that just occurred, we believe things are on track for the year. Of course, things were not on track for the year, which is why the stock was a fairly chronic disappointer on Wall Street.

The problem with Caterpillar isn't so much that it is a bad company. Actually, Caterpillar is a decent company. It just so happens that the firm sells big, expensive stuff—the kind of stuff that nobody wants to buy when the economy is bad and you're more worried about keeping your company afloat than buying the latest and greatest earthmover. Sure, the story always seems attractive—lots of government spending on highways, demand from overseas as a result of emerging countries joining the 21st century, and so forth. However, what usually happens is that the story stalls out at some point—state and federal budgets go through a downturn and emerging countries blow up.

Caterpillar is also captive to another cyclical influence—the dollar. Since the company derives more than half of its revenue from overseas (Caterpillar, like a lot of Dow stocks, has big overseas exposure), the ups and downs of the dollar versus foreign currency can create wide swings in profitability. Not surprisingly, Caterpillar's stock price has experienced wide swings over the years, although a clear pattern tends to emerge. For example, you would have made a lot of money buying Caterpillar in the 30s and selling in the high 50s over the last 8 years.

Could Caterpillar break out of this trading range? I suppose it could. The stock traded in the teens in the early '90s before launching into a solid 5-year run in the mid-'90s. But remember that the stock's price advance accompanied arguably the longest period of economic growth in the nation's history. Although I would love to see that growth streak resurrected, the odds of that happening, at least in the next few years, seem slim. Thus, I can't get too excited about Caterpillar's appreciation prospects.

BOTTOM LINE: Caterpillar has been among the Dow's 10 worst performers four times since it joined in 1991. In three of those four instances, the stock beat the Dow the next year. Given the stock's usual big swings and given its nice advance in 2003—the stock pushed into the 70s during the year—I wouldn't be surprised to see the stock revert to the mean and underperform the Dow, possibly by a wide margin, in 2004.

Caterpillar (NYSE: CAT)

Citigroup Inc. (NYSE: C)
399 Park Avenue
New York, NY 10043
(212) 559-1000
www.citigroup.com

Company's roots date to:
1812
First joined the Dow: 1997
Weighting in Dow: 3.5
percent
Value of $10,000 invested
5 years ago: $16,173

BUSINESS PROFILE: Citigroup is a leading banking and financial services firm. The company's Salomon Smith Barney unit is a leading brokerage and investment banking company. You would be hard-pressed to find a financial services company as dominant as Citigroup. The firm has a strong global presence, with offices in over 100 nations and more than 200 million customer accounts worldwide. Per-share profits have advanced nicely in recent years, despite a variety of economic woes and Wall Street scandals that have plagued the financial services sector. True, the stock has shown periodic volatility, such as in 2002 when these shares traded from a high of $52 to a low of $24. Fortunately for shareholders, Citigroup has shown the ability to come back strongly from such downturns.

When investing in companies, we sometimes forget that we invest in people. On that score, Citigroup's Sanford Weill is considered one of the best minds on Wall Street. Weill has a history of creating share-holder value, and I expect to see that continue. I would expect Citigroup to at least keep pace with the Dow over the next several years. The company should continue to spread its wings globally, and the scandals that have hurt the stock in recent years should be a distant memory 24 months from now.

BOTTOM LINE: Citigroup has been one of the Dow's 10 worst-performing stocks only once (1998) since it joined in 1997. (The stock joined as Travelers that year, changing its name to Citigroup in 1998.) Interestingly, in 1999 (the year after Citigroup's poor showing), the stock returned 70 percent, far outpacing the Dow's 27 percent return that year. I consider Citigroup to be a core holding for long-term investors. The issue has excellent long-term prospects. For that reason, I am not holding my breath that these shares will be among the Dow's worst performers anytime soon.

Citigroup (NYSE: C)

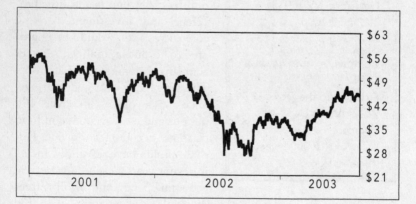

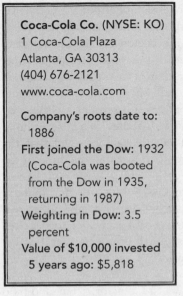

Coca-Cola Co. (NYSE: KO)
1 Coca-Cola Plaza
Atlanta, GA 30313
(404) 676-2121
www.coca-cola.com

Company's roots date to:
1886
First joined the Dow: 1932
(Coca-Cola was booted
from the Dow in 1935,
returning in 1987)
**Weighting in Dow: 3.5
percent**
**Value of $10,000 invested
5 years ago: $5,818**

BUSINESS PROFILE: Coca-Cola is the world's largest producer of soft drinks. Brands include Coke, Diet Coke, Sprite, Barq's, TAB, Fresca, PowerAde, Minute Maid, Hi-C, and Fruitopia. We can thank an Atlanta pharmacist, John Pemberton, for Coke. In 1886, in search for a cure for headaches, Pemberton created a caramel-colored liquid. When he was done, he carried the concoction a few doors down to Jacobs' Pharmacy. Here the mixture was combined with carbonated water. Pemberton's bookkeeper, Frank Robinson, named the mixture Coca-Cola. In the first year, the company sold about nine glasses of Coke a day.

Unfortunately for Pemberton, he didn't realize he was sitting on a fizzy gold mine. He sold the company to Asa Candler over the course of 3 years (1888 to 1891) for about $2,300. Today, every 10 seconds some 126,000 people reach for one of the company's brands. Unfortunately, not enough investors have been reaching for Coca-Cola stock in recent years. After peaking at $89 in 1998, the stock has been on a fairly steady decline.

The problem with Coca-Cola is that it is a busted growth stock—that is, it stopped growing. Wall Street doesn't like to see growth stocks (that sport growth stock–like price/earnings ratios) stop growing. The stocks usually get creamed. Coca-Cola is a good example of what can happen to a busted growth stock. After showing huge earnings growth through the '80s and the early part of the '90s, Coca-Cola hit a wall. Earnings were flat to lower for 5 years beginning in 1997. Not surprisingly, once the growth stopped, so did the stock price.

It is worth noting, however, that despite the stock getting hammered in recent years, it is difficult to call Coca-Cola a cheap stock. True, the company still has one of the strongest brand names in the world, which is certainly worth something. And the company's return on invested capital, although down considerably from the early '90s, still ranks high relative to most of corporate America.

Still, at the end of the day, how much growth can you expect to see in beverage consumption—3 percent per year? Five percent per year? I know that Coca-Cola is more than just soft drinks. The firm has Dasani and Evian water, PowerAde sports drink, and Minute Maid orange juice. Still, the consumer market is saturated with beverage brands. And while Coca-Cola is always touted as a great international story, the last few years have clearly demonstrated that the demand curves overseas are as vulnerable to weakness as those in the United States.

Investors often point to one major stockholder—Warren Buffett's Berkshire Hathaway, which owns 8 percent of the company—as reason enough to own these shares. However, I can't get too excited about the company and doubt that its growth prospects over the next few years will justify its still-rich valuation.

BOTTOM LINE: I am not a buyer of Coca-Cola for a buy-and-hold account. If it got obliterated in a particular year, it is the sort of stock that would be appealing as a worst-to-first stock. Beyond that, however, the stock doesn't interest me.

Coca-Cola (NYSE: KO)

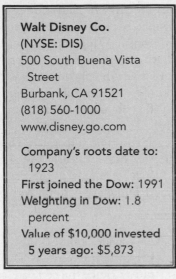

Walt Disney Co.
(NYSE: DIS)
500 South Buena Vista
  Street
Burbank, CA 91521
(818) 560-1000
www.disney.go.com

Company's roots date to:
  1923
First joined the Dow: 1991
Weighting in Dow: 1.8
  percent
Value of $10,000 invested
  5 years ago: $5,873

BUSINESS PROFILE: Walt Disney is a major entertainment company with businesses in television broadcasting (ABC, ESPN), movies, and theme parks. Disney was founded in 1923 in the rear of a small office occupied by a Los Angeles real estate company. In 1928, Mickey Mouse was born. (Did you know that Mickey's original name was Mortimer? Walt Disney's wife felt the name was too stuffy, so Walt changed the name to Mickey.) What put the company on the map was its 1937 full-length animated feature, *Snow White and the Seven Dwarfs*. In 1955, Disney opened its first theme park, Disneyland, in Anaheim, California. The company expanded its theme-park business when it opened Florida's Disney World in 1971.

Is there any magic left in Disney? Judging from the stock's performance in recent years, skeptics abound. That wasn't always the case. Disney posted a higher high every year but one from 1991 through 2000, topping out at nearly $44 per share in 2000. The stock benefited from the go-go growth markets of the '90s and investors being drawn to sexy stories. And make no mistake—the Disney story had sex appeal. Strong brand names. Big opportunities to expand overseas. Attractive media and entertainment assets. What's not to like?

Unfortunately, what happened to Disney was that its bottom line began to buckle, and the firm has yet to see profits recover to previous levels. To be sure, Disney has been fighting considerable headwinds. First, it was 9/11 and its impact on travel in the United States. Second, the slowdown in the economy crimped travel and entertainment spending. Third, the SARS scare affected global travel, including to the United States. Fourth, the war in Iraq curbed advertising, impacting Disney's network broadcasting business.

Of course, the big question is whether Disney can rekindle support on Wall Street. I happen to think that it can. Indeed, Disney still has the sort of consumer brand name that is the envy of many corporations. Its theme-park business should bounce back with an improved economy and reduced fears concerning terrorism. While its ABC unit remains a laggard, history has shown that networks can turn around rather quickly with just a few hit shows (witness the phoenix-like act of CBS in recent years). On the film side, the company has been generating more hits than misses lately, and that should continue going forward.

What is most appealing about Disney at this time is its price. The shares trade at a hefty discount to their 2000 high of nearly $44 per share. Although a return to that level does not seem to be in the cards over the next 12 to 24 months, I do expect Disney to perform better in line with an improving market.

BOTTOM LINE: Disney is a bull-market stock. If you are optimistic about the overall market, Disney would be a stock to own. Interestingly, Disney is not a stranger to the worst-to-first strategy. Since the company's inclusion in the Dow in 1991, the stock has been among the 10 worst-performing Dow stocks in 5 years.

Walt Disney (NYSE: DIS)

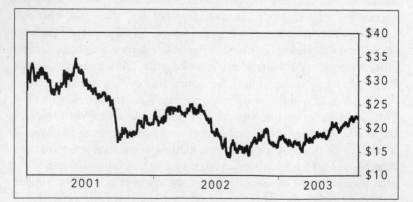

DuPont (E.I.) de Nemours & Co.

(NYSE: DD)
1007 Market Street
Wilmington, DE 19898
(302) 774-1000
www.dupont.com

Company's roots date to:
  1802
First joined the Dow: 1935
Weighting in Dow: 3.0
  percent
Value of $10,000 invested
  5 years ago: $6,443

BUSINESS PROFILE: DuPont is among the largest chemical companies in the world. DuPont's origins date back to 1802, when Frenchman E. I. du Pont built his first powder (as in gunpowder) factory in the United States. Today, DuPont has an extremely broad line of chemicals and materials. For example, the firm is the world's largest maker of fibers, with such brand names as Stainmaster (carpets) and Lycra (spandex).

This chemical company tried to remake itself into a growth company in the 1990s and early 2000s by focusing on its pharmaceutical business. However, profits were weak, and the firm ended up dumping its drug products to focus on specialty chemicals. This remake looks like it may take. Indeed, DuPont is making headway in specialty materials, which is a better place to be than simply low-margin commodity chemicals. Profits should rebound over the next few years, especially as the economy improves.

DuPont traded in the 70s in 1999 and 2000, so it has plenty of ground to recoup. Still, while I'm not a huge fan of chemical stocks, I like DuPont's prospects among the more cyclical stocks in the Dow.

BOTTOM LINE: DuPont has been a frequent visitor to the worst-to-first list, having been among the Dow's 10 worst performers in 4 of the last 10 years. The stock truly has been a trader's dream stock in recent years, consistently topping out in the high 40s and bottoming in the low 30s. Although I wouldn't be surprised to see the stock jump out of this range over the next few years, I don't think the 70s are in the cards anytime soon.

DuPont (NYSE: DD)

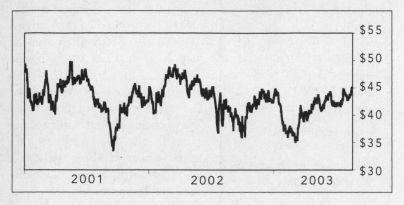

Exxon Mobil Corp.

(NYSE: XOM)

5959 Las Colinas Boulevard
Irving, TX 75039
(972) 444-1000
www.exxonmobil.com

Company's roots date to:
1882
First joined the Dow: 1928
(as Standard Oil Company
of New Jersey)
Weighting in Dow: 2.9
percent
Value of $10,000 invested
5 years ago: $11,288

BUSINESS PROFILE: Exxon Mobil is the largest publicly traded oil company in the world. The firm serves customers in some 200 countries. Exxon Mobil is the reunion of two companies that were once part of John D. Rockefeller's Standard Oil Trust that was formed in 1882. In 1911, the U.S. Supreme Court ordered the dissolution of the trust, resulting in the spin-off of 34 companies, including Standard Oil Company of New Jersey (the predecessor to Exxon) and Standard Oil Company of New York (the predecessor to Mobil). In 1999, Exxon and Mobil merged to form Exxon Mobil.

Exxon is one of the best-managed companies in the Dow. In an era when most megamergers have led to disappointing results and little reward for shareholders, Exxon's marriage with Mobil has been a huge success. The company has done a masterful job of wringing cost savings from the deal.

I call Exxon Mobil an easy hold stock. The stock is not likely to show up at the top of the leader board in any given year. However, these shares also tend to hold up relatively well during tough market environments. One reason for the resiliency is Exxon's broad-based business portfolio, which allows the firm to fend off weakness in any one geographic area.

To be sure, Exxon's bottom line is linked tightly to the price of oil, and oil prices have fluctuated significantly in recent years. Those fluctuations have caused swings in the company's profits. However, the stock's performance has been amazingly consistent over the years.

BOTTOM LINE: As evidence of the stock's fairly consistent performance over the years, these shares have been among the Dow's 10 worst performers only twice since 1990. I have owned Exxon Mobil for several years and have rarely been disappointed. The company combines decent appreciation potential with an above-average yield. I feel comfortable owning these shares and would recommend them for any portfolio.

Exxon Mobil (NYSE: XOM)

General Electric Co.
(NYSE: GE)
3135 Easton Turnpike
Fairfield, CT 06431
(203) 373-2211
www.ge.com

Company's roots date to:
  1876
First joined the Dow: 1896
Weighting in Dow: 2.1
  percent
Value of $10,000 invested
  5 years ago: $10,350

BUSINESS PROFILE: GE is truly a conglomerate. The firm has a multitude of businesses ranging from financial services (GE Capital), medical equipment, and broadcasting (NBC television network) to airplane engines, utility plants, appliances, and specialty materials. The common thread between these seemingly unrelated businesses is that GE usually maintains either the first or second position in every market. This is not by coincidence. Over the years, especially under the leadership of Jack Welch, GE made the decision to either be a leader or to exit the industry.

General Electric has the distinction of being the only stock currently in the Dow that was among the original 12 Dow stocks when the index was initiated in 1896. However, GE has not been continuously in the Dow. The company was removed from the Dow in 1898. It returned to the Dow in 1899 only to be removed in 1901. (Yes, there was quite a lot of movement in Dow stocks in the index's early years.) GE rejoined the Dow for good in 1907.

The founder of GE was one of the greatest inventors of all time, Thomas Alva Edison. By 1890, Edison organized his various businesses and research ventures into Edison General Electric Company. A number of Edison's early businesses are still part of GE today, including lighting, transportation, and medical equipment. GE Capital's origins date to the 1930s, when the finance company helped consumers purchase GE appliances during the Depression.

GE's tenure in the Dow has been, for the most part, a profitable one for longtime shareholders. The 1990s were especially lucrative for shareholders. Indeed, GE rose from a split-adjusted price of $7 in 1993 to $60 in 2000. The company had become a "must have" among institutional investors, and that demand, coupled with the company's solid track record of growth, drove these shares higher.

More recently, the landscape has changed for the company. Jack

Welch is no longer at the helm, giving way to Jeffrey Immelt in late 2001. While Immelt inherited a strong company, he also inherited a lousy economy. The slowdown in the economy in recent years has hurt GE's more economically sensitive businesses, which in turn has slowed down growth in the bottom line. Given that GE had sported price/earnings ratios in the high 20s and even 30s and 40s, these shares had a lot to give back when growth slowed, falling to $21 in 2003.

There is some doubt as to whether GE will be able to jump-start its growth. Bears on the stock point out the many acquisitions and the complexity of the company's operating structure as providing lots of cover to work accounting magic to show big profit gains. The problem is whether the revenue line will be able to grow again.

I think these are valid concerns. However, I also believe GE is a well-managed company that will make the right decisions going forward. Thus, I am optimistic about a turnaround for these shares. However, investors should not expect a big rebound much before 2005, as profits over the next 12 months are likely to show only moderate growth.

BOTTOM LINE: I expect GE to at least match the Dow over the next several years. The stock has not been a frequent visitor to worst-to-first portfolios. GE was among the Dow's 10 worst performers in 2002. You have to go back to 1988 to find the last time the stock was among the top 10 losers in the Dow. Interestingly, following its slump in 2002 (the stock fell 38 percent), these shares rebounded smartly in 2003, rising 30 percent.

General Electric (NYSE: GE)

General Motors
(NYSE: GM)
300 Renaissance Center
Detroit, MI 46265
(313) 556-5000
www.gm.com

Company's roots date to:
1897
First joined the Dow: 1915
(GM was dropped in
1916, returning to the
Dow to stay in 1925)
Weighting in Dow: 3.2
percent
Value of $10,000 invested
5 years ago: $7,786

BUSINESS PROFILE: General Motors is the world's largest auto manufacturer. Cyclical companies don't change their stripes, no matter how much investors argue that they do. I say this because over the years Wall Street has forgotten that General Motors is a cyclical stock. And it usually happens right at the top.

For example, go back to 1999 and 2000. GM was earning more than $8 and $6 per share, respectively. The company was getting high marks for improving the quality of its cars, introducing improved styles, and becoming a worthy competitor to foreign automakers. The firm also had a kicker in its ownership of Hughes, the owner of DirecTV. This is a different General Motors, said the GM bulls—one with a fast-growing satellite business and an improved position in an auto industry that seemed to defy skeptics by showing steady demand for much of the 1990s.

So what happened? What always happens with General Motors—the economy slows, demand subsides, profits sink, and the stock follows suit. Per-share profits went from over $6 in 2000 to less than $2 in 2001. The stock fell from nearly $95 in 2000 to $39 in 2001 to $30 in 2002.

While some of GM's problems are related to the economy, some seem to be self-inflicted. For example, to spur demand in recent years, U.S. automakers have resorted to aggressive financing plans, including 0 percent financing. Such deals did keep buyers buying, but it also had two negative effects. First, the company's financing arm lost out on big profits. Second, the price discounting and easy financing dollars conditioned buyers to buy only when deals were good. This same pitfall occurred in the airline sector, with discounting turning all buyers into, well, cheapskates, buying tickets at low prices.

The drop in the stock market, which played havoc on many companies' pension liabilities, also hurt GM. Keep in mind that GM, as is the case with a lot of the Dow stocks, has huge liabilities in the form of pension and health care obligations. And funding these billions of dollars of liabilities requires the stock market to do well. When the stock market does not do well, GM is on the pan to kick in more money to meet its obligations. These costs, coupled with legacy health care costs for retired workers, are a huge drag on GM. In fact, at the end of 2002, GM had an underfunded pension liability of more than $22 billion and a health care liability of $51 billion. Those are big, big numbers. GM will be forced to somehow account for these liabilities, which could present some challenges if the economy and stock market remain weak.

In some respects, the type of environment we had in the 1990s—rising stock prices and a strong economy—was the perfect climate for GM. What we are seeing now, however, is a more traditional bust cycle. If you look at previous bust cycles for GM, usually there is a dividend cut—the firm cut its dividend from $3 per share in 1990 to $0.80 in 1993—and red ink on the bottom line. GM has maintained its $2 dividend since 1997, but investors should not regard the dividend as a lock going forward.

BOTTOM LINE: GM dipped below $30 in the early '90s, so investors should be slow to call a bottom in these shares. Having said that, history has shown that these shares provide the perfect worst-to-first stock—a cyclical stock with a history of huge price swings.

General Motors (NYSE: GM)

Hewlett-Packard Co.
(NYSE: HPQ)
3000 Hanover Street
Palo Alto, CA 94304
(650) 857-1501
www.hp.com

Company's roots date to:
1939
First joined the Dow: 1997
Weighting in Dow: 1.6
percent
Value of $10,000 invested
5 years ago: $9,513

BUSINESS PROFILE: Hewlett-Packard is a major player in a variety of technology segments, from personal computers and printers to computer services and servers. Hewlett-Packard was the first true garage success story in the tech sector. Bill Hewlett and Dave Packard developed their first product—an audio oscillator used by sound engineers—in a Palo Alto garage. One of Hewlett-Packard's first customers was Disney, which purchased eight oscillators to develop and test a sound system for the movie *Fantasia*. The company has come a long way from those early days. Today, the firm produces everything from electronic equipment to a variety of printers and computers.

You would be hard-pressed to find a single acquisition in the technology sector that has rewarded investors over the last decade. Hewlett-Packard is attempting to buck this trend. The firm acquired Compaq Computer in May 2002. You might recall that many investors were not all that excited about a Compaq–Hewlett-Packard marriage, including family members of the company founder. However, with her job on the line, CEO Carly Fiorina kept pushing until the merger was a done deal.

While Fiorina displayed impressive political and leadership skills to get shareholders to approve the deal, her greatest challenge still lies ahead: making the merger work. On this count, I am not so optimistic. Rare is the case when you can take two underperformers in one sector—and both Hewlett-Packard and Compaq played second fiddle to Dell in the PC market—and create a single powerhouse. I don't think that is going to be the case this time around, either. Dell remains the dominant leader in the PC market, with everyone else playing for second place. And playing for second place in this cutthroat market usually means little profits and lousy profit margins.

To be sure, Hewlett-Packard has not had a great environment in which to test its newfound muscles. Technology spending in recent years has been weak, and it is tough to see much of an improvement in tech spending before 2005. Furthermore, Dell's move into printers can only hurt Hewlett-Packard's leadership in this segment. Cost cutting has helped H-P's bottom line in recent quarters, but that will only take things so far.

The technology sector kind of got this image as a true growth sector in the 1990s, when corporate America went on a huge spending spree, in part, to ready for the Y2K conversion (remember that?). Also, money was cheap, capital was everywhere, and the mantra in the corporate world was to spend, spend, spend on the latest and greatest tech equipment. In recent years, companies have been forced to take inventory of what they got for their tech spending and are coming to the conclusion that perhaps much of the spending was wasteful. As hard as it might be to believe, tech stocks at one time were considered fairly cyclical creatures. Indeed, I can remember Dell and other techs sporting price/earnings ratios of just 10 before the Internet exploded and demand for computers soared. I think you are going to see technology stocks continue to lose that cache as growth stocks and become more cyclical performers again. That will not help the Hewlett-Packards of the world. The firm will also suffer from the difficult task of trying to register consistent growth on a revenue base now exceeding $70 billion.

BOTTOM LINE: Hewlett-Packard is now like so many Dow stocks: a cyclical performer that becomes an attractive rebound play when it periodically gets mauled by Wall Street. The stock fell all the way to $10 in 2002 after reaching nearly $78 in 2000. I don't see these shares at $70 anytime soon. However, I would feel comfortable playing the worst-to-first strategy with the stock should the opportunity arise.

Hewlett-Packard (NYSE: HPQ)

Home Depot Inc.
(NYSE: HD)
2455 Paces Ferry Road NW
Atlanta, GA 30339
(770) 433-8211
www.homedepot.com

Company's roots date to:
 1978
First joined the Dow: 1999
Weighting in Dow: 2.5
 percent
Value of $10,000 invested
 5 years ago: $12,226

BUSINESS PROFILE: Home Depot is a leading retail chain providing building supply/home improvement products to contractors and do-it-yourself markets. Home Depot is the youngest of all the current Dow stocks. The firm, founded in Atlanta, Georgia, in 1978, fairly quickly became the world's largest home improvement retailer. The rapid growth was a major engine behind the stock's swift rise. Indeed, the stock climbed from a split-adjusted price of $7 in 1992 to $70 at the beginning of 2000. Unfortunately, Home Depot's stock price began to develop some leaks. The stock fell 33 percent in 2000. After rebounding slightly in 2001, the stock collapsed in 2002, plummeting 53 percent. That decline in 2002 gave Home Depot the prize as the Dow's worst performer for the year.

A slowdown in the company's same-store sales hurt Home Depot's stock price. The retailing sector is one of those areas where what truly matters to Wall Street is not gross revenue. After all, a retail chain can boost revenue simply by adding new outlets. To get a gauge on the health of the underlying retail concept, investors focus on same-store sales—that is, how are sales growing at outlets that have been in existence for at least 12 months. It is this metric that was the cause of Home Depot's downfall. While profits and overall revenue have continued to climb for the company, same-store sales growth declined and even turned negative in recent years.

What ails Home Depot? The competition is pretty strong in this part of the retail segment. Lowes Companies has been carving into Home Depot's leadership position. Also, regional players, such as Menards, have been competing aggressively for market share. Home Depot is losing out to what appears to be consumer fatigue for warehouse shopping formats. The firm is trying to address this issue by improving the attractiveness of its outlets, but such improvements take time.

What the firm does have going for it is a still-strong brand name, which is worth a lot in the retailing game. Since Home Depot was the worst performer in 2002, you would expect the stock to come back nicely in 2003. And that has been the case. Indeed, the stock posted a total return of 49 percent in 2003 versus a 28 percent gain in the Dow.

Of course, the big question is: Does Home Depot have much more on the upside? Admittedly, righting the ship in the retail sector is not easy—just ask Sears, Kmart, J.C. Penney, and any of the many wounded retailers over the last decade. Still, Home Depot is in a part of the retail sector that should continue to experience good demand. And the firm's back-to-basics move should help restore shoppers.

BOTTOM LINE: I don't think you'll see Home Depot at the price levels of the late 1990s anytime soon. I do believe, however, that these shares offer at least average appreciation potential going forward.

Home Depot (NYSE: HD)

Honeywell International Inc.
(NYSE: HON)
101 Columbia Road
Morristown, NJ 07962
(973) 455-2000
www.honeywell.com

Company's roots date to: 1885
First joined the Dow: 1925 (joined that year as Allied Chemical; became Honeywell International in 2002 after merger of AlliedSignal and Honeywell)
Weighting in Dow: 2.4 percent
Value of $10,000 invested 5 years ago: $6,662

BUSINESS PROFILE: Honeywell is a leading provider of aerospace, automation and controls, specialty materials, and transportation equipment. Honeywell kind of back-doored its way into the Dow via the merger of AlliedSignal and Honeywell in 1999. AlliedSignal, which had been a longtime resident of the Dow (it entered the index as Allied Chemical in 1925), actually was the acquirer of Honeywell. But the merged company chose to use the Honeywell moniker after the merger.

Honeywell's largest business is aerospace, accounting for around 40 percent of sales. In this segment, Honeywell manufactures propulsion engines, avionic controls, and aftermarket services. The firm's automation and controls unit (around one-third of total sales) produces home and building control and safety systems and facility equipment management. Transport and power services and specialty materials make up the remainder of sales. In transport and power services, Honeywell produces turbochargers, truck brakes, and consumer products. Specialty materials include polymers, plastics, and fibers.

Honeywell stock has taken a nosedive since the marriage of AlliedSignal and Honeywell. These shares plummeted from more than $68 per share in 1999 to $19 in 2002. Profits have been hurt by a soft economy and industry-specific issues, such as a downturn in commercial aerospace. Honeywell will get some relief from an improved economy. However, the company lacks a real catalyst for growth, which means these shares will likely become much more cyclical over the next 10 years.

I don't consider Honeywell a lock for remaining in the Dow. A fair amount of overlap exists in terms of businesses between Honeywell and such Dow components as General Electric and United Technologies. And Honeywell's lackluster performance in recent years hasn't exactly given the Dow keepers lots of reasons to keep the company.

BOTTOM LINE: Given the big price decline over the last 4 years, I wouldn't be surprised if Honeywell turns in a decent performance in 2004. Having said that, I can't get too excited about owning these shares in a long-term account. I do expect the stock to be a fairly frequent visitor to worst-to-first portfolios (the stock was the ninth-worst performer in the Dow in 2002) over the next few years.

Honeywell International (NYSE: HON)

Intel Corp.
(NASDAQ: INTC)
2200 Mission College
  Boulevard
Santa Clara, CA 95052
(408) 765-8080
www.intel.com

Company's roots date to:
  1968
First joined the Dow: 1999
Weighting in Dow: 1.9
  percent
Value of $10,000 invested
  5 years ago: $11,368

BUSINESS PROFILE: Intel is the world's largest producer of microprocessors for personal computers. The firm controls approximately 80 percent of the market. Intel has been branching out into chips for other technology applications, including telecom, mobile communications, and game consoles. Intel joined the Dow in 1999. The company, along with fellow Dow newcomer Microsoft, represent the first two Nasdaq-traded stocks ever in the Dow.

I kind of chuckle whenever I hear Wall Street say that Intel's competitors have the company on the ropes. Sure, Advanced Micro Devices occasionally comes out with a chip that gets lots of praise. But technology is truly a game about innovation, and nobody has the horses in the semiconductor business to innovate like Intel. The firm spends more than $4 billion per year on research and development. To put that number in perspective, Intel spends more on research and development each year than chief competitor Advanced Micro Devices reports in revenue.

That research and development spending is fueled by a pristine balance sheet. Intel has very little debt and cash assets in the billions of dollars. Such strong finances give the company lots of flexibility in terms of either creating products in-house or buying products via acquisitions.

To be sure, even a company as strong as Intel cannot fend off negative industry trends. And that has been the story for the company in recent years. The tech meltdown and the slowdown in tech spending by corporations hampered profits. Intel's per-share profits fell to $0.51 per share in 2002 after peaking at $1.53 per share at the height of the tech craze. The bottom line has been improving over the last four quarters or so, but it may take another 12 to 24 months or more before Intel sees its profits return to pre-2001 levels.

Intel was not immune to the selling in tech stocks, with these shares falling from $75 in 2000 to $13 in 2002. The big question for Intel, as is the case with other tech companies, is: When will the good times return? On the one hand, it could be argued that what happened in the 1990s was truly the best of times for the group. You had a strong economy spurring unprecedented demand from both consumers and corporations. You had a dramatic drop in the cost of computers, which fueled demand. You had the emergence of the Internet, which gave virtually everyone a reason to own a computer. And you had constant innovation, which reshaped the demand curve given that everyone had to have the latest and greatest computer and computer chips. Quite honestly, it is difficult to foresee such an environment returning anytime soon. Nevertheless, there will be the next big thing someday, and Intel has the financial firepower, research expertise, and management know-how to make sure it gets a big piece of whatever comes next.

BOTTOM LINE: I own Intel in a buy-and-hold account and expect these shares to outperform the Dow over the next several years. And if this stock is ever among the Dow Underdogs, you would do well to jump on it. Actually, Intel was the second-worst performer in the Dow in 2002, down 50 percent. And, in true worst-to-first fashion, the stock was the best performer in the Dow in 2003; up 106 percent.

Intel (NASDAQ: INTC)

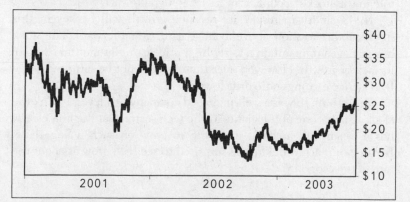

International Business
Machines Corp.
(NYSE: IBM)
New Orchard Road
Armonk, NY 10504
(914) 499-1900
www.ibm.com

Company's roots date to:
1911
First joined the Dow: 1932
(IBM was removed from
the Dow in 1939 and rein-
stated in 1979)
Weighting in Dow: 6.3
percent
Value of $10,000 invested
5 years ago: $14,783

BUSINESS PROFILE: IBM is a world leader in computer and technology products. The company has a huge computer services division in addition to its computer hardware and software products. IBM's roots date back to 1911 and the merger of the International Time Recording Company, the Computing Scale Company, and the Tabulating Machine Company to form the Computing-Tabulating-Recording Company. C-T-R was renamed International Business Machines in 1924.

IBM is the poster child for boosting profits via cost cutting and share buybacks. Per-share profits have gone from $1.23 in 1994 to around $4 in recent years. What is interesting, however, is that while profits have been growing, revenues have been flat to lower. In fact, IBM's 2002 revenue of $81.2 billion was below 1998 levels and only slightly above 1997 revenue. The inability to grow revenue is one reason Wall Street has cooled a bit on the stock in recent years. The tech meltdown, of course, also played a role in the stock's decline from its 1999 high of nearly $140.

IBM's ability to restart its revenue growth will be key in this stock's ability to show above average gains going forward. The stock has managed to maintain a fairly high price/earnings multiple despite its lack of growth. However, over time I would not be surprised to see IBM's price/earnings ratio drift lower.

Yes, I think IBM is a well-managed company. And, yes, I think the stock remains one of the giants in the tech sector. But the firm clearly has a tough task at hand in trying to grow on such a large base. Because of that, I wouldn't be surprised to see IBM grow at about the rate of the economy.

Among Dow technology stocks, I would much rather own Microsoft or Intel than IBM. Still, I don't expect IBM to be a dreadful performer going forward.

BOTTOM LINE: IBM has been among the Dow's 10 worst performers twice since the end of 1993. My guess is that these shares will match the Dow over the long term.

International Business Machines (NYSE: IBM)

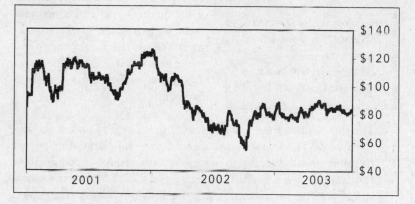

**Johnson & Johnson
(NYSE: JNJ)**
One Johnson & Johnson
  Plaza
New Brunswick, NJ 08933
(732) 524-0400
www.jnj.com

Company's roots date to:
  mid-1880s
First joined the Dow: 1997
Weighting in Dow: 3.5
  percent
**Value of $10,000 invested
  5 years ago:** $14,938

BUSINESS PROFILE: Johnson & Johnson is a broad-based health care company. The firm has consumer products (Tylenol), pharmaceuticals (Procrit), medical technology products (Cypher drug-coated stents), and orthopedics (DePuy).

Johnson & Johnson may not be at the top of the leader board every year. But the stock usually does well in up markets and holds up relatively well in down markets, making it one of the better long-term investments in the Dow. The secret of Johnson & Johnson's success is threefold:

1. The firm is one of the few companies that actually makes acquisitions work. The firm's modus operandi is to supplement its potent research and development program with strategic acquisitions. Biotechnology has been the more recent focus of the firm's acquisition activity. In recent years, the firm purchased ALZA and Centocor. In 2003, Johnson & Johnson followed up those deals with the purchase of Scios, another biopharmaceutical firm. I expect J&J to continue its acquisitive ways in the future. It certainly has the financial firepower for acquisitions.
2. Johnson & Johnson has a knack for turning out revolutionary products. A good example is the firm's drug-coated stent. J&J's Cypher-coated stent is used to prop open clogged blood vessels. One problem with traditional metal stents is restenosis, or the reclogging of vessels after they have been opened. Restenosis happens in up to 30 percent of traditional stents. J&J's coated stent, however, has shown to be effective in eliminating restenosis in up to 90 percent of cases. The firm hopes to generate annual revenue of $3 billion or more from this product.
3. The company's broad-based exposure in the health care segment helps shield it from downturns in any one area. The company is a

powerhouse in pharmaceuticals, with such popular drugs as Remi-
cade for rheumatoid arthritis and Procrit for anemia. In consumer
health care markets, J&J sells such popular products as Band-Aids,
Monistat, Neutrogena, Reach, Stayfree, and Tylenol. In medical
technology, J&J sells a variety of surgical instruments and diagnos-
tic products.

Johnson & Johnson has one of the most consistent track records
among the Dow stocks. Revenue has increased for 70 consecutive
years. And the firm has boosted its dividend annually for 41 consecutive years.

Of course, nothing can grow forever, which is one of the concerns
with Johnson & Johnson. The firm generates annual sales of roughly
$40 billion, making it much tougher to show big growth on such a siz-
able revenue base. Nevertheless, while growth may slow a bit going
forward, my guess is that investors should still do just fine owning this
blue-chip stock.

BOTTOM LINE: Since entering the Dow in 1997, Johnson & Johnson has
only once (2003) been among the 10 worst-performing Dow stocks.

Johnson & Johnson (NYSE: JNJ)

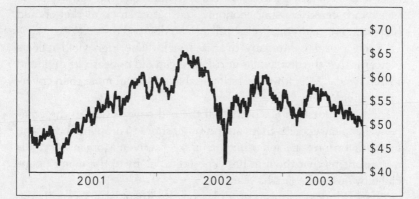

J.P. Morgan Chase & Co.
(NYSE: JPM)
270 Park Avenue
New York, NY 10017
(212) 270-6000
www.jpmorganchase.com

Company's roots date to:
  1838
First joined the Dow: 1991
Weighting in Dow: 2.8
  percent
Value of $10,000 invested
  5 years ago: $8,009

BUSINESS PROFILE: Formed by the December 2000 merger of J.P. Morgan and Chase Manhattan, J.P. Morgan Chase is the second-largest banking institution in the country. J.P. Morgan Chase ran into all sorts of problems in recent years. For starters, the downturn in the financial markets hurt the firm's investment banking and underwriting businesses. Second, Morgan was a party to the research scandal that rocked Wall Street and damaged reputations. Morgan also had its share of unwanted exposure to the Enron fallout. These factors led to the stock getting decimated, from a high of $67 in 2000 to a low of $15 in 2002.

On the positive side, Morgan still has reasonably strong banking franchises that should generate profits. Also, the major factors crimping the stock should have a finite life. True, the company will need help from the overall market in order for its investment banking and asset management businesses to return to normal. However, when the headwinds cease, a rising economy and better stock market should help improve credit quality as well as loan demand.

One appeal is Morgan's oversized yield. The high yield reflects concerns that the dividend is at risk. Morgan did not earn its dividend in 2001 and 2002. However, estimates have Morgan more than covering its dividend by 2004.

The big question is whether all the bad news is out on the company. People wonder if there are yet other shoes to drop, including the lingering Enron issue and other credit issues. Given Morgan's size, it is not surprising that the firm has exposure to many of the major financial blowups of the last 10 years.

I see Morgan as more of a play on the financial markets. If the stock market is lackluster, it will be hard for these shares to muster much interest. In contrast, more robust debt and equity markets will help investors forget about the company's past sins.

BOTTOM LINE: Morgan was the seventh-worst performer in the Dow in 2002, falling 31 percent. Not surprisingly, the stock rebounded nicely in 2003, up 60 percent. These shares traded for more than $67 in 2000. Still, the easy money has been made in the stock, in my opinion. I prefer Citigroup among Dow banking issues.

J.P. Morgan Chase (NYSE: JPM)

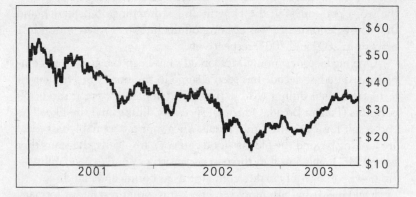

McDonald's Corp.
(NYSE: MCD)
One McDonald's Plaza
Oak Brook, IL 60523
(630) 623-3000
www.mcdonalds.com

Company's roots date to:
1955
First joined the Dow: 1985
Weighting in Dow: 1.9
percent
Value of $10,000 invested
5 years ago: $6,626

BUSINESS PROFILE: McDonald's is the world's largest fast-food restaurant company.

Ray Kroc didn't set out to become a restaurant mogul. Rather, he mortgaged his home and invested his entire life savings to become the exclusive distributor of a five-spindled milk-shake maker called the Multimixer. In an attempt to find a big market for his mixer, Kroc went to California to visit Dick and Mac McDonald's restaurant. What Kroc initially saw was a big market for his mixer if the McDonald's boys decided to expand. When the brothers wondered who they could get to open restaurants for them, Kroc (so the story goes) answered, "What about me?" Kroc opened his first McDonald's in Des Plaines, Illinois, in 1955. First day revenue—$366.12.

McDonald's daily revenue is a bit higher today—around $42 million. But that revenue number has had a tough time growing, which has been a problem for the stock. Indeed, McDonald's has left a bad taste in the mouth of investors in recent years. The stock was one of the worst performers in the Dow in 2002 (dropping 38 percent), and that lousy performance was coming off declines of 15 percent and 21 percent in 2000 and 2001, respectively.

One big factor crimping McDonald's has been the growth in competitors. The last decade has seen a surge in the number of restaurant formats—casual dining (Ruby Tuesday's, Applebees, etc.), sandwich concepts (Panera Bread, Quiznos), specialty dining, and the like. The end result has been that individuals who want a reasonably fast meal are looking beyond the old fast-food category. Ironically, the traits that served McDonald's well in the past—consistency and dependability—are now spun by McDonald's competitors as boring and bland.

McDonald's has attempted to break into other restaurant formats. But success has been limited. In particular, the company's acquisition of Boston Market yielded no obvious benefits. Another factor that has hurt McDonald's has been a slowdown in its major growth engine: overseas business. Between Mad Cow scares, SARS, and a global economic slowdown, McDonald's international business has not met expectations.

To address its problems, McDonald's is putting the brakes on expansion plans. The company has dropped the number of new outlets. The firm is also concentrating on improving the quality of its food as well as its service. Time will tell whether these moves can help revenue numbers improve.

On the positive side, McDonald's financial position remains decent. Thus, McDonald's has time on its side. It may boil down to shrinking its way to greatness—that is, foregoing a growth strategy and streamlining the number of outlets to focus on its most profitable restaurants. This strategy is often difficult for former growth companies like McDonald's to pursue. However, restless investors may force the company's hand on this matter.

BOTTOM LINE: It is tough to build an appetite for these shares. True, McDonald's has had some bad luck on the international front that could take a turn for the better over time. McDonald's was a solid worst-to-first performer in 2003, rising 56 percent after cratering in 2002. However, the big gains have returned the stock to a level that may provide some upside resistance over the next 12 months. I think the stock will be an average performer at best over the next few years.

McDonald's (NYSE: MCD)

Merck & Co. (NYSE: MRK)
One Merck Drive
P.O. Box 100
Whitehouse Station, NJ
  08889
(908) 423-1000
www.merck.com

Company's roots date to:
  1889
First joined the Dow: 1979
Weighting in Dow: 3.0
  percent
Value of $10,000 invested
  5 years ago: $9,996

BUSINESS PROFILE: Merck & Co. is one of the largest drug companies in the world. Major brand names include Zocor (cholesterol), Mevacor (cholesterol), Vioxx (antiinflammatory), Crixivan (HIV), Fosamax (osteoporosis), Prilosec (antiulcer), and Singulair (asthma and allergy). Big pharmaceutical companies, such as Merck, have been in Wall Street's sick bay in the last few years. Investors are concerned about a number of issues affecting the group:

- Generic competition and a political climate that seemingly favors generics over brand-name drugs
- Limited blockbuster product introductions
- Worries over increased regulation of health care costs
- Patent expirations for big-selling products

Merck's bottom line has been feeling the pinch. After steady growth in the bottom line through the 1980s and 1990s, results stalled in 2002. While profits are getting back on the growth track, growth rates will not likely match the heady gains of decades past.

On the plus side, Merck's valuation is relatively modest compared to the past. That Wall Street does not appear to be expecting much from the stock puts Merck in the position to surprise analysts.

I have been a fan of Merck over the years. The firm has a reputation for being well managed, and its research and development program has historically been strong. However, industry headwinds can take down even good companies. Still, demographics in this country will continue to fuel strong demand for health care. Further, Merck's yield and dividend growth should remain a cut above the average Dow stock. I would feel comfortable owning Merck in a long-term portfolio and taking advantage of any opportunities should these shares be among the Dow Underdogs in any given year.

BOTTOM LINE: Merck has been among the Dow's 10 worst performers five times since 1992. In three of those five times, the stock handily beat the Dow the following year.

Merck & Company (NYSE: MRK)

MRK

BUSINESS PROFILE: Microsoft is the world's largest provider of software. Microsoft, along with Intel, were the first stocks to cross over into the Dow from the Nasdaq market. Up until these two technology giants joined the Dow in 1999 the index had maintained its exchange purity; no stock from the Nasdaq had ever been part of the Dow. However, the keepers of the Dow could not ignore one of the world's most valuable companies (Microsoft's market cap is $280 billion).

> **Microsoft Corp.**
> (NASDAQ: MSFT)
> One Microsoft Way
> Redmond, WA 98052
> (425) 882-8080
> www.microsoft.com
>
> Company's roots date to:
> 1975
> First joined the Dow: 1999
> Weighting in Dow: 1.7
> percent
> Value of $10,000 invested
> 5 years ago: $9,494

Interestingly, Microsoft has not exactly been a boon to the Dow since becoming a member. In fact, these shares are down considerably from their 1999 high of $60. Suffice it to say that the tech wreck of recent years did not leave Microsoft unscathed. Fortunately, investors now have the opportunity to buy these shares, not exactly at bargain prices but at greatly reduced levels.

I'm a bull on the stock for several reasons. For starters, the strong usually get stronger during weak industry periods. Microsoft, with much of the antitrust hullabaloo behind it, is now in the position to flex its muscles. And the firm has been doing just that, building strong market positions in everything from the Internet (via its MSN unit) to server and database software, to gaming consoles (its Xbox). These new ventures have allowed the company to continue to grow its revenue despite the tough technology markets. Profits have continued to move higher as well, and I expect that trend to continue.

One factor that concerns analysts—ironically—is that Microsoft has accumulated a cash war chest of $60 billion. Microsoft decided in early 2003 to share its largess by initiating a dividend, and in 2004, the firm is paying out a special dividend of $3 per share. However, the company's huge cash flow will keep that cash asset base swelling. Obviously, the big question is: What is Microsoft going to do with all of that money? Sure, the firm could make acquisitions, or at least try to make acquisitions. But how likely is it that the Department of Justice is going to allow its poster child for monopoly power to buy another company, especially a big company. And Microsoft only has so many growth opportunities in which to invest. The company can buy back more stock, which is a real possibility if the stock remains depressed. Or, another likelihood is that it could generate some hefty dividend increases.

Actually, I find it a bit ironic that Wall Street is worrying over a company that has too much cash. It seems what has been a bigger problem for firms in recent years is not having enough cash. I remain confident that Microsoft's top management—all of which have a huge interest in seeing the stock price get back to former levels—will use its cash haul wisely to enhance shareholder value.

Owning technology stocks has been a fairly adventurous exercise in recent years. That's why I believe the investors who want tech exposure going forward will preference the giant, well-financed players in the field. That preference for size, quality, and financial strength works to the advantage of Microsoft.

BOTTOM LINE: I own Microsoft and believe these shares will outpace the Dow over the long term. Microsoft has been a Dow Underdog twice since being added in 1999, including in 2003.

Microsoft (NASDAQ: MSFT)

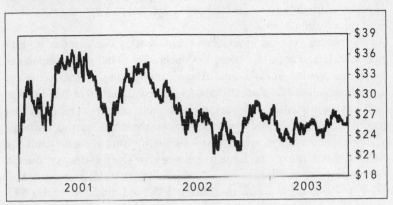

Pfizer, Inc. (NYSE: PFE)
235 E. 42nd Street
New York, NY 10017-9393
(212) 573-2323
www.pfizer.com

Company's roots date to:
1849
First joined the Dow: 2004
Weighting in Dow: 2.4
percent
Value of $10,000 invested
5 years ago: $9,967

BUSINESS PROFILE: Pfizer is a leading pharmaceutical company.

Pfizer has a stable of well-known pharmaceutical products. Brand names include Zoloft (antidepressant), Lipitor (cholesterol), Zyrtec (antihistamine), Celebrex (rheumatoid arthritis), and Viagra (impotence). Of course, the key to a successful drug company is its ability to generate a steady stream of products. And that requires big research and development spending. Pfizer spends more than $7 billion per year on R&D spending. Such hefty spending is one reason the company's medicines library includes approximately 2 million compounds. In addition, Pfizer's product pipeline holds more than 160 projects in development and over 300 projects in discovery research in 18 therapeutic areas. This R&D scope is unmatched in the industry.

Also unmatched in the industry is the company's financial firepower. Impressive cash flow, coupled with its growing bottom line, has afforded Pfizer the ability to make important acquisitions in the sector. The strong finances have also allowed the company to raise its dividend on a regular basis.

Big pharmaceutical stocks have not exactly been stellar investments of late. Pfizer has been no exception. The stock underperformed the market in 2003, and investor interest in the stock remains, to be nice, subdued. True, drug stocks face a number of headwinds, from an unfavorable political climate and patent expirations to generic competition and limited blockbuster drugs in the industry pipeline. Nevertheless, when you look at the long-term demand for drugs in this country, you have to believe that the top drug producers will continue to see their revenue and profits expand. Pfizer was a $50 stock in 1999, a $49 stock in 2000, a $46 stock in 2001, and a $42 stock in 2002. Thus, these shares have quite a bit of catching up to do.

BOTTOM LINE: Despite the sector's near-term problems, I'm confident investors will eventually return to quality drug stocks like Pfizer. I expect these shares to outperform the market over the next 3 to 5 years.

Pfizer (NYSE: PFE)

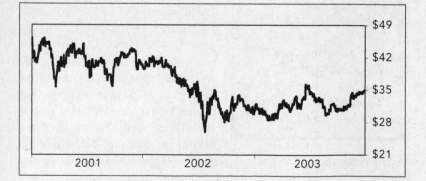

Procter & Gamble Co.
(NYSE: PG)
1 Procter & Gamble Plaza
Cincinnati, OH 45202
(513) 983-1100
www.pg.com

Company's roots date to:
1837
First joined the Dow: 1932
Weighting in Dow: 7.2
percent
Value of $10,000 invested
5 years ago: $10,774

BUSINESS PROFILE: Procter & Gamble is a leading consumer products company. Brands include Crest toothpaste, Tide detergent, Pampers diapers, and Charmin toilet paper. William Procter and James Gamble started making and selling soap and candles in 1837. On August 22 of that year, they formalized the relationship, each of them putting up $3,596.47. The partnership was signed on October 31, 1837. Since then, P&G has grown to a giant multinational firm with more than 100,000 employees and annual revenue of more than $40 billion.

Procter & Gamble has done what few firms its size have been able to accomplish: rekindle growth. Indeed, for much of the 1990s, Procter & Gamble was really a financial engineering play—that is, the company did a decent job of manufacturing profit growth by cutting costs. But organic revenue growth was limited.

Obviously, a company can only play the cost-cutting game for so long. At some point, you need revenue growth to drive earnings. Unfortunately for a lot of consumer products companies, revenue growth has been tough to achieve. That was the case for Procter & Gamble, too, under previous CEOs. The situation changed when current CEO Alan Lafley entered the picture in 2000. By focusing on new products—for example, the company's Crest White Strips—Procter & Gamble has been able to resume growing revenue at a 5 to 7 percent rate. Wall Street has responded to the better volume and profit growth. Indeed, Procter & Gamble posted positive total returns of 3 percent and 11 percent in 2001 and 2002, respectively, when the Dow showed losses.

BOTTOM LINE: Procter & Gamble's recent success does raise the bar for future quarters. And a company of P&G's size will find it increasingly difficult to grow. Still, I think there's enough gas in the tank to drive steady growth over the next few years. And that growth should be enough to drive these shares higher. I own P&G in a buy-and-hold portfolio and don't expect to see these shares among the Dow's losers over the next few years.

Procter & Gamble (NYSE: PG)

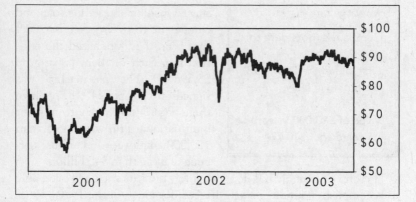

SBC Communications Inc.
(NYSE: SBC)
175 E. Houston
San Antonio, TX 78205
(210) 821-4105
www.sbc.com

Company's roots date to:
1875
First joined the Dow: 1999
Weighting in Dow: 1.7
percent
Value of $10,000 invested
5 years ago: $7,301

BUSINESS PROFILE: SBC Communications was one of the seven regional Bell companies spun off from AT&T at the end of 1983. The company, the second-largest local telephone service provider, serves customers in 13 states: California, Illinois, Michigan, Ohio, Texas, Missouri, Indiana, Connecticut, Wisconsin, Kansas, Arkansas, Oklahoma, and Nevada. The firm also has operations in the cellular market via its 60 percent–owned Cingular joint venture.

SBC is a relative newcomer to the Dow, joining the index just 5 years ago. The firm is also one of the youngest companies in the Dow, formed at the end of 1983 as part of the breakup of AT&T. However, the company's roots go back more than 100 years to the beginning of the Bell telephone system. Since the AT&T breakup, SBC has expanded its operations significantly. The firm bought fellow Baby Bell Pacific Telesis in 1997 and followed that up with the purchase of another Baby Bell, Ameritech, in 1999.

After peaking at nearly $60 in 1999, the stock went on a slide, falling to under $20 in 2002. The telecom blowup and poor profits were responsible for the massive selling in these shares. Wall Street continues to look at telecom stocks with a somewhat jaundiced eye. Prices on virtually every type of phone service—long distance, cellular, and even local—have been flat to lower. Too much competition and capacity remain in the system. Demand has not risen much, if at all, in recent years. That has made profit growth basically a function of cost cutting. SBC Communications, like all telecom players, has been cutting costs. But cost cutting can only go so far. At some point, you need revenue growth to spur long-term earnings growth.

On the plus side, SBC is one of the most financially sound players in this sector, which puts the firm in the position to buy assets on the cheap. One long-rumored target of telecom companies is AT&T. The problem is that regulators may look twice at any deals because of SBC's size.

The main appeal of these shares is the yield. The dividend appears well covered by earnings, and I suspect SBC Communications will even increase the dividend modestly going forward.

BOTTOM LINE: I have liked SBC Communications over the years. Having said that, it is difficult to see a catalyst that will fuel long-term growth for the company. Thus, my guess is that SBC will be a relatively flat performer going forward.

SBC Communications (NYSE: SBC)

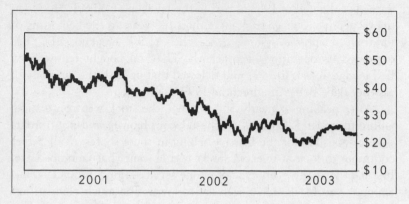

3M Co. (NYSE: MMM)
3M Center
St. Paul, MN 55144
(651) 733-1110
www.mmm.com

Company's roots date to:
1902
First joined the Dow: 1976
Weighting in Dow: 5.6
percent
Value of $10,000 invested
5 years ago: $17,600

BUSINESS PROFILE: 3M is a diversified manufacturer of more than 50,000 industrial and technology-based products. Under the direction of former General Electric exec W. James McNerney, 3M is trying to become a growth company again. But converting a $16 billion firm situated in many mature markets into a growth engine will be no small feat. It would appear, however, that the firm is off to a good start. Indeed, volume gains in recent quarters have been surprisingly strong for the company.

True, what has helped earnings jump sharply higher over the last few years has been cost cutting, and that game has probably been played out. Still, 3M is moving aggressively into more growth markets. The health care sector, in particular, seems to be a focus of the company's plans. 3M has some interesting products in this segment, including immune response modifiers that stimulate the body's immune system to help fend off infections.

3M's mature businesses throw off lots of cash flow, which gives the firm the ammunition to make acquisitions. And 3M has been fairly active in the acquisition market. My guess is that you'll see the company make a bold acquisition move over the next 12 months, probably in the health care or technology sectors.

My problem with 3M has been one of valuation. Wall Street is putting a lot of faith in McNerney's ability to make the right moves to keep the growth streak alive. At the time of this writing, 3M was sporting a price/earnings ratio that rivaled Microsoft's, which I'm not sure is warranted.

BOTTOM LINE: I'm not a big bull on 3M. I think the stock has had its big run, and future gains will be more measured.

3M (NYSE: MMM)

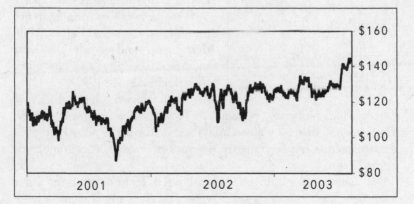

> **United Technologies Corp.**
> (NYSE: UTX)
> United Technologies
>   Building
> Hartford, CT 06101
> (860) 728-7000
> www.utc.com
>
> **Company's roots date to:**
> 1853
> **First joined the Dow:** 1930
> (the stock was removed
> from the Dow in 1932,
> returned in 1933, removed
> again in 1934, and
> returned to stay in 1939)
> **Weighting in Dow:** 6.1
> percent
> **Value of $10,000 invested
> 5 years ago:** $16,398

BUSINESS PROFILE: United Technologies operates in four main areas: aerospace (Pratt & Whitney); heating, ventilating, and cooling (Carrier); elevators (Otis); and flight systems (Sikorsky helicopters). United Technologies has a fairly similar profile to another Dow company, Honeywell. Of the two, however, United Technologies is the superior company. Despite the economic slowdowns and softness in many of its markets, United Technologies has not failed to boost profits in recent years. Other factors that separate the company from its peers are its solid financial position, strong brand names (Carrier, Otis), and steady dividend increases (the dividend has more than doubled since 1995).

Wall Street has taken notice of the relative resiliency of United Technologies' business model. Though these shares are down from their 2001 peak of more than $87, the damage has not been nearly as severe as at some other companies in the Dow.

To be sure, it is difficult to see United Technologies growing a whole lot over the next several years. The company is mature, large (nearly $30 billion in annual revenue), and cyclical. Sure, the firm could buy growth via acquisitions, but Wall Street has shown that it is not all that enamored with companies trying to buy growth. More likely, United Technologies will use its cash flow to raise its dividend and buy back stock.

BOTTOM LINE: Since 1992, United Technologies has been among the Dow's 10 worst performers only twice: 1992 (down 8 percent) and 1997 (up 12 percent in what was a good year for most Dow stocks). In the years immediately following the rough showing, the stock moved sharply higher (up 33 percent in 1993 and 52 percent in 1998).

United Technologies (NYSE: UTX)

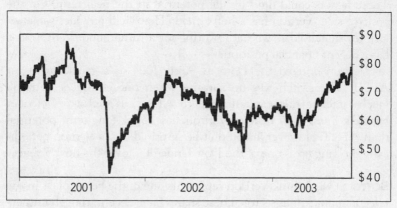

Verizon Communications (NYSE: VZ)
1095 Avenue of the
  Americas, 36th Floor
New York, NY 10036
(212) 395-2121
www.verizon.com

Company's roots date to:
  1875
First joined the Dow: 2004
Weighting in Dow: 2.5
  percent
Value of $10,000 invested
  5 years ago: $10,113

BUSINESS PROFILE: Verizon is one of the largest telecommunications firms in the world.

Verizon was formed in June of 2000 with the merger of Bell Atlantic and GTE. Bell Atlantic was one of the original seven "Baby Bells," which were spun off from AT&T at the beginning of 1984.

Verizon has leading positions in a variety of telecommunications markets. The company is one of the largest providers of wireline and wireless communications in the United States. Verizon is also the largest directory publisher in the world. The firm's international presence includes wireline and wireless communications operations and investments, primarily in the Americas and Europe.

Verizon faces a lot of the same pressures that have crimped most communications providers—tough pricing and plenty of competition. Those factors could limit upside potential in the near term. On the positive side, Verizon has a hefty yield. That yield provides some solace for shareholders who are waiting for a turnaround. Verizon also has a decent financial position.

Verizon entered the Dow in April 2004 as a replacement for AT&T. The switch was no surprise when one considers Verizon's much larger market capitalization to AT&T, as well as its broader business lines. I do believe Verizon has better long-term potential than AT&T. However, I wouldn't be surprised to see Verizon periodically showing up as one of the Dow Underdogs over the next 5 years.

BOTTOM LINE: I think Verizon represents one of the better plays in the telecommunications sector. These shares have decent, though unspectacular, total-return potential. However, I don't consider the stock a "must-have" holding for a long-term, buy-and-hold portfolio.

Verizon Communications (NYSE: VZ)

Wal-Mart Stores Inc.
(NYSE: WMT)
P.O. Box 116
Bentonville, AR 72716
(479) 273-4000
www.walmart.com

Company's roots date to:
1962
First joined the Dow: 1997
Weighting in Dow: 3.9
percent
Value of $10,000 invested
5 years ago: $18,119

BUSINESS PROFILE: Wal-Mart is the largest retailer in the world. The company's outlets include its namesake Wal-Mart Stores and Sam's Club warehouse-style outlets. Although it seems like it has been around forever, Wal-Mart is still a fairly young company by Dow standards. The first Wal-Mart store was opened in Rogers, Arkansas, in 1962; the first Sam's Club in 1983; and the first Supercenter in 1988. Today, the company employs more than 1.3 million people worldwide.

Wal-Mart continues to defy the law of big numbers. It's easy, for example, for a $5 million company to grow by 10 percent a year; the company is starting from a relatively small base. However, it's extremely difficult for a $5 billion company to grow at 10 percent annually. The reason is that you need big, big ideas to generate 10 percent growth at a $5 billion company. That's what makes Wal-Mart such an impressive company. The firm continues to generate solid revenue growth on a sales base of nearly one-quarter of a *trillion* dollars.

How does the company do it? One strength of Wal-Mart is its size, which allows the firm to dictate terms to its suppliers. That's the good news/bad news scenario of being a Wal-Mart vendor. The good news is obvious: access to millions and millions of shoppers. The bad news is that Wal-Mart basically owns you since you need that access. Thus, the firm can cut deals with vendors that no other retailer can make.

Another reason for the company's strength is that Sam Walton recognized very early that what matters in the retailing world is information—information that tells you what products are selling and what products aren't, information that tells you when to reorder goods and when to trim a slow-selling product, information that allows you to maximize your store shelves. Wal-Mart spent aggressively on technology, putting the company light-years ahead of once dominant discounters, such as Kmart, and once dominant middle-market retailers, such as Sears and J.C. Penney.

Can Wal-Mart continue its magic act? I wouldn't bet against the company. Yes, the firm occasionally has some hiccups, but they usually don't last long. And while it only feels like there is a Wal-Mart on every corner, the fact is that the firm still has plenty of real estate left uncovered. Exporting the Wal-Mart success story overseas is another important growth avenue for the company. No retailing format is safe from the Wal-Mart shadow. For example, the firm has quickly become a major player in the grocery market. Finally, the Wal-Mart brand name has become so embedded in this country that it would not be surprising to see Wal-Mart become more of a player in consumer finance markets.

BOTTOM LINE: Wal-Mart had been a fairly consistent performer before joining the Dow in 1997. While I suppose that could change down the road, I wouldn't be surprised if the stock continues to perform reasonably well relative to its Dow peers.

Wal-Mart Stores (NYSE: WMT)

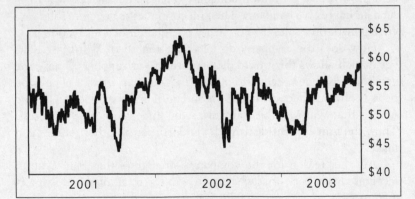

PART III

THE STRATEGY—
BASIC AND ADVANCED
WORST-TO-FIRST STRATEGIES

4

WORST TO FIRST—BASIC STRATEGIES

You now understand the logic and concepts underlying my worst-to-first strategies. You now are familiar with the investment vehicle (the 30 stocks in the Dow Jones Industrial Average) used to implement the worst-to-first strategies. It's time to make some money. The following is a step-by-step blueprint for implementing your very own worst-to-first strategy.

STEP 1: DETERMINE THE STRATEGY'S FIT IN YOUR OWN PORTFOLIO

One of the beauties of my worst-to-first strategies is that they fit nicely into a variety of broader investment approaches. As discussed in Chapter 7, you can use a worst-to-first approach as a complement to a broad portfolio. You can use the worst-to-first strategy as a stand-alone portfolio. You can take parts of the strategy (e.g., buying the worst-performing stock in the Dow instead of the five worst-performing stocks) to include in a portfolio of many stocks. You can use a worst-to-first strategy to balance other investments that you are buying and holding.

In any case, the first step in creating a worst-to-first portfolio is determining just how much money you want to invest in the strategy. Of course, an investor with $1 million may want to invest more than an investor who has $25,000. Fortunately, the capital requirements of my worst-to-first strategies are such that virtually any investor, regardless of the size of his or her portfolio, should be able to invest money using this approach. If you are looking for a specific percentage of a portfolio that should be focused on worst-to-first strategies, I would feel comfortable devoting 10 to 30 percent of the equity portion of the portfolio on a worst-to-first strategy.

STEP 2: ESTABLISH A RELATIONSHIP WITH A BROKERAGE FIRM

In order to implement my worst-to-first strategies, you'll need to buy stocks through a broker. That means establishing a brokerage account. Here are some things to consider when choosing a broker:

- *The cheapest brokerage commissions are usually available online.* Most brokerage firms give substantial breaks on online commissions versus telephone orders.

- *The smaller your investment stake, the greater the impact of fees.* If you have $50,000 devoted to a worst-to-first portfolio, spending $50 per trade will not have nearly the impact on your portfolio's performance as if you have $5,000 to devote to the strategy.

- *Brokerage firms differ in the amount required to open an account.* Some brokerage firms will let you open an account with little ($500) or even nothing down. Other brokerage firms may require a minimum of $5,000 or $10,000 in investments and cash.

- *Many brokerage firms have inactivity fees and other fees that can add up over time.* Brokerage firms have been quick to levy a variety of fees on customers, including inactive account fees (i.e., a fee for not making a minimum number of trades per year), transfer fees, termination fees, and so on. Make sure you are aware of all the fees before signing up.

What brokerage firm works best for my worst-to-first strategies? Well, since you don't need any advice or research—you (or, rather, the strategy) make all the buy and sell decisions—a full-service broker is probably overkill. You may already have a relationship with a full-service broker. If you do, check with the broker to see what kind of trading fees he or she will give you if you want to put some money into my worst-to-first strategies. If you are a big shooter with your broker, my guess is that the broker will give you cheap commission rates in order to keep your other business.

If you don't already have a relationship with a broker, search for a discount brokerage firm that provides the best combination of cheap commissions and affordable minimums. Also, if you aren't currently online, most discount brokers allow trades to be made via the telephone. However, as I've already mentioned, be prepared to pay higher commissions for phone trades.

One final point to check with your broker is the amount of interest paid on cash held in your trading account. My historical results for the worst-to-first strategies assume that all dividends are reinvested. However, as a practical matter, you may not be able to reinvest dividends. Thus, your account will likely receive dividends as they are paid on your stocks. Double-check with your broker to make sure you earn at least some interest on that cash. The following is a list of popular discount brokers and contact information:

- **Ameritrade** (800-454-9272; www.ameritrade.com)—$2,000 minimum to open an account; $10.99 per online trade
- **Brown & Co.** (800-822-2021; www.brownco.com)—$15,000 minimum to open an account; $5 per online trade
- **Charles Schwab** (800-372-4922; www.schwab.com)—$10,000 minimum to open an account; $21.95 per online trade
- **E*Trade** (800-786-2575; www.etrade.com)—$1,000 minimum to open an account; $22.95 per online trade
- **Interactive Brokers** (877-442-2757; www.interactivebrokers.com)—$2,000 minimum to open an account; $0.01 per share commission up to 500 shares ($1 minimum), $0.005 per share above 500 shares. Minimum account charge per month is $10.
- **Scottrade** (800-619-7283; www.scottrade.com)—$500 minimum to open an account; $7 per online trade
- **TD Waterhouse** (800-934-4410; www.tdwaterhouse.com)—$1,000 minimum to open an account; $17.95 per online trade

Getting Online

If you aren't online but would like to get online to take advantage of lower commissions, you'll need the following items:

- Computer and monitor
- Modem or some other mode of linking to the Internet
- Internet service provider

You can purchase a decent computer/monitor package these days for surfing the Internet for less than $1,000. If you are looking to purchase a computer, I'd stick with Dell or one of the other major manufacturers (Gateway, Hewlett-Packard). In addition to a computer, you'll need something to link you to the Internet. The most common communication device is a modem. It allows your computer to access the Internet via your phone line. Other ways to access the Internet include cable modem and DSL (digital subscriber line). Cable modems are available via your cable company. For DSL availability, you might want to check with your local telephone service provider.

If you use a dial-up modem, you'll need an Internet service provider to connect you to the Internet. Popular Internet access companies include America Online, Juno, Earthlink, Microsoft's MSN service, and AT&T's Worldnet. These services offer Internet access for prices in the $9 to $20 per month range. If you use a cable modem, your Internet access provider is your cable company. Expect to pay $50 or so for cable Internet service. Keep in mind, however, that the increased price reflects the superior speeds at which you'll access the Web. Typical DSL service will likely run you $30 or more per month.

Once you can access the Internet, trading through an online broker is easy. Just type in the broker's Web address, which is usually www.(broker name).com. If you don't know the brokerage firm's Web address, use one of the many search engines on the Internet. My favorite is Google (www.google.com). Google is a supremely user-friendly search engine that can lead you to information on virtually any topic. Just plug in the name of the broker in Google's search engine, and you'll be taken to links to the broker's Web site.

Most brokerage firms have fee information and account applications online. Once you have established an online account, trading through the account is easy. You will also be able to access your account online anytime to check the performance of your investments.

Buying Dow Stocks Without a Broker

If you don't have a broker and don't want to open a brokerage account, yet still want to try your hand at a worst-to-first approach, there is another way. Direct-purchase plans allow investors to buy stock directly from companies, the first share and every share. Direct-purchase plans are an offshoot of dividend reinvestment plans. Dividend reinvestment plans have been around for more than three decades. These programs allow investors to buy stock in two ways: (1) with reinvested dividends and (2) with optional cash investments that can be sent directly to the companies.

The problem with traditional dividend reinvestment plans is that in order to buy stock directly from the company you already have to be a shareholder of at least one share. Fortunately, more and more companies are taking their DRIP plans to the next level by allowing investors to purchase even initial shares directly. These direct-purchase plans (I also call them no-load stocks since you purchase them without a broker, just like a no-load mutual fund) have been growing in big numbers over the last decade. Today there are more than 300 U.S. companies as well as more than 300 foreign companies whose shares trade as American Depositary Receipts (ADRs) on U.S. exchanges that allow any investor to buy stock directly, the first share and every share, without a broker.

Direct-purchase plans differ between companies. Indeed, Exxon Mobil's minimum initial investment is $250. IBM's minimum initial investment is $500, while Microsoft's minimum is $1,000. Fees will differ between plans. For example, Exxon Mobil doesn't charge any purchase fees, while Disney charges a fee of $5 plus 4 cents per share per purchase. Thus, if you buy 100 shares of Disney stock, you'll pay a fee of $9 ($5 flat fee plus $4 share fee).

The appeal of direct-purchase plans is twofold. First, the purchase fees, in most cases, will be lower than you would pay via most brokers. Second, the small dollar amounts are affordable for virtually any investor. In fact, if your investment is not enough to buy a full share of stock, the plan will buy you a fractional share of stock, and that fractional share is entitled to a fractional part of the dividend. Thus, these plans are extremely easy for divvying up an investment program based on equal investments.

The downside of these plans—and it is a big one when it comes to a worst-to-first strategy—is that you don't have the execution speed when buying and selling stock through a direct-purchase plan that you have via a broker. True, direct-purchase plans have become better in terms of speed. You can now make an investment in most plans in just a couple of days, and selling via the plans has become easier and quicker via toll-free sell lines. Still, if you want to buy or sell stock in these plans *right now at the current price*, you can't.

Two other issues that make direct-purchase plans less than optimal for implementing a worst-to-first strategy are:

1. *Selling fees.* Although the plans have low or no fees on the buy side, selling fees can get expensive. Most plans charge a flat fee of $10 to $15 plus a per-share fee of 10 cents to 15 cents. Thus, selling larger share amounts could get pricey.

2. *Availability.* Because only 16 of the 30 Dow stocks offer a direct-purchase plan, chances are pretty good that a Dow Underdog in a particular year will not have a plan. In 2002, for example, the five worst-performing stocks were Home Depot (–53 percent), Intel (–50 percent), McDonald's (–38 percent), General Electric (–38 percent), and International Business Machines (–35 percent). Out of these five stocks, all but Intel offered a direct-purchase plan. In 2001, two of the five worst performers—Merck and American Express—offered direct-purchase plans.

Still, for investors who may not be able to scrounge up the minimum to open a brokerage account, direct-purchase plans offer a possible, albeit imperfect, way to implement a worst-to-first investment program. To obtain enrollment information for the plans, call the toll-free numbers below. If you prefer, you can usually download enrollment information online at the company's Web site or the Web site of the firm's transfer agent. (Companies hire transfer agents to administer these plans.) If you visit the firm's Web site, follow the links to the "investor relations" section of the site.

Dow Stocks with Direct-Purchase Plans

Name	Min. Initial Investment ($)	Phone
Altria (www.altria.com)	500	(800) 442-0077
American Express (www.americanexpress.com)	1,000	(800) 842-7629
Caterpillar (www.cat.com)	250	(800) 842-7629
Disney (Walt) (www.disney.go.com)	1,000	(818) 553-7200
Exxon Mobil (www.exxonmobil.com)	250	(800) 252-1800
General Electric (www.ge.com)	250	(800) 786-2543
Home Depot (www.homedepot.com)	250	(877) 437-4273
IBM (www.ibm.com)	500	(888) 426-6700
McDonald's (www.mcdonalds.com)	500	(800) 621-7825
Merck (www.merck.com)	350	(800) 831-8248
Microsoft (www.microsoft.com)	1,000	(800) 842-7629
Pfizer (www.pfizer.com)	500	(800) 733-9393
Procter & Gamble (www.pg.com)	250	(800) 764-7483
SBC Comm. (www.sbc.com)	500	(800) 351-7221
Verizon (www.verizon.com)	1,000	(800) 631-2355
Wal-Mart (www.walmart.com)	250	(800) 438-6278

STEP 3: KNOW YOUR INVESTMENT OPTIONS— THE DOW JONES INDUSTRIAL AVERAGE

At this point, you'll want to examine each of the components of the Dow Jones Industrial Average. The Dow components are listed daily in *The Wall Street Journal* on page C2. You'll find the listing in the middle of the page. Also, you can check out the Dow components at www.dowjones.com.

Here is a listing of the current stocks in the Dow Jones Industrial Average, along with their stock symbols and exchanges where the stocks are listed (NYSE—New York Stock Exchange; NASDAQ—Nasdaq Market):

AT&T *(NYSE: T)*

Alcoa *(NYSE: AA)*

Altria Group *(NYSE: MO)*

American Express *(NYSE: AXP)*

American Internationl Group *(NYSE: AIG)*

Boeing *(NYSE: BA)*

Caterpillar *(NYSE: CAT)*

Citigroup *(NYSE: C)*

Coca-Cola *(NYSE: KO)*

Disney *(NYSE: DIS)*

DuPont *(NYSE: DD)*

Exxon Mobil *(NYSE: XOM)*

General Electric *(NYSE: GE)*

General Motors *(NYSE: GM)*

Hewlett-Packard *(NYSE: HPQ)*

Home Depot *(NYSE: HD)*

Honeywell International *(NYSE: HON)*

Intel *(NASDAQ: INTC)*

International Business Machines *(NYSE: IBM)*

Johnson & Johnson *(NYSE: JNJ)*

J.P. Morgan Chase *(NYSE: JPM)*

McDonald's *(NYSE: MCD)*

Merck & Co. *(NYSE: MRK)*

Microsoft *(NASDAQ: MSFT)*

Pfizer *(NYSE: PFE)*

Procter & Gamble *(NYSE: PG)*

SBC Communications *(NYSE: SBC)*

3M *(NYSE: MMM)*

United Technologies *(NYSE: UTX)*

Verizon *(NYSE: VZ)*

Wal-Mart Stores *(NYSE: WMT)*

STEP 4: ANALYZE THE DOW— FINDING THE 12-MONTH PERCENTAGE PRICE CHANGE

Once you have identified the Dow stocks, the next step is determining the percentage price change of each Dow stock over the last 12 months. You will use this information to choose the stocks for the basic worst-to-first strategy.

If you plan to institute a worst-to-first strategy at the beginning of each year, an easy (and low-tech) source for the 12-month percentage price change for each component is *The Wall Street Journal*. Take a look at a quote from *The Wall Street Journal*. Notice that each stock quote has a wealth of information. (The stock quote pages usually start on page C2 or C3 of the *Journal*.) Each listing provides the stock's price range over the last 52 weeks, the stock name, symbol, dividend (this dividend is usually an annual dividend based on the payment in the most recent quarter), price/earnings ratio, trading volume, closing price, and net change from the previous close.

Also notice the very first listing: YTD % CHG. This represents the year-to-date price change for the stock. Now, if you look at a stock quote in the first issue of *The Wall Street Journal* of the year 2003, the stock quote represents the trading on the last day of 2002. (This is important to remember when using *The Wall Street Journal*—the stock quotes are always from the previous trading day's action. I know this sounds silly to emphasize, but it is actually easy to make a mistake if you are looking for historical prices. For example, in order to find the closing price on June 30, 2003, you'll want to look in *The Wall Street Journal*'s July 1, 2003, issue, not the June 30 issue.)

Thus, if you are planning to implement a strategy on the first trading day of the year, you can simply look up each of the 30 Dow components in *The Wall Street Journal* to get their 12-month price change. (Since you are using the year-end closing price, the YTD price change is equal to the 12-month price change.) Make sure you use the *Journal* published on the first day of the new year to get the previous 12-month price change numbers.

It will probably be helpful to create a worksheet for this process. A spreadsheet on your computer would work nicely. You'll need just two columns: company name and percentage price change. Fill in the company name, and enter the 12-month price change from *The Wall Street Journal*. You'll need to look up each Dow stock in the stock quote pages. With the exception of Intel and Microsoft (which are found on the Nasdaq Market stock quote pages), all of the Dow stocks trade on the New York Stock Exchange. The stock quote pages in the *Journal* list companies by alphabetical order, so you should have no trouble finding the information for most of the companies. The following are a few tricky placements of Dow stocks in the *Journal*'s stock quote pages:

- **Walt Disney** is located in the D section, not the W section.

- **IBM** is located in the I section, where International Business Machines would be alphabetically.
- **J.P. Morgan** is located in the J section, near the beginning.
- **3M** is located in the T section, where Three M would be alphabetically.

Once you have your worksheet completed, sort the list from the worst-performing stock to the best-performing stock. Remember that the sort is based on the 12-month *price change*, not the 12-month *total return* numbers. The worst-to-first strategy uses price change data.

If you have a computer and Internet access, an easier way to find the 12-month price change for the stocks in the Dow is to go to my Web site: www.dowunderdogs.com. At this Web site, I maintain the 12-month price changes for all 30 Dow stocks on a daily basis. Another online source is Yahoo's Finance Web site: http://finance. yahoo.com. Once you arrive at this site, follow these steps:

1. Enter a stock symbol.
2. On the next page, you should see "Historical Prices" along the left hand side of the page. Click on this link.
3. You are now on a page that provides historical price information for the stock. To find the 12-month price change, enter the "start" and "end" dates over the last year. Make sure you show "daily" quotes. Click "Get Data."
4. You should now see daily price data for this stock.
5. To determine the percentage change, subtract the end price from the start price and divide by the start price. For example, if the starting price was $20.50 and the price on the last day was $27.25, the percentage change is 32.92 percent ($6.75—the difference between the start price and the end price—divided by $20.50— the start price). Now, if the end price is below the start price (e.g., if the start price is $27.25 and the end price is $20.50), you would take the difference and divide by the start price to obtain the negative return. In this example, a stock that declines from $27.25 to $20.50 over the course of 12 months has a price change of −24.7 percent.

6. If you use Yahoo historical prices, make sure you take into account any corporate actions (stock splits, spin-offs) that will affect the stock price. Yahoo provides the adjustments for stock splits and spin-offs.

Again, if you have online access, the fastest way to get 12-month price changes for all Dow stocks—whether you implement the strategy at the beginning of the year or anytime during the year—is to visit my Web site: www.dowunderdogs.com.

Once you have found the 12-month price change for each Dow stock, rank them in order from the worst performer to the best performer. It is possible, though unlikely, that you'll have a tie between two stocks. If two stocks appear to be tied, start taking the percentage change past one or two decimals. The percentage change in *The Wall Street Journal* goes to one decimal point, which should be adequate in most cases. My Web site—www.dowunderdogs.com—takes the 12-month percentage change for each Dow stock out three decimal points.

STEP 5: PICK YOUR BASIC WORST-TO-FIRST STRATEGY— ONE STOCK, THREE STOCKS, FIVE STOCKS, OR TEN STOCKS

The next step is to choose which portfolio of worst-to-first stocks to own. I have run the numbers on worst-to-first portfolios holding the worst-performing Dow stock, the 3 worst-performing Dow stocks, the 5 worst-performing Dow stocks, and the 10 worst-performing Dow stocks. Here is what I've found (a complete history of all basic worst-to-first strategies is provided in Chapter 5):

- Over the last 5-year period, all of these basic strategies handily outperformed the Dow. The best of the bunch was owning the single worst-performing Dow stock. Over the last 5 years, the strategy of owning the worst-performing Dow stock grew a $1,000 investment to $4,676—a 5-year gain of 368 percent. That's an annualized return of 36 percent compared to a Dow Jones Industrial Average that grew $1,000 to just $1,251—a 25 percent gain and an annualized return of less than 5 percent.

- Over the last 10-year period, all of these strategies outperformed the Dow as well.

- Over the last 20-year period the 1-, 3- and 5-stock strategies handily outperformed the Dow; the 10-stock strategy underperformed slightly. Once again, the single-stock portfolio had the strongest showing, outperforming the Dow by nearly threefold.

- Over the last 30-year period, the 3-, 5-, and 10-stock strategies all outperformed the Dow. Curiously, the 1-stock strategy failed to beat the Dow over the last 30 years.

Bottom line: History says that adopting any of the basic worst-to-first strategies gives you a pretty good chance of beating the Dow over time. However, one important point to remember is that the fewer stocks you hold, the greater the volatility of the portfolio. I talk more about portfolio volatility and risk in Chapter 9. For now, you need to realize that the more stocks in the portfolio, the lower the portfolio volatility. If you tend to be more risk averse, you'll probably want to look at a portfolio containing the 5 or 10 worst performers rather than a 1-stock portfolio.

If I had to pick one portfolio that is suitable for most investors, I would choose the 5-stock portfolio. A portfolio of the 5 worst-performing Dow stocks has beaten the Dow over the last 1-, 5-, 10-, 20-, 30-, 50-, and 74-year holding periods. Furthermore, it has beaten the Dow at a risk level that is palatable for most investors.

Another reason that 5 stocks make sense is they are enough to reduce portfolio volatility, yet the number is small enough to maximize the power of the strategy. Remember that what makes this strategy work is reversion to the mean. You need to own stocks that have reached extreme price levels on the downside relative to other stocks in the Dow. The more stocks you include in the strategy, the more your total portfolio starts to migrate from the extreme ends toward the average. Thus, the performance of the 10th-*worst*-performing Dow stock may not be all that different from the performance of the 10th *best*-performing Dow stock. At that point, you are likely to be including stocks that are probably close to achieving average returns in that particular year. You don't want average performers in your worst-to-first portfolios; you want terrible performers—stocks whose performance is well below that of the average. That's how you achieve the type of spread that enhances returns as reversion to the mean occurs.

STEP 6: BUY THE STOCKS

Once you have decided on the size of the portfolio and which Dow Underdogs to buy, it's time to buy the stocks. You will want to divide your money equally among the stocks. For example, if you choose the 5-stock portfolio (the 5 worst-performing stocks) and you have $10,000 to invest, you should invest $2,000 in each of the 5 stocks. Since it is highly unlikely that all 5 stocks will be trading at the exact same price, your $2,000 will buy different share amounts. That's not important. What is important is that you have relatively equal *dollar* amounts invested in each company.

At this point, it is probably worthwhile to cover the various trading orders you can give when buying stock. A *market* order will buy stock at the prevailing market price. What is that market price? Every stock carries two prices: a *bid* price and an *ask* price. The bid price represents the price you'll receive if you sell a stock at the market price. The ask price is the price you'll pay if you buy a stock at the market price. The difference between the bid and ask prices—that is, the *spread*—goes to the broker and/or market maker.

The spread is affected by trading volume—that is, stocks usually have big spreads if they don't trade often. Indeed, it is not uncommon for small companies to have spreads of $0.50 or more. Because of such large spreads, the best way to purchase smaller companies is by placing a *limit* order specifying the exact price at which you are willing to buy the stock.

Let's say you want to buy a stock with a bid price of $10 and an ask price of $11. If you put in a market order, you will probably pay around $11 (or worse if the market is moving), thus building in a loss of $1. (Remember, if you bought this stock and immediately sold it, you would buy at the ask—$11—and sell at the bid—$10—thus locking up a $1 loss.) Instead of paying such a large spread, you decide you don't want to buy unless the stock falls to $10.25. Thus, you put a limit order with your broker instructing him or her to buy only if the stock falls to $10.25.

The problem with placing a limit order is that there is no guarantee you will ever buy the stock. Indeed, the stock could jump sharply and never look back. That is the danger of using limit orders in my worst-to-first strategies. You may set a limit that is never met. Thus, you lose the opportunity of owning a big gainer because you wanted to save yourself a few pennies.

Because the worst-to-first strategies in this book focus on big, highly liquid Dow stocks, the spreads between the bid and ask prices are usually very, very small. Thus, I would feel comfortable placing market orders when buying the stocks, ensuring I buy the stocks I want to own. True, you may pay a few pennies more by placing a market order, but the benefits of owning the Dow Underdogs should more than compensate, especially over time.

WHAT ABOUT USING STOPS?

One strategy geared toward protecting downside risk is placing a *stop* order on stocks you own. A stop order automatically becomes a market order to sell when the stop price is met. Let's say you decide on a single-stock worst-to-first portfolio. But to protect yourself from a big loss—after all, it is a 1-stock portfolio—you place a stop order when you make your purchase. Thus, you put a market order to buy but place a stop order 15 percent below your purchase price. Now, if the stock falls 15 percent to your stop price, your broker will automatically sell the shares, thus limiting your loss.

Keep in mind that stops are risk-reduction tools. While they do provide protection on the downside, they may also boot you out of stocks that decline sharply only to rebound. Also be aware that stops do not guarantee that you will get out at your stop price. In fast-moving markets, when stocks are melting down, it is entirely possible that your stop order at, say, $15 may not get filled until the stock drops to $10 or $11 if sell orders are swamping the market. People who had stops on their investments during the market collapses in

1987 and 1989 felt the potential pitfalls firsthand of having stops on their stocks.

Fortunately, because you are dealing with big, highly liquid Dow stocks, the chances of selling well below your stop price are fairly remote. And if you are worried about such an event happening, you can place a *stop-limit* order, which says that you will sell at that price and only that price. Thus, in the preceding example with the stop-limit price at $15 instead of a stop order, you would not have sold at $10. Of course, you will wish you had sold if the stock goes to $5. However, at least you won't sell at a price below your stop. With a stop-limit order at $15, you will sell at $15 and only $15.

All of this talk about stops and stop-limit orders begs the question: Do stops make sense for worst-to-first strategies? I think the answer depends on how aggressive you are with the strategies. If I were buying just one stock, I would probably use a stop to limit my risk. If I were buying 10 Dow Underdogs, I would be less likely to use stops.

Also, if the worst-to-first strategy represented my only investment nest egg, I would want to protect it from a calamitous decline by using stops. If, however, the worst-to-first strategy represented a fairly small portion of my investment dollars, I would be inclined to worry less about setting stops.

Remember that the risk you run using stops is that a stock may have a quick decline—perhaps the overall market is tanking—only to rebound quickly after you have been stopped out. If you do use stops, I would give the stocks plenty of room to maneuver and not set the stop too snug. I would probably not want to set a stop closer than 15 to 20 percent or so from my purchase price.

STEP 7: HOLD THE STOCKS FOR 12 MONTHS (AND MAYBE AN EXTRA DAY OR TWO)

Once you have selected your stocks and made your purchases, you need to do nothing else except wait 12 months or so. Actually, instances may arise when you'll want to hold the portfolio for 12 months and 1 day. By holding your investments for one year and a day, you receive favorable tax treatment on your capital gains.

Turning short-term gains into long-term gains by holding an extra day may be a huge deal if you are holding your Dow Underdogs in a taxable account. Let's say you are in the 35 percent tax bracket. Thus, any realized gains on investments held 12 months or less will be taxed at 35 percent. However, if you hold the investment for the extra day, that tax on profits drops to just 15 percent.

To put that into numbers, say you have a worst-to-first portfolio of $10,000 and you make 20 percent on your money (or a gain of $2,000) at the end of 12 months. If the gain is short term, (i.e., you sell the investments after holding them 12 months or less), you will lose 35 percent of that profit, or $700, to taxes. Your after-tax profit is $1,300. If the gain is long term, however, your taxes are just $300, giving you an after-tax profit of $1,700. You pocket an extra $400—or 4 percent of your original investment—by waiting one extra day to sell your positions.

Of course, this strategy of holding an extra day is not without its risks. Indeed, if the stock gets hammered on the last day, you may have been better off selling and paying taxes on the short-term gain. When you run the numbers to see whether it makes sense to hold the extra day for capital gains purposes, you need to take into account the following:

- *The size of your initial investment.* A bigger investment in the strategy will generate bigger gains during years that the strategy is successful. Shielding those gains from ordinary tax rates will make more sense.

- *The strategy's performance in a given year.* For years in which the strategy loses money (and, yes, any strategy can lose money in a given year), you may want to create a short-term loss rather than a long-term loss for tax reasons. Thus, in this instance, you may want to sell after 12 months and not hold the extra day. In years when the strategy works well, the after-tax profit will be significantly greater if you hold the extra day before selling.

- *Your tax bracket.* Obviously, a person in the 35 percent tax bracket will get a bigger bang for his or her dollar waiting the extra day—

and incurring the extra day's risk that the stock could drop—than a person in the 15 percent tax bracket.

Also keep in mind that while you run the risk of the stock declining on the extra day, probabilities suggest that the stock could rise on the extra day, thus enhancing returns.

Remember that in order to receive favorable tax treatment of long-term capital gains, you'll need to hold your investment for at least 12 months and 1 day. For example, if you buy on February 15, the earliest you can sell and receive favorable capital gains tax treatment is February 16 (or whatever the next trading day is following the 15th) of the following year.

Bottom line: The decision to hold for 12 months or 12 months and 1 day will largely depend on whether turning short-term results into long-term results has a big impact on your after-tax returns. All things equal, it will probably make sense in most cases to take advantage of favorable long-term capital gains treatment by holding the extra day.

Of course, if you hold your worst-to-first investment in a tax-preferenced account, such as a Roth IRA, the distinction between long-term and short-term gains is moot. For those accounts, I would be inclined to hold for exactly 12 months to keep the system on a consistent starting point each year.

One final point worth mentioning: What do you do if a stock you own is booted from the Dow during the year? Continue to hold the stock. True, stocks that get booted from the Dow usually see some short-term selling pressures as Dow indexers sell the stock that has been booted and buy the stock that is being added. However, I recommend that you maintain positions for simplicity sake. The historical returns provided in Chapter 5 and throughout the book assume a 12-month holding period regardless of whether the stock was booted from the Dow.

Another issue may come up if a Dow company spins off a firm to shareholders. For example, in 1996, AT&T spun off Lucent and NCR to AT&T shareholders. What should you do with the spin-off company? I suggest keeping the spin-off until the end of the 12-month holding period, then selling it (assuming, of course, that the spin-off does not join the Dow).

STEP 8: SELL AND CREATE A NEW WORST-TO-FIRST PORTFOLIO

Once your holding period has expired, it is time to rebalance your portfolio. Before selling any shares, however, run a new listing of the 12-month price performance of the 30 Dow stocks to see what new Dow Underdogs you need to own. The chance exists that one or more of your stocks may still be Dow Underdogs, in which case you would continue to hold the stocks. Sell the stocks that no longer are among the Dow Underdogs and buy the new Underdogs.

Remember that you need to have an equal-weighted portfolio each year. You need to make sure that you keep the dollar investments fairly equal among the worst-to-first stocks. If you are keeping some stocks from the prior year, you may have to add more dollars to those investments in order to get the weightings reasonably equal. Again, when you are through rebalancing, you'll want to have equal dollar investments in each of the stocks in the portfolio.

When fine-tuning your portfolio to achieve equal dollar investments in the stocks, be practical. Weigh the trading costs. Indeed, it may not make sense to incur a lot of trading costs to bring the weightings exactly in line if your investment in each stock differs by just a few hundred dollars. When selling, I would opt for placing market orders. This assures that you will sell the stock and have the proceeds readily available to put into your next worst-to-first portfolio.

STEP 9: COMPUTE YOUR RETURN

To compute your portfolio return for a given year, simply take your starting investment and subtract it from the total value of your portfolio on the last day of the holding period. Make sure you include the value of the entire portfolio, including cash. Take that amount and divide by the starting value, and that is your return. Let's say you start with $10,000. At the end of the holding period, the value of your account (including cash/dividends) is $11,000. Your profit is $1,000 ($11,000 − $10,000), or 10 percent total return ($1,000 divided by the starting value of $10,000).

CONCLUSION

Simple strategies are the best. They are easy to understand, easy to implement, easy to monitor, and easy to rebalance. My basic worst-to-first strategies are about as simple as they come. You have only 30 stocks from which to choose, and information is easily found on the stocks online or in *The Wall Street Journal*. You only have to figure out the 12-month price change for each company. My Web site (http://www.dowunderdogs.com), *The Wall Street Journal*, and Yahoo Finance (http://finance.yahoo.com) all provide this information. Once you buy your investments, you don't have to do anything for 12 months. And taking stock of the strategy's gains/losses each year is easy. Best of all (as you'll soon read in Chapter 5), this simple strategy of buying the Dow's worst performers has produced the type of returns that would make any Wall Street professional jealous.

CHOOSING THE DOW UNDERDOGS—A WORKSHEET

I thought it would be useful to provide a specific example of picking the Dow Underdogs in a given year. Below is a worksheet showing the 30 Dow stocks as of the end of 2002, along with their 12-month price changes. I've ranked the stocks from worst performer to best performer. As you can see, the two worst-performing stocks in 2002 (and this information was readily available in the January 2, 2003, issue of *The Wall Street Journal*) were Home Depot (down 52.9 percent) and Intel (down 50.5 percent). The best-performing Dow stock was Eastman Kodak (up 19.1 percent).

Dow Component Performance in 2002 (%)

HOME DEPOT INC	–52.9
INTEL CORP	–50.5
MCDONALDS CORP	–39.3
GENERAL ELECTRIC CO	–39.2
INTERNATIONAL BUSINESS MACHS COR	–35.9
ALCOA INC	–35.9

Dow Component Performance in 2002 (%)

J P MORGAN CHASE & CO	−34.0
S B C COMMUNICATIONS INC	−30.8
HONEYWELL INTERNATIONAL INC	−29.0
A T & T CORP	−28.4
CITIGROUP INC	−25.7
GENERAL MOTORS CORP	−24.2
MICROSOFT CORP	−22.0
DISNEY WALT CO	−21.3
HEWLETT PACKARD CO	−15.5
BOEING CO	−14.9
INTERNATIONAL PAPER CO	−13.3
CATERPILLAR INC	−12.5
WAL MART STORES INC	−12.2
PHILIP MORRIS COS INC	−11.6
EXXON MOBIL CORP	−11.1
JOHNSON & JOHNSON	−9.1
COCA COLA CO	−7.0
UNITED TECHNOLOGIES CORP	−4.2
MERCK & CO INC	−3.7
AMERICAN EXPRESS CO	−1.0
DU PONT E I DE NEMOURS & CO	−0.3
3M CO	4.3
PROCTER & GAMBLE CO	9.5
EASTMAN KODAK CO	19.1

Let's say you wanted to implement a worst-to-first strategy on the first day of trading in 2003. You've already determined how much money you planned to invest in the strategy ($10,000). And you've opened a brokerage account. All that's left is choosing which basic strategy you want to implement for 2003 and the stocks for that portfolio.

- If you chose the 1-stock portfolio, you invested all of your money in Home Depot, which was the worst-performing stock in the Dow.

- If you chose the 3-stock portfolio, you purchased the three worst-performing stocks in the Dow in 2002: Home

Depot, Intel, and McDonald's. In order to keep the port-folio equal weighted, you'll need to invest equal dollar amounts (as close to $3,333 per company as possible) in each stock.

- If you chose my favorite basic worst-to-first strategy—the 5-stock portfolio—you bought $2,000 worth of each of the following stocks: Home Depot, Intel, McDonald's, General Electric, and IBM. (When you take the results out to the second decimal, IBM posted a greater negative price change than Alcoa.)

- And if you chose the 10-stock portfolio of Dow Under-dogs, you bought $1,000 each of the following stocks: Home Depot, Intel, McDonald's, General Electric, IBM, Alcoa, J.P. Morgan Chase, SBC Communications, Honey-well, and AT&T.

For the record, here is how each of these portfolios per-formed in 2003, relative to the Dow Jones Industrial Average:

- 1-stock portfolio: +49.0 percent
- 3-stock portfolio: +70.8 percent
- 5-stock portfolio: +52.7 percent
- 10-stock portfolio: +42.1 percent

Dow Jones Industrial Average: +28.3 percent

5
—

WORST TO FIRST—THE TRACK RECORD

This book is not an attempt to promise you the moon when it comes to investment performance. I am not out to convince you that you can turn $1,000 into $1 million in 1 year. I am proposing a strategy that has stood the test of time, not just in the short run but also in the long run. Not just for 1 year or 5 years but for 50 and 74 years.

But make no mistake, I am not talking about beating the market by 20 or 30 percentage points per year, year in, year out. That can't be done, regardless of what you read elsewhere. I'm talking about beating the market by a percent or two or five per year every year. That's really all you need.

For example, the average annual return of the basic worst-to-first strategy (i.e., owning the five worst performers each year) since 1931 is 11 percent versus 10 percent for the Dow. Although that doesn't seem like much, 1 percent difference adds up to a rather staggering dollar amount over a long period of time. Indeed, at 11 percent per year for 74 years, a $1,000 investment becomes $2 million. How much difference does 1 percent make per year? Since 1931, a $1,000 investment in the Dow growing at 10 percent per year turned into just over $1 million. Generating an additional 1 percent per year over 74 years means that you double your money.

Of course, what matters more to investors are shorter time frames. On this account, the result of my worst-to-first strategies have been quite impressive. Over the last 30-, 20-, and 10-year holding periods the basic worst-to-first strategy (owning the five worst-performing

5-Stock (Worst to First) versus Dow Industrials—74 Years

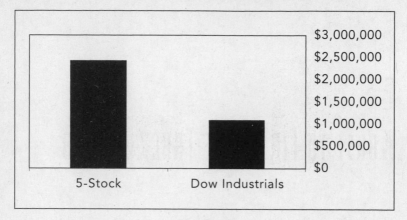

stocks) has beaten the Dow by roughly 1 percentage point per year. In fact, all of my worst-to-first strategies based on annual price change—1-stock, 3-stock, 5-stock, and 10-stock portfolios—have beaten the Dow over the last decade.

5-Stock (Worst to First) versus Dow Industrials—30 Years

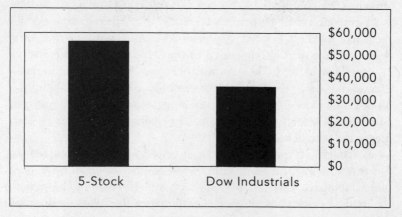

5-Stock (Worst to First) versus Dow Industrials—20 Years

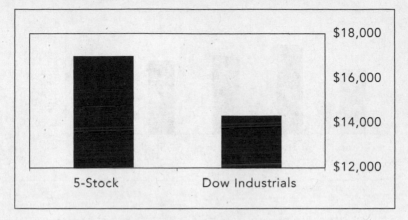

5-Stock (Worst to First) versus Dow Industrials—10 Years

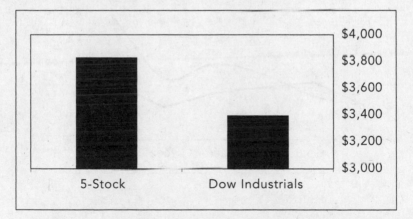

And the performance of the strategy over the last 5 years has been nothing short of amazing. Indeed, while the Dow Jones Industrial Average has posted an average annual return of a little over 4 percent, my 5-stock worst-to-first portfolio has posted average annual returns of 15 percent. To put that performance into raw numbers, check out what has happened to a $1,000 investment in the 5-stock worst-to-first portfolio versus the Dow over the last 5 years (see next page).

And if you had decided to go with any of the other worst-to-first

All Worst-to-First Portfolios versus Dow Industrials—10 Years

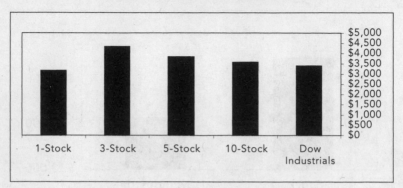

5-Stock (Worst to First) versus Dow Industrials—5 Years

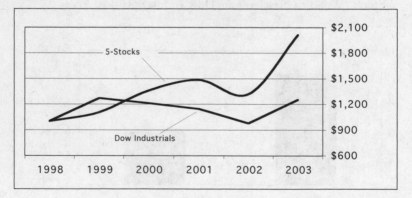

portfolios, you would have generated big returns versus the Dow. For example, over the last 5 years, owning the single worst-performing Dow stock would have generated a 36.1 percent annual return on your investment versus 4.6 percent for the Dow.

All of these worst-to-first strategies not only handily outperformed the Dow but also all of the various Dogs of the Dow strategies over that time frame. (See Chapter 8 for more on how my worst-to-first strategies stack up against the Dogs of the Dow strategies.)

1-Stock (Worst to First) versus Dow Industrials—5 Years

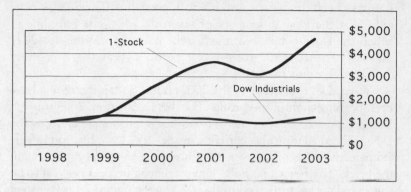

PERFORMANCE BY THE DECADE

Not only has the performance of the worst-to-first strategies been solid over both the short and long term but also it has been decent during the decades of the 1930s, 1940s, 1950s, 1960s, 1970s, 1980s, and 1990s. Here is a performance breakdown of the various worst-to-first strategies by decade, along with the performance of the Dow during the same time frames (these are annualized return numbers):

Performance of Worst-to-First Portfolios, by Decade (annualized returns)

Decade	1 Stock (%)	3 Stocks (%)	5 Stocks (%)	10 Stocks (%)	Dow Return (%)
1931–1939	−10.6	2.9	4.2	7.6	4.1
1940–1949	22.4	17.8	14.7	11.2	8.3
1950–1959	14.3	15.6	17.6	19.5	18.5
1960–1969	14.7	6.1	7.7	5.9	5.2
1970–1979	−8.9	0.3	2.3	6.5	5.2
1980–1989	15.1	19.6	19.6	19.0	17.6
1990–1999	3.5	7.4	11.3	13.2	18.2
2000–2003	38.0	28.6	16.2	8.0	−0.4

The most consistent performers among the worst-to-first portfolios have been the 5-stock and 10-stock portfolios. The 5-stock portfolio beat the Dow in four out of seven decades. The only one in which the Dow soundly beat the 5-stock portfolio was the decade of the '90s. The 10-stock worst-to-first portfolio beat the Dow every decade except one: the 1990s.

What does the decade of the 2000s hold? So far, the results have been nothing short of spectacular. For the 4 years from 2000 through December 31, 2003, all of the worst-to-first strategies are crushing the Dow. Indeed, during the current decade, the Dow has lost nearly 0.5 percent per year. However, all of my worst-to-first portfolios are in the black. The 1-stock portfolio is averaging 38 percent per year so far this decade. The 3-stock portfolio is averaging almost 29 percent per year. The 5-stock portfolio is averaging around 16 percent per year. And the 10-stock portfolio is averaging around 8 percent per year. To put those returns in perspective, the *worst-performing* worst-to-first portfolio so far this decade (10-stock portfolio) is still beating the Dow by an average of more than 8 percentage points per year.

WHAT DOES AVERAGE ANNUAL RETURN MEAN?

Whenever someone starts throwing around average annual return numbers at you, the first question you should ask is: How are those numbers being computed? Here's a simple example that shows how annual performance numbers can be misleading. Let's say you have a $1,000 investment.

- In year 1, the investment rises 100 percent.
- In year 2, the investment declines 50 percent.
- In year 3, the investment rises 100 percent.
- And in year 4, the investment falls 50 percent.

What is your average annual return? Well, if you simply added up the individual returns and divided by 4, you would come up with the following: 100 percent – 50 percent + 100 percent – 50 percent = 100 percent. The average over the four periods is 25 percent.

Thus, your average annual return is 25 percent, right? Not exactly. Let's see what happened to your $1,000 over that 4-year period. In year 1, your investment rose 100 percent, meaning your $1,000 became $2,000. In year 2, your investment lost 50 percent, meaning your $2,000 became $1,000. In year 3, your investment rose 100 percent, meaning your $1,000 became $2,000. In year 4, your investment lost 50 percent, meaning your $2,000 became $1,000.

You started with $1,000 and you ended with $1,000—that is, you made *zero* on your money in those 4 years. That doesn't sound like an average annual return of 25 percent to me. And it shouldn't to you, either.

The average annual return numbers I use in this book take into account the *annualized* returns based on the growth of the original investment. Thus, an investment that grows from $1,000 in year 1 to $2,000 by the end of year 7 has an average annual return of approximately 10 percent over that 7-year period. In our example, the $1,000 investment in year 1 that is still worth only $1,000 at the end of year 4 has an annualized return of 0 percent.

Don't be confused by individuals professing huge average annual returns. What matters is what happens to your money over the time period.

WHEN WORST TO FIRST DOESN'T WORK—AND WHY

It's worthwhile to look not only at periods when the worst-to-first strategy performs well but also at periods when the strategy has not worked so well. By looking at the losing periods, you will likely learn things about the strategy that can be useful when implementing it going forward.

The decade of the 1990s was arguably the worst, relative to the Dow, for virtually all of the worst-to-first strategies. To be sure, all of the strategies made money during the decade. Still, none of them kept pace with the 18 percent average annual return turned in by the Dow Jones Industrial Average.

In some respects, I'm glad the one decade in which the strategy failed to outperform was the '90s. The '90s were unique. They were years of outrageous valuations on the part of many stocks. We had the Internet bubble, the technology bubble, the growth-stock bubble. You couldn't give away stocks that paid dividends. In short, the 1990s were truly an anomaly, a once-in-a-lifetime period of sweeping change, volatility, and excess. Many tried-and-true investment styles and strategies were crushed under the weight of momentum investing.

That my worst-to-first strategies didn't beat the Dow during the 1990s is, in retrospect, not surprising. Remember that my strategies rely on reversion to the mean, on stocks returning to their long-run equilibrium periods. In the 1990s, reversion to the mean didn't happen (that is, until 2000). Expensive stocks kept getting more expensive each year. And laggards kept getting cheaper as money was rushing out of them into the high fliers.

Thus, lousy performers in one year often followed up that poor performance with another down year. For example, Woolworth was among the top four worst performers in 4 out of 5 years beginning in 1991. Another killer stock was Bethlehem Steel, which followed up its showing as the Dow's worst performer in 1995 (down 23 percent) by being the worst-performing Dow stock in 1996 (down 36 percent). The inability of stocks like Woolworth and Bethlehem Steel to revert to the mean during the 1990s was a result of momentum investors chasing growth stocks—with no money left to support laggards—as well as investors wanting to avoid companies in financial distress.

Remember that the bane of any mean-reversion strategy is financial distress. You need time for mean reversion to occur. As I've said, financial distress steals time. That Woolworth and Bethlehem Steel were not exactly financial superpowers did not help their ability to snap back from bad years.

I don't expect a decade like the 1990s anytime soon. Investors are still smarting from the hangover, and my guess is that the excesses of the roaring 1990s still haven't been totally purged.

THE NEED FOR EXTREMES

Worst-to-first strategies work because Wall Street clearly demonstrates that it loves some stocks and hates some stocks—that is, worst-to-first strategies depend on extremes. Extreme prices create the greatest snapback. Think of our rubber band analogy. If the band is stretched to near the breaking point, the ensuing snapback is much greater than if the rubber band is barely stretched.

Market environments that are flat, with the market treating all stocks with equal disdain, are a problem for worst-to-first strategies. If little or no performance spread exists between the Dow's winners and losers, any mean reversion will likely be rather timid.

I generally like to see large spreads between the 10 worst performers (and especially the 5 worst performers) versus the Dow's performance. For example, in 2000, the average Dow stock was down 6 percent. The Dow's two worst performers, AT&T and Microsoft, were down 66 percent and 63 percent, respectively. That's the kind of spread that should generate some powerful mean reversion. And that was the case in 2001, when Microsoft and AT&T were the best and third-best performers among the Dow, rising 53 percent and 36 percent, respectively.

To be sure, a big spread may not be enough to help lousy performers that are in financial distress. Indeed, during the 1990s, the spreads for stocks such as Bethlehem Steel and Woolworth were fairly high, yet these stocks tended to have back-to-back dour performances. If financial distress is not an issue, however, I would expect at least some mean reversion.

CONCLUSION

This chapter shows two things:

1. The worst-to-first strategies have turned in decent gains relative to the Dow over many different time periods and during very different types of markets.
2. The worst-to-first strategies don't work every year and have had extended periods of underperformance versus the Dow.

What that means to investors is twofold:

1. You should feel comfortable putting some of your investment dollars into these strategies.
2. You should not bet the farm on this or any other investment strategy.

Indeed, nothing is infallible. Every strategy can have a bad year. If you have a limited investment time horizon, a couple of bad years can permanently deep-six your portfolio. Thus, as confident as I am in these strategies, I also recognize that investors need to diversify across a variety of investments and investment styles. For ideas on how to incorporate worst-to-first strategies into a broad-based investment program, see Chapter 7.

The following tables are a complete statistical analysis of the various worst-to-first strategies going back to 1931. To view the worst-to-first stocks each year, see the complete year-by-year statistics in the Appendix.

This table shows the annual percentage gain/loss of the worst-to-first portfolios (1-stock, 3-stock, 5-stock, and 10-stock worst-to-first portfolios) versus the annual percentage gain/loss of the Dow Industrials. These are annual total return numbers (dividends included). For example, the total return of the 10-stock worst-to-first portfolio in 1935 was 43.5 percent versus 42.9 percent in the Dow.

Performance of Worst-to-First Portfolios

Year	1 Stock (%)	3 Stocks (%)	5 Stocks (%)	10 Stocks (%)	Dow Return (%)
1931	−54.2	−57.4	−49.4	−48.4	−47.6
1932	−71.4	−16.8	−13.0	0.7	−17.1
1933	122.2	113.1	83.3	84.7	72.4
1934	25.9	7.4	12.1	16.2	7.8
1935	−5.5	43.1	36.4	43.5	42.9
1936	21.1	14.0	13.3	16.4	29.7
1937	−37.3	−30.9	−27.3	−25.0	−27.9
1938	79.9	57.0	50.7	45.0	32.2
1939	−23.2	−9.5	−5.5	−4.6	1.0

Performance of Worst-to-First Portfolios

Year	1 Stock (%)	3 Stocks (%)	5 Stocks (%)	10 Stocks (%)	Dow Return (%)
1940	−11.0	−12.7	−11.9	−10.2	−8.0
1941	19.9	18.8	11.3	−0.1	−9.6
1942	175.7	95.6	62.9	39.7	13.4
1943	16.6	14.5	11.8	17.8	19.1
1944	14.3	11.6	14.4	15.9	16.9
1945	31.3	26.5	28.1	25.9	31.0
1946	−6.0	−18.1	−13.4	−11.4	−4.3
1947	41.2	34.9	21.8	13.0	7.4
1948	−15.1	4.3	5.5	3.2	4.2
1949	30.2	36.6	35.9	30.6	20.1
1950	37.2	31.0	42.4	41.3	25.7
1951	2.6	10.5	11.3	16.8	21.3
1952	5.6	10.9	14.4	16.1	14.2
1953	−13.4	−11.5	−9.6	−1.7	1.8
1954	28.8	59.3	52.3	62.5	50.2
1955	32.0	17.2	17.7	18.1	26.1
1956	−0.6	8.1	6.5	6.1	7.0
1957	−8.0	−11.2	−10.3	−8.6	−8.4
1958	40.7	40.6	56.6	44.7	38.6
1959	35.0	19.1	14.9	16.6	20.0
1960	−1.0	−4.8	−1.3	−3.4	−6.2
1961	29.2	14.3	20.3	20.8	22.4
1962	−14.2	−10.1	−10.3	−14.0	−7.6
1963	26.7	13.9	15.2	18.5	20.6
1964	59.3	32.0	29.6	25.7	18.7
1965	27.1	10.9	14.8	9.1	14.2
1966	8.4	−12.3	−12.4	−18.8	−15.6
1967	91.4	46.4	40.2	28.3	19.0

Performance of Worst-to-First Portfolios

Year	1 Stock (%)	3 Stocks (%)	5 Stocks (%)	10 Stocks (%)	Dow Return (%)
1968	10.2	4.5	3.4	10.7	7.7
1969	−38.4	−17.6	−9.1	−5.7	−11.6
1970	−24.5	−16.8	0.3	8.3	8.8
1971	−24.4	−13.7	−3.2	2.2	9.8
1972	2.2	18.3	6.2	11.8	18.2
1973	−38.0	−31.3	−31.3	−14.5	−13.1
1974	−48.2	−10.4	−2.3	−8.7	−23.1
1975	42.9	78.7	62.4	51.2	44.4
1976	32.7	22.8	31.6	37.7	22.7
1977	−38.4	−26.5	−18.3	−14.3	−12.7
1978	−2.8	4.3	−8.3	−5.9	2.7
1979	84.0	17.6	13.0	15.6	10.5
1980	23.5	37.5	32.6	17.4	21.4
1981	−72.2	−11.6	−10.0	−5.7	−3.4
1982	−40.4	−8.1	−7.2	15.5	25.8
1983	170.6	100.7	68.8	56.2	25.7
1984	−9.2	−1.6	8.9	1.4	1.1
1985	106.9	34.1	23.8	21.0	32.8
1986	31.7	−9.4	2.2	5.7	26.9
1987	168.0	52.3	48.5	30.6	6.0
1988	26.0	38.6	32.6	30.5	14.9
1989	−11.8	5.5	17.8	29.4	31.7
1990	−41.9	−11.5	−22.7	−15.8	−0.6
1991	187.2	69.2	59.9	38.0	23.9
1992	−22.3	−15.5	0.2	3.5	7.4
1993	15.6	2.0	12.1	9.7	16.7
1994	9.2	−4.7	4.4	4.0	5.0
1995	−12.5	18.0	29.1	29.6	36.5

Performance of Worst-to-First Portfolios

Year	1 Stock (%)	3 Stocks (%)	5 Stocks (%)	10 Stocks (%)	Dow Return (%)
1996	−36.0	14.3	20.5	27.4	28.6
1997	−2.1	19.0	23.2	16.9	24.8
1998	21.8	−5.0	−5.0	9.9	18.0
1999	28.8	9.0	10.5	18.4	27.1
2000	105.2	37.1	22.9	4.8	−4.7
2001	37.2	22.7	9.2	4.5	−5.4
2002	−13.5	−4.8	−11.1	−12.5	−14.9
2003	49.0	70.8	52.7	42.1	28.3

This table shows the annual growth of a $1,000 investment in each of the worst-to-first portfolios, beginning in 1931, versus growth of a $1,000 investment in the Dow Industrials over the same time frame. For example, since 1931, a $1,000 investment in the five-stock worst-to-first portfolio grew to $2,417,333 versus $1,266,742 for the Dow.

Value of $1,000 Invested
Prior Year Price Action

Year	1 Stock ($)	3 Stocks ($)	5 Stocks ($)	10 Stocks ($)	Dow Return ($)
1931	458	426	506	516	524
1932	131	354	440	520	435
1933	291	755	807	960	749
1934	366	811	905	1116	807
1935	346	1160	1234	1601	1154
1936	419	1322	1399	1864	1497
1937	263	914	1017	1399	1078
1938	473	1435	1532	2028	1425

Value of $1,000 Invested
Prior Year Price Action

Year	1 Stock ($)	3 Stocks ($)	5 Stocks ($)	10 Stocks ($)	Dow Return ($)
1939	363	1299	1447	1934	1440
1940	323	1134	1274	1736	1325
1941	388	1347	1418	1734	1198
1942	1069	2634	2311	2422	1358
1943	1246	3014	2583	2853	1617
1944	1424	3364	2956	3308	1891
1945	1870	4256	3785	4166	2477
1946	1757	3488	3277	3689	2372
1947	2481	4705	3992	4168	2548
1948	2107	4909	4213	4299	2656
1949	2744	6705	5725	5613	3189
1950	3765	8784	8151	7934	4008
1951	3863	9709	9070	9268	4863
1952	4079	10767	10374	10759	5551
1953	3532	9529	9375	10580	5648
1954	4548	15176	14276	17188	8482
1955	6004	17785	16808	20305	10697
1956	5966	19227	17906	21535	11443
1957	5488	17072	16058	19678	10477
1958	7723	23995	25154	28465	14515
1959	10427	28585	28899	33203	17411
1960	10323	27204	28524	32080	16332
1961	13332	31085	34318	38749	19990
1962	11439	27936	30774	33319	18467
1963	14489	31812	35457	39500	22269
1964	23083	42006	45939	49655	26426
1965	29329	46574	52730	54184	30166

Value of $1,000 Invested
Prior Year Price Action

Year	1 Stock ($)	3 Stocks ($)	5 Stocks ($)	10 Stocks ($)	Dow Return ($)
1966	31780	40853	46171	43986	25446
1967	60822	59807	64748	56456	30291
1968	67023	62508	66967	62521	32633
1969	41256	51501	60865	58974	28847
1970	31146	42857	61050	63847	31373
1971	23551	36971	59092	65272	34445
1972	24069	43732	62746	72952	40717
1973	14911	30030	43121	62356	35375
1974	7728	26902	42143	56961	27188
1975	11044	48072	68432	86142	39261
1976	14656	59022	90032	118601	48180
1977	9033	43370	73576	101631	42059
1978	8784	45253	67440	95660	43190
1979	16160	53211	76237	110555	47735
1980	19951	73164	101056	129801	57957
1981	5547	64658	90906	122464	55987
1982	3309	59407	84370	141398	70427
1983	8954	119227	142402	220873	88511
1984	8126	117338	155145	223934	89443
1985	16811	157366	192013	270906	118761
1986	22139	142599	196160	286445	150728
1987	59334	217114	291319	374078	159797
1988	74757	300978	386268	488046	183574
1989	65924	317509	454880	631390	241783
1990	38278	281021	351593	531398	240392
1991	109954	475380	562271	733192	297928
1992	85427	401921	563549	759122	319835

Value of $1,000 Invested
Prior Year Price Action

Year	1 Stock ($)	3 Stocks ($)	5 Stocks ($)	10 Stocks ($)	Dow Return ($)
1993	98746	409850	631678	832695	373378
1994	107792	390767	659577	865799	391879
1995	94310	461275	851695	1122453	534880
1996	60324	527187	1026037	1429490	687730
1997	59050	627448	1263940	1671561	857958
1998	71942	596128	1200890	1837504	1012479
1999	92641	649906	1326738	2176240	1286425
2000	190114	890882	1630215	2280675	1226206
2001	260876	1092898	1780531	2384080	1159788
2002	225782	1040455	1583060	2086682	987328
2003	336415	1777097	2417333	2965175	1266742

This table shows the growth of a $1,000 investment in each of the worst-to-first portfolios over the last 50 years (beginning in 1954). For example, a $1,000 investment in the 10-stock worst-to-first portfolio at the end of 1953 grew to $280,274 by the end of 2003.

50 Years to Present (1954–2003)
Value of $1,000 Invested
Prior Year Price Action

Year	1 Stock ($)	3 Stocks ($)	5 Stocks ($)	10 Stocks ($)	Dow Return ($)
1954	1288	1593	1523	1625	1502
1955	1700	1866	1793	1919	1894
1956	1689	2018	1910	2035	2026
1957	1554	1792	1713	1860	1855
1958	2187	2518	2683	2691	2570

50 Years to Present (1954–2003)
Value of $1,000 Invested
Prior Year Price Action

Year	1 Stock ($)	3 Stocks ($)	5 Stocks ($)	10 Stocks ($)	Dow Return ($)
1959	2953	3000	3083	3138	3083
1960	2923	2855	3043	3032	2892
1961	3775	3262	3661	3663	3539
1962	3239	2932	3283	3149	3270
1963	4103	3338	3782	3734	3943
1964	6536	4408	4900	4694	4679
1965	8305	4888	5625	5122	5341
1966	8999	4287	4925	4158	4505
1967	17223	6276	6907	5336	5363
1968	18979	6560	7144	5910	5778
1969	11682	5405	6493	5574	5108
1970	8820	4498	6512	6035	5555
1971	6669	3880	6303	6170	6099
1972	6815	4589	6693	6896	7209
1973	4222	3151	4600	5894	6263
1974	2188	2823	4496	5384	4814
1975	3127	5045	7300	8142	6952
1976	4150	6194	9604	11210	8531
1977	2558	4551	7849	9606	7447
1978	2487	4749	7194	9042	7647
1979	4576	5584	8132	10450	8452
1980	5649	7678	10780	12269	10262
1981	1571	6785	9697	11575	9913
1982	937	6234	9000	13365	12470
1983	2535	12512	15190	20877	15672
1984	2301	12314	16550	21167	15837

50 Years to Present (1954–2003)
Value of $1,000 Invested
Prior Year Price Action

Year	1 Stock ($)	3 Stocks ($)	5 Stocks ($)	10 Stocks ($)	Dow Return ($)
1985	4760	16514	20482	25607	21028
1986	6269	14965	20925	27075	26688
1987	16801	22784	31076	35359	28294
1988	21168	31585	41204	46131	32504
1989	18667	33320	48523	59680	42810
1990	10839	29491	37505	50229	42564
1991	31135	49887	59979	69303	52751
1992	24190	42178	60115	71754	56630
1993	27961	43010	67382	78708	66110
1994	30523	41008	70358	81837	69386
1995	26705	48407	90852	106096	94706
1996	17082	55324	109449	135118	121769
1997	16721	65846	134827	157999	151910
1998	20371	62559	128101	173684	179269
1999	26233	68202	141526	205702	227774
2000	53834	93491	173898	215574	217112
2001	73871	114691	189933	225348	205352
2002	63934	109187	168868	197237	174816
2003	95262	186491	257861	280274	224288

This table shows how much a $1,000 investment in the various worst-to-first strategies has grown over the last 30 years.

30 Years to Present (1974–2003)
Value of $1,000 Invested
Prior Year Price Action

Year	1 Stock ($)	3 Stocks ($)	5 Stocks ($)	10 Stocks ($)	Dow Return ($)
1974	518	896	977	913	769
1975	741	1601	1587	1381	1110
1976	983	1965	2088	1902	1362
1977	606	1444	1706	1630	1189
1978	589	1507	1564	1534	1221
1979	1084	1772	1768	1773	1349
1980	1338	2436	2344	2082	1638
1981	372	2153	2108	1964	1583
1982	222	1978	1957	2268	1991
1983	600	3970	3302	3542	2502
1984	545	3907	3598	3591	2528
1985	1127	5240	4453	4345	3357
1986	1485	4749	4549	4594	4261
1987	3979	7230	6756	5999	4517
1988	5013	10023	8958	7827	5189
1989	4421	10573	10549	10126	6835
1990	2567	9358	8154	8522	6796
1991	7374	15830	13039	11758	8422
1992	5729	13384	13069	12174	9041
1993	6622	13648	14649	13354	10555
1994	7229	13013	15296	13885	11078
1995	6325	15360	19751	18001	15120
1996	4046	17555	23794	22925	19441

30 Years to Present (1974–2003)
Value of $1,000 Invested
Prior Year Price Action

Year	1 Stock ($)	3 Stocks ($)	5 Stocks ($)	10 Stocks ($)	Dow Return ($)
1997	3960	20894	29311	26807	24254
1998	4825	19851	27849	29468	28622
1999	6213	21642	30768	34900	36366
2000	12750	29666	37805	36575	34664
2001	17495	36394	41291	38234	32786
2002	15142	34647	36712	33464	27911
2003	22562	59177	56059	47552	35810

20 Years to Present (1984–2003)
Value of $1,000 Invested
Prior Year Price Action

Year	1 Stock ($)	3 Stocks ($)	5 Stocks ($)	10 Stocks ($)	Dow Return ($)
1984	908	984	1089	1014	1011
1985	1878	1320	1348	1227	1342
1986	2473	1196	1378	1297	1703
1987	6627	1821	2046	1694	1805
1988	8349	2524	2713	2210	2074
1989	7363	2663	3194	2859	2732
1990	4275	2357	2469	2406	2716
1991	12280	3987	3948	3320	3366
1992	9541	3371	3957	3437	3614
1993	11029	3438	4436	3770	4218
1994	12039	3277	4632	3920	4427
1995	10533	3869	5981	5082	6043
1996	6737	4422	7205	6472	7770
1997	6595	5263	8876	7568	9693

20 Years to Present (1984–2003)
Value of $1,000 Invested
Prior Year Price Action

Year	1 Stock ($)	3 Stocks ($)	5 Stocks ($)	10 Stocks ($)	Dow Return ($)
1998	8035	5000	8433	8319	11439
1999	10347	5451	9317	9853	14534
2000	21233	7472	11448	10326	13854
2001	29137	9167	12504	10794	13103
2002	25217	8727	11117	9447	11155
2003	37573	14906	16976	13424	14312

10 Years to Present (1994–2003)
Value of $1,000 Invested
Prior Year Price Action

Year	1 Stock ($)	3 Stocks ($)	5 Stocks ($)	10 Stocks ($)	Dow Return ($)
1994	1092	953	1044	1040	1050
1995	955	1125	1348	1348	1433
1996	611	1286	1624	1717	1842
1997	598	1531	2001	2007	2298
1998	729	1455	1901	2207	2712
1999	938	1586	2100	2613	3445
2000	1925	2174	2581	2739	3284
2001	2642	2667	2819	2863	3106
2002	2286	2539	2506	2506	2644
2003	3406	4337	3827	3561	3392

5 Years to Present (1999–2003)
Value of $1,000 Invested
Prior Year Price Action

Year	1 Stock ($)	3 Stocks ($)	5 Stocks ($)	10 Stocks ($)	Dow Return ($)
1999	1288	1090	1105	1184	1271
2000	2643	1494	1358	1241	1211
2001	3626	1833	1483	1297	1145
2002	3138	1745	1318	1136	975
2003	4676	2980	2013	1614	1251

This table shows the annualized total returns of the various worst-to-first portfolios over the last 30 years, 20 years, 10 years, 5 years, 3 years, 1 year, and since 1931. For example, over the last 10 years, the 5-stock worst-to-first portfolio posted an average annual return of 14.4 percent versus a 13.0 percent return in the Dow Industrials over the same time period.

Annualized Returns to Present (2003)
Prior Year Price Action

Years	1 Stock (%)	3 Stocks (%)	5 Stocks (%)	10 Stocks (%)	Dow Return (%)
1	49.0	70.8	52.7	42.1	28.3
3	20.9	25.9	14.0	9.1	1.1
5	36.1	24.4	15.0	10.0	4.6
10	13.0	15.8	14.4	13.5	13.0
20	19.9	14.5	15.2	13.9	14.2
30	10.9	14.6	14.3	13.7	12.7
Since 1931	8.3	10.8	11.3	11.6	10.3

6

Worst to First—Advanced Strategies

One of the strengths of the basic worst-to-first strategies—buying the worst-performing Dow stocks, holding them for a year, and rebalancing—is its simplicity. Having said that, a number of additional ways exist to exploit mean reversion in an investment strategy focusing on Dow stocks. For the more adventuresome investors, here are some advanced worst-to-first techniques.

Dow Stocks Trading Below Their 200-Day Moving Average

If you think about it, reversion to the mean implies that some long-run equilibrium exists for most stocks—that is, although stocks may bounce all around the place in the short run, they tend to revert over time to some steady state, the "golden mean," if you will. We exploited this tendency for mean reversion in the basic worst-to-first strategies—buying the worst-performing stocks in the Dow. The thinking here, obviously, is that a stock that has been beaten up dramatically in one year is probably due for a bounce-back.

The potential problem with simply using the worst-performing stocks as a barometer for mean reversion is that the worst performers may actually not be trading well below their long-run average. If you were trying to think of what would constitute a stock's equilibrium range, you would probably want to look at a stock's average trading level over some period of time. One fairly common time frame that investors use when evaluating stocks is a 200-day moving average. A stock's 200-day moving average line is computed by taking the average price of the stock's last 200 trading days to obtain the first point on the line. To get the second point, drop a day and add a day, and take the average . . . and so on.

As you can see, a stock's 200-day moving average line takes into account a fairly long period of stock prices. For that reason, I think the 200-day moving average represents a worthwhile benchmark for a stock's long-run equilibrium level.

Now, if you buy into the fact that a stock's 200-day moving average is a reasonable surrogate for its long-run equilibrium level, mean reversion says that anytime a stock is trading well above or well below that 200-day moving average, you would expect the stock to eventually migrate back to its long-run equilibrium point. Thus, an alternative way to employ a mean-reversion investment strategy in the Dow is to buy the Dow stocks trading the greatest percentage below their 200-day moving average. In that way, an investor truly is owning the stocks that would be expected to have the biggest rebounds according to mean reversion.

Is the 200-day moving average a better tool for mean reversion than the stock's 12-month price change? As we have seen, the latter metric works exceedingly well in pinpointing rebound stocks. And, not surprisingly, in many cases the worst-performing stock will also be the stock trading the most below its 200-day moving average. For example, in 17 of the 20 years (1983 through 2002), the worst-performing Dow stock was also among the top two Dow worst performers in terms of its 200-day moving average.

Still, you may improve your odds of investing in stocks that are ready to rebound by incorporating the 200-day moving average analysis into your worst-to-first strategies, if nothing else but to validate that the worst-performing stock (in terms of 12-month price change) truly has moved to an extreme level below its equilibrium range. How well would you have done if you bought the Dow stocks trading the greatest percentage below their 200-day moving average? To test the 200-day moving average, I (with the help of the Center for Research in Security Prices at the University of Chicago) went back to 1963 and looked at the year-end ratio of price to 200-day moving average for all 30 Dow components. I then back-tested a strategy of simply buying the stocks trading the farthest below their 200-day moving average. I discovered that an investor who bought the single Dow stock trading below its 200-day moving average would have made huge money over the last 10-, 20-, and 30-year holding periods.

30 Years	Value of $1,000 Invested	30 Years	Value of $1,000 Invested
1974	518	1989	3447
1975	724	1990	2002
1976	1131	1991	2335
1977	697	1992	1814
1978	671	1993	2097
1979	772	1994	2058
1980	1180	1995	2645
1981	328	1996	4476
1982	196	1997	4381
1983	354	1998	5338
1984	425	1999	6874
1985	879	2000	14105
1986	1150	2001	19356
1987	3103	2002	24315
1988	3909	2003	38126
		Dow (30 year): 35810	

2003

20 Years

1984	1199
1985	2480
1986	3267
1987	8754
1988	11030
1989	9727
1990	5648

2003

20 Years

1991	6589
1992	5119
1993	5917
1994	5808
1995	7463
1996	12629
1997	12362
1998	15061
1999	19395
2000	39801
2001	54615
2002	68610
2003	107580
	Dow (20 year): 14312

2003

10 Years

1994	981
1995	1261
1996	2134
1997	2089
1998	2545
1999	3278
2000	6726
2001	9230
2002	11595
2003	18181
	Dow (10 year): 3392

2003	
5 Years	
1999	1288
2000	2643
2001	3626
2002	4555
2003	7142
	Dow (5 year): 1251

In fact, an investor who bought the Dow stock trading the farthest below its 200-day moving average on the last trading day of the year, and held it for 1 year and rebalanced, would have turned $1,000 at the end of 1983 into $107,580 by December 31, 2003. That huge gain was more than seven times greater than the gain of the Dow Jones Industrial Average. It was also nearly three times better than simply buying the worst-performing Dow stock.

Of course, any investment strategy that focuses on a single stock has lots of risk. Indeed, a single-stock portfolio may experience huge volatility as a result of stock-specific risk. Also, if the company is trading below its 200-day moving average because it is in financial distress, there's no assurance that mean reversion will kick in if finances go from bad to worse. Thus, if you plan to exploit this strategy of buying the Dow stock that is trading the greatest percentage below its 200-day moving average, make sure you use some protective stop to help limit downside risk.

I'm sure some of you are wondering where you can find a stock's price relative to its 200-day moving average. The easiest place to obtain this information is from my Web site: www.dowunderdogs.com. I maintain it on a daily basis for all Dow stocks. Another source is the Yahoo Finance Web site: http://finance.yahoo.com. At that site, you can create a portfolio of Dow stocks by hitting the "create" button near the top of the page and inputting the stock symbols for the 30 components. Once you've created the Dow portfolio, you can "edit" the "performance" of the portfolio to include various metrics. One of those metrics is "Pct Chg From 200-day Moving Average." Once you

**1-Stock (200-Day Worst to First) versus Dow Industrials—
20 Years**

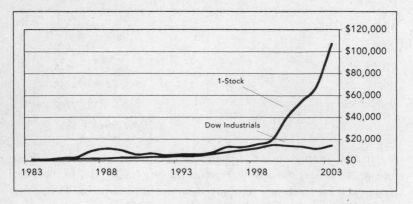

include this metric, you can see just how each Dow component is trading relative to its 200-day moving average.

In order to put this strategy into practice, follow these steps:

1. On the last day of the year (or quarter, or whenever you plan to put this strategy into effect), look at each of the 30 Dow stocks and determine where the current price is relative to its 200-day moving average price.
2. Buy the Dow stock (or, if you want a more diversified portfolio, the 3 or 5 or 10 Dow stocks) trading the greatest percentage below its 200-day moving average.
3. Hold that investment (or investments) for 1 year and 1 day.
4. At the end of the year, sell the stock(s) and buy the new Dow stock(s) that is trading the greatest percentage below its 200-day moving average.

Example: Below are the 30 Dow stocks as of the end of 2002, along with the ratio of each stock's year-end price to its 200-day moving average. Remember that the smaller the ratio, the greater the stock is trading below its 200-day moving average. As you can see, the Dow stock trading the greatest percentage below its 200-day moving average was McDonald's, followed by Home Depot, Intel, General Motors, and Honeywell. If you wanted to follow this strategy for 2003, you would have bought McDonald's on the first trading day of 2003 and held it for the year. An alternative would be to buy the five stocks with the smallest ratios (McDonald's, Home Depot, Intel, General Motors, and Honeywell International) and hold those for the year. If you wanted to limit your downside in any one stock, you would set protective stop orders with your broker.

2002 Dow Component Performance	Ratio Price
MCDONALDS CORP	0.68
HOME DEPOT INC	0.70
INTEL CORP	0.75
GENERAL MOTORS CORP	0.76
HONEYWELL INTERNATIONAL INC	0.78
ALCOA INC	0.81
GENERAL ELECTRIC CO	0.83
BOEING CO	0.85
DISNEY WALT CO	0.86
PHILIP MORRIS COS INC	0.86
COCA COLA CO	0.86
J P MORGAN CHASE & CO	0.87
INTERNATIONAL PAPER CO	0.90
WAL MART STORES INC	0.93
JOHNSON & JOHNSON	0.94
EXXON MOBIL CORP	0.94
S B C COMMUNICATIONS INC	0.94
AMERICAN EXPRESS CO	0.96
UNITED TECHNOLOGIES CORP	0.96
CITIGROUP INC	0.96
PROCTER & GAMBLE CO	0.97
CATERPILLAR INC	0.98
DU PONT E I DE NEMOURS & CO	0.99
MICROSOFT CORP	0.99

2002 Dow Component Performance	Ratio Price
INTERNATIONAL BUSINESS MACHS COR	1.00
3M CO	1.00
A T & T CORP	1.05
MERCK & CO INC	1.08
HEWLETT PACKARD CO	1.08
EASTMAN KODAK CO	1.10

How did the stocks at the top of the list perform in 2003? Here is the performance of the top five stocks through December 31, 2003, compared to the Dow:

- McDonald's: +56.8 percent
- Home Depot: +49.0 percent
- Intel: +106.5 percent
- General Motors: +52.7 percent
- Honeywell International: +43.3 percent

Dow Jones Industrial Average: +28.3 percent

A fair question at this point would be: Why 200 days? Why not look at a stock's 250-day moving average, or its 400-day moving average? Actually, a good argument could be made that a better proxy for a stock's long-run equilibrium range would be a moving average of at least 1 to 2 years. Since there are approximately 250 trading days per year, perhaps looking at a stock's 250-day or 500-day moving average would provide better results.

I would maintain that using a stock's 200-day moving average, as my results show, has been extremely productive in generating big portfolio profits. Nevertheless, I cannot tell you that using a 250-day or a 500-day moving average would not yield better results. The appeals of using a 200-day moving average are that it does represent a fairly lengthy period of time and it is readily obtainable. As mentioned, anyone can find out a stock's 200-day moving average price by visiting my Web site (www.dowunderdogs.com) or using the feature provided on the Yahoo Finance Web site. Determining the 250-day or the 500-day moving average is not impossible but a bit more complicated for the average investor. If you want to use different moving average prices, here is a way to obtain the necessary data:

1. Log on to the Yahoo Finance Web site (http://finance.yahoo.com).
2. Type the symbol of a stock of interest and hit "enter."
3. You'll be taken to an information page on that stock. Notice the link "Historical Prices." Click on that link.
4. You'll be taken to a page that allows you to input specific dates for the stock. Let's say that you want to compute a stock's 2-year moving average price. You would enter the dates that would provide a full 2 years worth of prices.
5. Once you enter dates, specify you want daily prices, and hit "enter," you'll be taken to a series of pages that show the daily high, low, and close for the stock of interest.
6. Notice that you can download this pricing information into a Microsoft Excel spreadsheet. Follow the directions to do so.
7. Once you have downloaded the pricing information into Excel, you can manipulate the data to determine the stock's average closing price over the 2-year period.
8. Once you have determined the moving average price, you can determine its relationship to the stock's current price simply by taking the current price and dividing by the 2-year moving average price.

Again, one reason I use a stock's 200-day moving average is that the data are readily available. However, for investors who want to implement a mean-reversion strategy in the Dow by using periods that are different from a 200-day moving average, the Yahoo Finance Web site provides an excellent resource for customizing moving average studies.

Long-Short Program

Another strategy that takes advantage of the concept of mean reversion uses both the worst-performing stock and the best-performing stock in the Dow. Remember that reversion to the mean applies not only to stocks that have fallen and are due to rebound but also to stocks that have surged and, under mean reversion, are expected to pull back to their long-run equilibrium range.

While the basic worst-to-first strategy focuses exclusively on buying stocks, an investor who feels comfortable shorting stocks can also take advantage of mean reversion. Short sellers focus on stocks they believe are headed lower. A short seller sells the stock that he or she doesn't actually own with the hope of buying back the stock at a lower price, thus pocketing the difference in price.

Let's say you believe Boeing, which is trading for $40 per share, is overvalued at current prices. If you believe Boeing is headed lower, you can go to your broker (provided you have established an account that allows you to sell stocks short) and actually sell shares of Boeing that you don't own. By selling the stock, you lock up a $40 per share sale price. At some point, short sellers must close out their position, which means they must buy back the stock in the future. Let's say you are right about Boeing and the stock declines to $25. You can then close out your position by buying back the Boeing stock at $25. In this instance, you would have made $15 per share in profit (sold at $40, bought back at $25, for a $15 difference), minus trading commissions.

This example shows what can happen when short selling works to your advantage. Keep in mind, however, that short selling can expose you to losses. Why? Suppose you were wrong about Boeing, and the stock surged to $60. Where does that leave you? You would be showing a paper loss of $20 per share on your holding. Now, you would not necessarily have to close out your position by buying back the stock. However, you would probably have to pony up more money to cover your margin, or the collateral (cash and/or stocks in your brokerage account) that you must have with your broker in order to sell short.

Short selling can lead to big losses because the loss potential is unlimited. When you buy stock, your loss potential is the amount of your investment. When you short a stock, however, your losses are unlimited since the stock can (in theory at least) rise to infinity.

More daring investors can play both ends of the mean-reversion concept with the Dow by implementing a *long-short* program. In this strategy, investors go long (or buy) stocks in the Dow that have performed the worst over the last 12 months (or are trading the greatest percentage below their 200-day moving average) while selling short the Dow stocks that have performed the best over the last 12 months (or are trading the greatest percentage above their 200-day moving average). Let's return to the end of 2002 to provide a concrete example:

	Closing Price	200-Day Average Price	Ratio	Annual Price Change (%)
HOME DEPOT	24.02	34.54	0.70	−52.9
INTEL	15.57	20.79	0.75	−50.5
MCDONALDS	16.08	23.50	0.68	−39.3
GE	24.35	29.20	0.83	−39.2
IBM	77.50	77.77	1.00	−35.9
ALCOA	22.78	28.03	0.81	−35.9
J P MORGAN CHASE	24.00	27.64	0.87	−34.0
S B C COMM.	27.11	28.78	0.94	−30.8
HONEYWELL	24.00	30.65	0.78	−29.0
A T & T	26.11	24.96	1.05	−28.4
CITIGROUP	35.19	36.53	0.96	−25.7
GENERAL MOTORS	36.86	48.19	0.76	−24.2
MICROSOFT	25.85	26.13	0.99	−22.0
WALT DISNEY	16.31	18.93	0.86	−21.3
HEWLETT PACKARD	17.36	16.07	1.08	−15.5
BOEING	32.99	38.82	0.85	−14.9
INT'L PAPER	34.97	38.95	0.90	−13.3
CATERPILLAR	45.72	46.83	0.98	−12.5
WAL MART STORES	50.51	54.26	0.93	−12.2
PHILIP MORRIS	40.53	47.05	0.86	−11.6
EXXON MOBIL	34.94	37.09	0.94	−11.1
J&J	53.71	57.20	0.94	−9.1
COCA COLA	43.84	50.69	0.86	−7.0
UNITED TECH.	61.94	64.53	0.96	−4.2
MERCK & CO	56.61	52.52	1.08	−3.7
AMERICAN EXPRESS	35.35	36.91	0.96	−1.0
DU PONT	42.40	42.90	0.99	−0.3
3M	123.30	123.55	1.00	4.3
PROCTER & GAMBLE	85.94	88.84	0.97	9.5
EASTMAN KODAK	35.04	31.79	1.10	19.1

One way to implement this long-short strategy would be to buy the worst-performing Dow stock (Home Depot) while shorting the best-performing Dow stock in 2002 (Eastman Kodak). Ideally, what you hope happens is that Home Depot rises a lot and Eastman Kodak declines a lot. In that way, you make big profits on your long position (Home Depot) while generating big profits on your short position (Eastman Kodak). At the very least, in order to generate a profit on the trade, you need Home Depot to rise more than Eastman Kodak. In that way, your long position covers the losses on your short position in Eastman Kodak.

Remember that one way to reduce your downside risk is to set stop orders. You can set stop orders in long and short positions. Here is a potential $10,000 long-short investment strategy for 2003 (based on year-end 2002 results for the Dow):

1. Buy $5,000 worth of Home Depot stock (208 shares) at $24.02 (the closing price of 2002). Set a stop at $20.40 (15 percent below the market price) in order to protect yourself on the downside.
2. Sell short $5,000 worth of Eastman Kodak (143 shares) at $35.04. Set a stop on the short at $40.25. (This stop is 15 percent above the purchase price. Remember that you lose on a short position when the stock rises, not falls.)
3. Hold for 1 year and 1 day.
4. At the end of the holding period, sell your Home Depot position while buying back (also known as *covering*) your short position in Eastman Kodak.

This strategy would have worked particularly well in 2003. Indeed, your long position in Home Depot rose 49 percent. And your short position (because Eastman Kodak declined around 25 percent) showed a 25 percent profit. Thus, the gain on Home Depot, coupled with the gain on the Eastman Kodak short, would have translated into a hefty 74 percent profit in 2003. For comparison, the Dow's return in 2003 was just 28.3 percent.

A variation of the long-short strategy would be to buy the five worst-performing Dow stocks while going short the five best-performing Dow stocks. Alternatively, an investor could go long the

Dow stock that is trading the greatest percentage below its 200-day moving average while shorting the Dow stock trading the greatest percentage above its 200-day moving average. If you followed this strategy at the end of 2002 for 2003, you would have gone long McDonald's (up 56.8 percent in 2003) while still shorting Eastman Kodak. For 2003, this long-short position would have yielded a positive return of around 82 percent—well ahead of the 28.3 percent gain in the Dow.

I reiterate that shorting stock does have its risks. That's why using some protective stop on your short position (remember to place the stop *above* the purchase price) would help limit your risk.

WORST-TO-FIRST STRATEGY USING OPTIONS AND LEAPS

Warning: What you are about to read deals with options. Option investing can entail substantial risks. Use options at your own peril.

Sorry for the overkill, but I think it is important to make sure you understand that the next advanced technique for exploiting the worst-to-first strategy entails the potentially high-risk world of options. Options are forms of derivative securities. Derivatives are financial instruments whose prices are derived from prices of other underlying securities, assets, or indexes. For example, a *call* option on a stock gives an investor the right to buy a stock at a set price. A *put* option gives an investor the right to sell a stock at a set price. Options provide a way for an investor to leverage a bet on the direction of the underlying stock.

Let's say that you really like American Express at $40 and believe the stock is destined for $50 within the next 6 months. To leverage your bet, an investor may choose to buy the underlying call option rather than the common stock. Here's why: Let's say you purchase a call option on American Express with a strike price of $40 with 9 months until expiration. Basically, that call option gives you the option of purchasing American Express stock at $40 anytime during that 9-month period. Of course, the call option is not free; you'll have to pay something to obtain the option. The price of an option is called a *premium*. Option premiums are determined by a variety of items, but an important driver of option premiums is the underlying volatility of the stock. The more volatile the stock, the higher the cost of the option. Now, let's say that you pay $5 to purchase one call option on American Express at $40. (Actually, options are priced in $100 increments. Thus, a $5 option will cost you $500.) You are now the owner of one call option on American Express, giving you the option to purchase 100 shares of American Express stock anytime over the next 9 months at $40 per share.

Now, let's say you were right about American Express. The stock soars from $40 to $50 in 4 months. What has happened to the value of your option? Well, if you have an option to buy American Express at $40 and the stock is currently trading for $50, the value of the option has to be worth at least $10. If its value was less than $10, an investor would exercise the option, buy American Express at $40, and immediately sell at $50 for a gain of $10 per share.

Actually, the call option will be worth more than $10 since the premium will reflect the fact that there are still 5 months remaining before the option expires. In this scenario, what happened to your initial $5 (actually $500) investment in the option? Its price has at least doubled to $10 ($1,000). In just 4 months, your investment has gained 100 percent or more.

Compare that to the gain had you bought the stock instead of the option. Your gain in American Express stock would be 25 percent (a $10 gain on a $40 purchase price)—a pretty good return for 4 months but not nearly as big as the gain on your call option.

Let's say that you think American Express is a dog and the stock is overpriced at $40. You think the stock will drop to $30 over the next 9 months. However, you are not comfortable selling short American Express. To leverage this bet, an investor may buy a put option. As mentioned, a put option gives an investor the right to sell a stock at a given price. Now, let's say you buy a put on American Express with a strike price of $40 with a 9-month life. That option gives you the right to sell 100 shares of American Express at $40 anytime during the next 9 months. Let's say you pay $5 for the put.

Instead of rising to $50, American Express drops to $30. What is the value of your put option? The option would be worth at least $10. Why? Again, the put option gives you the right to sell the stock at $40. However, you cannot sell something you don't own. Thus, let's assume you exercised the put option and sold the stock at $40. To cover that sell, you would have to buy back the stock. In this case, you would buy back the stock at $30. Thus, your profit would be $10 (selling at $40 and buying at $30). Your put option, then, would have to be worth at least $10.

As in the previous case, the value of your option doubled, from $5 (or $500) to $10 (or $1,000). Thus, your gain on the put option was 100 percent. Sound too easy? Actually, options can create huge profits for investors. But plenty of risks exist. For starters, remember that options have a limited life span. Think back to our examples. The longer the life of the option, the greater its value as a result of the time premium. However, as time elapses and the option gets closer and closer to its expiration date, the time premium shrinks and eventually disappears.

Return to our first example. Let's say you bought an American Express call option with a strike price at $40. If the stock trades for $39 at the end of the option's life, the option would expire worthless. That's because an option to buy a stock at $40 that is trading for $39 has no value at all.

Herein lies the rub with options. An investor has to be right about the direction of the underlying stock *and* has to see that idea come to fruition in a fairly limited period of time. Being right about a stock and right about timing is hard to do successfully over time. That's why most options expire worthless.

Still, for more aggressive investors who want to leverage a worst-to-first strategy, options do provide an interesting vehicle. Indeed, all 30 Dow stocks have call and put options available for purchase, which means that an investor who wants to implement any variation of the worst-to-first strategy could do so using put and call options rather than buying and shorting the underlying stocks.

Let's say that you wanted to employ the worst-to-first strategy in 2003 (choosing the five worst performers in 2002) but you wanted to buy options, not stocks. On the first day of trading in 2003, you purchased options on the following stocks:

Home Depot ($24.02)

Intel ($15.57)

McDonald's ($16.08)

General Electric ($24.35)

IBM ($77.50)

Remember that one option gives you the right to purchase 100 shares of the underlying stock. One appeal of using options instead of the stock, in addition to the increased leverage, is that it is a cheaper way to implement the strategy. Look at the prices of the five worst-to-first stocks for 2003. To buy 100 shares in each of the five stocks would entail an investment of more than $15,700. However, to purchase the equivalent of 100 shares in each of the companies via buying a single call option in each of the five companies (assuming you bought call options with a strike price that matched the current stock price) would have entailed a much smaller investment—as low as $1,000 if you purchased relatively short-term options (expiring within 3 months).

One relevant question is: What is the best option term to employ in the worst-to-first strategy? Since the holding period for our basic strategy is 12 months, I would opt for 12-month options. Now, most options have a maximum 9-month life. Fortunately, an option form exists that provides investors with an option life of more than 12 months. Best of all, many of the Dow 30 stocks have them.

LEAPS

In 1990, Long-Term Equity Anticipation Securities (LEAPS) were introduced to the options market. LEAPS are basically long-term call and put options. They are purchased on the various options exchanges the same way and in the same dollar increments as call and put options. For example, one LEAPS call is the equivalent of having an option to buy 100 shares of the underlying stock. One LEAPS put is the equivalent of having an option to sell 100 shares of the underlying stock.

LEAPS are attractive vehicles for implementing an aggressive worst-to-first strategy for several reasons:

• Most Dow stocks have LEAPS.

• LEAPS provide ample leverage for investors. Since LEAPS are options, gains in the underlying stock will create even bigger percentage gains in the LEAPS. (Of course, this leverage cuts both ways. Losses in the underlying stock will create even greater losses, on a percentage basis, in the LEAPS.)

- LEAPS have life spans of more than 1 year.

Buying LEAPS is as easy as buying common stocks or call and put options. One online brokerage firm with low commissions for options and LEAPS is Interactive Brokers (www.interactivebrokers.com). Interactive charges just $1 per option contract.

Step-by-Step Blueprint for Implementing LEAPS Worst-to-First Strategy

1. Open an account at a brokerage firm that allows you to trade LEAPS.
2. Determine the amount of money you want to invest in the strategy.
3. On the first day of each year, buy the LEAPS of the five worst-performing Dow stocks over the last 12 months. (Alternatively, if you wanted to be more aggressive, you could buy the LEAPS of the single worst-performing Dow stock, or the LEAPS of the Dow stock that is trading the greatest percentage below its 200-day moving average.) As much as possible, try to invest equal dollar amounts in each LEAPS.
4. Make sure you buy LEAPS that have a life span greater than 12 months. For example, if it is January 2004, make sure you buy LEAPS that expire in January 2005 or later. Basically, LEAPS expire after the third Friday of the expiration month. The last trading day for the LEAPS is the business day preceding that Saturday. This is also the case with regular call and put options.
5. Hold the LEAPS for 1 year and 1 day.
6. Sell the LEAPS and purchase LEAPS of the new Dow Underdogs.

Keep in mind that you don't necessarily have to implement this strategy on the first day of the year. You could implement a worst-to-first strategy anytime throughout the year if you know which Dow stocks have shown the biggest negative price change over the last 12

months or are trading at the greatest percentage change below their
200-day moving average. The key point is that you need to hold the
LEAPS for 1 year and 1 day.

Note that any worst-to-first strategy that you can do with stocks
you can do using LEAPS. Let's say you want to make a bet that the
worst-performing Dow stock will do well and the best-performing
Dow stock will decline. You can buy the LEAPS call on the worst performer and the LEAPS put on the best performer to simulate a long-
short strategy. You can also combine LEAPS and stocks. For example,
you can go long the worst performer (by buying the stock) while buying a LEAPS put on the best performer.

Two final cautions are in order. Yes, options and LEAPS will mag-
nify the gains that you would achieve in a worst-to-first strategy. But
options and LEAPS will also accentuate losses when the strategy
doesn't work. Indeed, it is quite possible that you could lose your
entire investment in options and LEAPS if the worst-to-first strategy
performs poorly for that 12-month time frame. Also, options and
LEAPS values reflect both a time premium and a price premium.
Thus, the closer the LEAPS is to expiration, the lesser the time premium in the LEAPS price.

In terms of taxes, options and LEAPS may not always be tax-
friendly relative to owning the underlying stocks. Indeed, all gains on
traditional call and put options (because they have a maximum life of
9 months) are taxed at ordinary income rates. And the tax rules gov-
erning LEAPS can get rather hairy in terms of short-term versus long-
term gains. The bottom line is that these strategies will tend to be less
tax-friendly than buying the underlying stocks and holding for more
than 12 months. For these reasons, investors should pursue an option/
LEAPS driven worst-to-first strategy only with higher-risk capital.

AN ENHANCED INDEX APPROACH TO THE DOW

In the late 1990s, I comanaged the Strong Dow 30 Value fund. The
fund was an enhanced index fund. An enhanced index fund attempts
to generate superior returns to the index while not straying too far
from the performance of the underlying index. In our fund, 50 percent
of the assets were pegged directly to the Dow. With the remaining 50
percent of the assets, my partner and I overweighted (relative to the

stock's weighting in the index) Dow stocks that we liked and under-weighted (relative to the stock's weighting in the index) Dow stocks that we didn't like. Our approach was well received by investors. Indeed, in less than 3 years, fund assets grew to more than $150 million.

One reason that enhanced indexes are appealing is that they allow you to have your cake and eat it, too. On the one hand, an enhanced index fund is usually going to perform close to the underlying index. Thus, an investor who doesn't want too much variation in returns over time from a particular index will feel comfortable owning an enhanced index fund. On the other hand, the fact that it is an enhanced index investment gives you the possibility of outperforming the index over time.

Investors who find an enhanced index approach to investing appealing can implement a simple Dow enhanced index approach by combining an investment in the Dow Jones Industrial Average with an investment in the worst-to-first stocks. The easiest way to make an investment in the entire Dow is by buying the Dow Diamond. The Diamond is an exchange-traded fund listed on the American Stock Exchange. Exchange-traded funds are a hybrid of a mutual fund and a stock. Like a traditional mutual fund, an exchange-traded fund is a single investment that allows an investor to buy a basket of stocks. Unlike a traditional open-end mutual fund, which does not trade on any stock exchange, exchange-traded funds trade just like stocks—that is, any investor can buy an exchange-traded fund simply by placing an order via a broker.

Exchange-traded funds, unlike options, have no finite life. Also, unlike open-end mutual funds, exchange-traded funds can be bought and sold intraday. Finally, the fees to own exchange-traded funds are rather small—the commission to purchase the exchange-traded fund and a fairly minimal annual expense fee.

As mentioned, the exchange-traded fund for the Dow is referred to as the *Diamond*. The trading symbol is DIA. An investor who simply wants to replicate the Dow can buy Diamonds and, in effect, buy the Dow.

If you want to try to beat the Dow but don't want your investment to stray too far from the Dow's performance, one strategy is to combine a Diamond with purchases of worst-to-first stocks or LEAPS.

Let's say you have $5,000 you want to devote to an investment in the Dow but are looking to "juice up" this investment a bit. One approach would be to take $4,000 and buy Dow Diamonds. With the remaining $1,000, you could buy LEAPS on one or more of the Dow Underdogs.

How would this strategy perform? Well, of course, it depends on the Dow's performance as well as the performance of the various worst-to-first strategies you employ. Let's assume that the Dow rises 8 percent over the year, and your worst-to-first strategy hits a home run—up 30 percent for the year. Your total $5,000 would grow to $5,620 (your $4,000 in the Diamonds multiplied by the 8 percent return *plus* the $1,000 investment in LEAPS multiplied by the 30 percent return)—a gain of 12.4 percent. Notice that your performance was more than 4 percentage points higher than the Dow's gain of 8 percent.

Now, let's say that the worst-to-first strategy you chose was a stinker for the year, losing 30 percent. Your $5,000 investment (assuming the same 8 percent return on the Dow) would have risen to just $5,020—a gain of 0.4 percent. In this instance, you would have done nearly 8 percentage points worse than the Dow. However—and this is important—you would have still made a few bucks even though one-fifth of your investment had declined 30 percent.

Obviously, you can tweak an enhanced index approach based on your risk parameters and your desire to stay close to the performance of the underlying index. The following is one enhanced index strategy using Dow Diamonds, LEAPS, and Dow Underdogs:

Enhanced Index Approach (assuming investment of $10,000)

1. Open a brokerage account. Make sure the account allows you to buy LEAPS.
2. Determine the portion of your money that you want indexed to the Dow and the portion you want to invest in enhancers. Obviously, the more dollars devoted to enhancers, the more divergence between the performance of the Dow and your investment performance. In this example, you have decided to go with $7,500 in Dow Diamonds and $2,500 in enhancers.
3. You purchase $7,500 worth of Dow Diamonds.
4. You purchase $1,250 in the long LEAPS (the *call* LEAPS) of the

Dow stock that is trading the farthest below its 200-day moving average and $1,250 in the short LEAPS (the *put* LEAPS) of the Dow stock that is trading the greatest percentage above its 200-day moving average. You want to buy the LEAPS with the strike price closest to the actual trading price of the underlying stock. Make sure the LEAPS you buy have a life span of at least 12 months.

5. Hold the Diamond and LEAPS for 1 year and 1 day.
6. Sell your positions and (hopefully) count your profits.

As you can see, this enhanced index approach uses a variation of the long-short approach discussed earlier in this chapter. But instead of going long the Dow Underdog and shorting the Dow winner, we use LEAPS puts and calls to replicate a similar bet.

CONCLUSION

The beauty of mean reversion is that you can apply the concept in a variety of ways and investment vehicles. Of course, each of these strategies has its own risks, and you need to decide how risky you want to be in implementing a worst-to-first approach with the Dow. With such vehicles as LEAPS and Diamonds, the nice thing is that investors who have fairly limited funds can implement any one of several techniques used to take advantage of the profit-making opportunities in the Dow Underdogs.

Part IV

The Portfolio—
Putting the Pieces Together

7

Worst to First—An Important Piece of the Portfolio Puzzle

If the last 3 years have taught us anything, it's that diversification matters. I've written a lot about diversification in recent years, for good reason. How your portfolio has been diversified has been the biggest driver of its performance. Quite frankly, that's why most investors have been bloodied over the last 3 years. Their portfolio diversification was horrible or, in too many cases, nonexistent.

What's especially sad, however, is that many investors still haven't learned from their mistakes. They still have portfolios that don't match up properly with their investment time horizon and risk parameters. There is no better time than the present to fix what's broken in your portfolio in terms of diversification. Fortunately, employing the worst-to-first strategy can give your investment portfolio a needed boost of diversification on several levels. Here's how.

Four Types of Portfolio Diversification

Diversification *Across* Asset Classes

Investors who owned nothing but stocks in the last 3 years felt the full force of the market's wrath. Investors who held investments in other asset classes, however, were cushioned a bit from the market's blow.

An investor who held an index fund that mimicked the S&P 500 Index saw his or her investment dollars decline 9 percent in 2000, nearly 12 percent in 2001, and 22 percent in 2002. However, had the investor diversified across asset classes—say, including 20 percent bonds in the mix—the damage would have been less severe. Indeed, a portfolio invested 80 percent in the S&P 500 and 20 percent in the Vanguard Total Bond Market Index fund (a reasonable proxy for the bond market) would have seen portfolio losses diminish to 4.9 percent in 2000, 7.9 percent in 2001, and 15.9 percent in 2002. Of course, that same investor holding bonds during the go-go '90s would have reduced returns relative to the S&P 500.

My point is that if you are as concerned about risk as you are returns—and you should be—you need to find the appropriate mix of stocks, bonds, cash, and other asset classes that provide the best opportunity to match your risk level with expected returns. If you have no clue about what an appropriate asset allocation is for your situation, a good rule of thumb is to subtract your age from 110, and that is the percentage of your portfolio that should be devoted to stocks. Thus, a 50-year-old should use a 60 percent weighting in stocks (110 – 50) as a starting point for determining equity exposure in a portfolio, with bonds and cash making up the remainder (perhaps 30 percent in bonds and 10 percent in cash).

The worst-to-first strategy provides a way to supplement the part of your portfolio devoted to stocks. Let's say that your appropriate asset allocation is 65 percent stocks, 25 percent bonds, and 10 percent cash. Among the 65 percent stock position, you would include some weighting in worst-to-first stocks. What would be an appropriate weighting? That would depend on your risk parameters. However, I would feel comfortable devoting 10 percent to 30 percent of the equity side of a portfolio to investments in the Dow Underdogs in a given year. Thus, for a portfolio with 65 percent of its assets in stocks, 6.5 percent (10 percent weighting in worst-to-first investments multiplied by the 65 percent equities weighting) to 19.5 percent (30 percent multiplied by 65 percent) of the entire portfolio could be devoted to various worst-to-first strategies.

Diversification *Within* Asset Classes

As mentioned, an investor who had all of his or her assets in an S&P 500 Index fund would have posted losses of 9 percent in 2000, nearly 12 percent in 2001, and 22 percent in 2002. However, an investor who had invested all of his or her money in a different stock index—the Nasdaq Composite—would have suffered much greater losses. Indeed, the Nasdaq Composite plummeted 39 percent in 2000, 20 percent in 2001, and 31 percent in 2002. This example shows very clearly how investments in the same asset class—in this case, stocks—can produce dramatically different results for investors. Because returns can diverge dramatically among investments in the same asset class, investors must consider diversification *within* asset classes when risk-proofing a portfolio.

A good way to think of diversification within asset classes is to break the asset class down into *style* boxes. In stocks, for example, style boxes are determined by company size (usually measured as market capitalization) and investment characteristics (usually growth or value). A large-cap growth style box would include companies with market capitalizations (market cap is a stock's per-share price multiplied by the number of outstanding shares) of $4 billion or more and also have earnings and revenue growth records exceeding those of the economy. A small-cap value style box would include stocks with market caps below $1 billion that have stock prices that may approximate or be below the company's intrinsic worth.

Among stocks, the seven primary style boxes are

1. Large-cap growth
2. Large-cap value
3. Mid-cap (market caps between $1 billion and $4 billion) growth
4. Mid-cap value
5. Small-cap growth
6. Small-cap value
7. International stocks

A variety of style boxes exist for fixed-income investments as well. For example, within the broad bond asset class, there are

1. Corporate bonds
2. Municipal bonds
3. International bonds
4. Mortgage-backed bonds
5. Zero-coupon bonds
6. Short-term bonds
7. High-yield ("junk") bonds
8. Treasury bonds

As an investor, your challenge is to cover as many style boxes as possible and, indeed, practical given your investment dollars. The reason you want to cover so many bases is that you never know what particular style box will perform the best/worst in a given year.

So how does a person diversify within asset classes? One easy way is to cover the various style boxes using both individual stocks and mutual funds. Concerning the latter, Morningstar (www.morningstar.com) provides clear style classifications for mutual funds and is an extremely useful resource for helping to diversify a portfolio of mutual funds.

How can you enhance diversification within asset classes using the worst-to-first strategy? For starters, the strategy focuses exclusively on the 30 stocks in the Dow Jones Industrial Average. These 30 stocks are almost always going to be large-cap issues. Thus, owning Dow Underdogs gives you exposure to the large-cap style box. As for value versus growth, there seems to be a slight bent toward value among the Dow Underdogs, although plenty of growth stocks find their way into worst-to-first portfolios. For example, Home Depot and Intel—stocks generally viewed more as growth stocks than value stocks—were the worst-performing stocks in 2002. Thus, investors who put some of their portfolio dollars in worst-to-first stocks will likely be covering both the large-cap value and, in many years, the large-cap growth style boxes.

Having exposure to large-cap value oftentimes pays big dividends during down markets. In the 1990s, it's a safe bet that most of you reading this book didn't have any money in large-cap value stocks. In fact, you probably didn't have any money in any value style box. Indeed, most investors loaded up on large-cap growth stocks (i.e., the tech giants like Cisco, Oracle, Yahoo, and the like) only to get rocked when large-cap growth stocks got creamed. The nice thing about the worst-to-first strategy is that it forces you to cover what was one of the best-performing style boxes during the bear market of 2000 to 2002: large-cap value.

If you are looking for a particular percentage of your portfolio to focus on each equity style box, consider this formula: divide your portfolio's allocation to stocks by 7 (the number of equity style boxes), and the result is the percentage of the overall portfolio to devote to that style box. For example, a portfolio with 65 percent equities would probably want somewhere around 9 percent of the portfolio focused on each of the seven style boxes. True, it would mean that small-cap stocks would receive the same weighting as large-cap stocks. If that concerns you—some investors get a little skittish owning smaller, unfamiliar companies—you could bias the large-cap style boxes a bit by stealing a few percentage points from small-cap and mid-cap style boxes. In the end, however, using Dow Underdogs to cover the large-cap value (and, perhaps, a little in large-cap growth) would mean an investment of around 9 percent to perhaps 20 percent in these stocks (based on a portfolio allocation of 65 percent equities). Interestingly, these percentages are similar to the percentage allocation (6.5 percent to 19.5 percent) that I suggested when we looked at diversification across asset classes in the earlier example.

Of course, this example is for the individual who has enough money to diversify across all seven style boxes. I realize that investors with limited investment dollars may not have this ability. In those instances, the worst-to-first portfolios may still be considered, but realize you are going without exposure to other style boxes.

Diversify Across *Time*

One form of diversification that often gets overlooked by investors is diversification across time. How do you effect time diversification? By spreading your investments over a period of time.

I know the academic books say that diversification across time is inefficient. If you have money to invest, get it all into the market as soon as possible. After all, the market trends higher over time. Anytime you are holding money on the sidelines is time you are wasting, time that your money is not taking advantage of the market's long-term uptrend.

The problem with lump-sum investing, of course, is that what works over the long run may produce horrific results in the short run. For example, an individual who came into a big inheritance at the end of 1999 and invested all of the money in April 2000 will not find much solace in the academic argument that what he or she did was the right thing. It is tough to believe you've done the right thing when your portfolio could be down 50 percent or more since you made the investment. True, you might be awfully glad you made the one-time investment 10 or 20 years from now. But you certainly don't feel like a smart investor right now.

What's more, what may happen by making a big one-time invest-ment—and getting killed in the short run—is that you won't stick around long enough to benefit from the market's long-term trend. You'll be long gone, taking your investment out of the market, licking your wounds, and swearing off the stock market forever. That, as I see it, is the biggest risk of lump-sum investing: the risk that you won't have the patience or the stomach to ride out potentially severe mar-ket downturns in the near term to reap the long-term benefits.

The other problem with lump-sum investing is that, aside from hitting the lottery, inheriting money, or rolling over a 401(k) plan, most of us don't really have the opportunity to invest a lump sum. Our money comes to us in regular streams, such as a paycheck. Thus, the argument to invest all at once or to spread out investments is really a moot point for many investors.

What I like about diversifying investment dollars over time is that it provides a much more palatable way for investors to get in the mar-ket and stay in the market. Consider the last few years. While you know that intuitively the best time to buy stocks is when they are down, it is awfully hard to muster up the courage to make big invest-ments in stocks when they are falling by the day. That's what makes a strategy employing time diversification a winner. You can divvy up your investment dollars and spread them over time, investing smaller amounts more frequently. This tends to be a bit easier on your psyche as an investor.

Perhaps the best-known strategy for diversifying over time is dollar-cost averaging (DCA). DCA takes emotion out of the invest-ment process. It requires you to make regular contributions to your investments, regardless of market levels.

Let's say that you own shares in an S&P 500 Index fund. Dollar-cost averaging says that you will invest some regular amount (e.g., $100) every month (or quarter or whatever time period you establish). Thus, regardless if the market is high or low, you will make that $100 investment every month.

The beauty of DCA is that the average cost of your investment will always be less than the average of the prices at the time the pur-chases were made. This is significant, for it means that dollar-cost averaging can make you money even if your investments, over time, show no net positive change.

Another form of time diversification, as well as a variation of dollar-cost averaging, is value averaging. Instead of making the same dollar investment each month in a stock or mutual fund, value aver-aging says that you vary the amount invested so that the value of the portfolio increases by a fixed sum or percentage each interval.

Let's say that instead of investing $100 per month, you want the value of your investment to rise by $100 per month. In month 1, the value of the investment rises $200. Under value averaging, you would *sell* $100 worth of your investment. (Remember, you want your invest-ment to rise $100 per month.) Now, what if your investment declined $100? Under value averaging, you would invest $200 that month in order for the value of the portfolio to increase $100.

In a nutshell, with value averaging you know how much your portfolio will be worth at the end of your investment time horizon, but you don't know how much it will cost out of your pocket. This dif-fers from dollar-cost averaging in which you know how much you'll invest, but the final value of your portfolio is uncertain.

Value averaging is considered a bit more aggressive strategy than dollar-cost averaging. Also, because of the need to rebalance the port-folio's value on a regular basis, value averaging is not as tax-friendly. Still, it does provide a different slant on time diversification and may be appealing to certain investors, especially those with larger amounts of money to invest.

How a worst-to-first strategy contributes to a portfolio's time diversification is subtle but significant. Employing a worst-to-first strategy each year ensures that you will have at least some money in the market. In fact, buying Dow Underdogs *forces* you to keep money in stocks, even if your emotions are telling you otherwise.

This may seem like a very minor benefit of employing worst-to-first strategies. But make no mistake. You will not get rich owning bonds or money market accounts. True, you will preserve your assets owning bonds and cash. But you will not get rich. You get rich owning stocks. Thus, any strategy that forces you to own stocks will pay huge dividends over time.

Diversify Across *Strategies*

Many different ways exist to beat the market, at least in the short run. I'm sure go-go growth investors who were making huge gains in the second half of the 1990s felt that the only way to invest in the market was to buy the fastest-moving stocks. Of course, this strategy crashed when momentum stocks died—but not until some investors made a lot of money.

And I'm sure value investors who cleaned up in the last few years believe value investing is the only way to true profits in the market. Of course, what these value investors don't tell you is how badly their portfolios trailed the major indexes in the 1990s. And day traders probably felt that the only way to make big money in the market was to hold stocks by the minute or the hour, not for years and years as buy-and-holders believe. Of course, both day traders and buy-and-holders have gotten their comeuppance in the last 3 years.

My point is that investment styles and strategies run in and out of favor, much like different investment sectors or different asset classes run in and out of favor. Since investors diversify across and within asset classes, why not diversify across investment styles? For example, I consider myself to be a buy-and-hold investor. I tend to buy stocks for long periods of time—10 years or longer is my typical holding period. I happen to believe that buying stocks for the long term is the best way to build wealth in the stock market. The tax system is too onerous on short-term gains to be trading stocks.

Having said that, I realize that buy-and-hold investing does not always provide big returns during all market periods. In fact, selling some stocks would have saved me a lot of money over the last few years. Thus, I think it makes perfect sense to balance out a buy-and-hold portfolio with investment funds that may be focused on more short-term investment strategies. To be sure, one strength of my worst-to-first strategies is that you still hold your investments long enough to enjoy long-term capital gains tax rates. Still, you are turning over most or all of your portfolio every 53 weeks or so, which is a lot shorter time frame than most buy-and-hold investors use.

What I like about balancing a long-term investment strategy with a worst-to-first strategy is that you will be forced in part of your portfolio to take some profits off the table each year (providing, of course, the strategy does its job that year). Taking profits is not necessarily a bad thing and can be a very good thing during choppy market periods when short-term strategies tend to do better than long-term strategies. And if you are a short-term trader, employing a worst-to-first strategy presents a way to balance your trading strategy with investments in an approach that, while certainly not long term, does allow you to protect at least some of your profits by taxing them at long-term capital-gains rates.

WHICH INVESTMENT ACCOUNT?

Diversification is not the only question to answer when building portfolios. An investor must consider tax issues, especially when it comes to placing investments in the account that is best suited from a tax standpoint. For example, you shouldn't put municipal bonds in your Individual Retirement Account. Why? Because municipal bonds are already tax exempt; it makes no sense to put tax-exempt investments in a tax-exempt account. You want to shelter your investments with the greatest potential tax consequences in a tax-exempt account. That's how you maximize the tax break.

Likewise, if you own both bonds (or bond mutual funds) and stocks (or stock mutual funds), you are usually better off putting the bonds in tax-exempt accounts, where the high-income streams can be sheltered from taxes. Finally, if you have one stock account that is geared for short-term trading (in which you'll likely generate lots of short-term gains or losses) and one equity account in which you buy and hold investments, you are probably better off putting the short-term trading account within an IRA framework. In that way, your short-term gains—which are taxed at high rates relative to long-term gains—can be protected from taxes. (This example, of course, presumes you are good at trading stocks and generate gains. Obviously, if you are a lousy trader, you will wish the trading account were taxable, where you could at least take advantage of the losses.)

This discussion begs the question: What account is best suited for housing a worst-to-first strategy? Actually, I can see arguments for holding a worst-to-first portfolio in either taxable or tax-exempt accounts.

Argument for Holding in a Taxable Account

With the 2003 tax legislation that reduces the maximum tax rate on dividends and long-term capital gains to 15 percent, keeping investment dollars in a worst-to-first strategy in a taxable account makes more sense. After all, any dividends and long-term capital gains (and remember, as long as you hold the investment for 1 year and 1 day, your gains are taxed at long-term rates) will be taxed at just 15 percent. Also, in the years the strategy fails, you have booked losses that you can use to offset gains in that year and, depending on the size of the losses, future years. Finally, you have more flexibility and access to the funds if they are in a taxable account than if they are in a tax-exempt account. Pulling money out of most tax-exempt accounts, such as an IRA, may leave you vulnerable to penalties and a big tax hit.

Argument for Holding in a Tax-Exempt Account

When deciding what account is best for a worst-to-first strategy, you have to start with the premise that you will make more money than you will lose using the strategy. Even though your gains will be taxed at long-term rates (maximum 15 percent), you will still be generating lots of potential tax liabilities if you use this strategy over several years. In effect, you will lose 15 percent of your gains roughly every year if you hold your worst-to-first investments in a taxable account. Conversely, if you hold those same investments in a tax-exempt account (e.g., a Roth IRA), you will be able to shelter your worst-to-first profits from any tax liabilities (capital gains and dividend income) for as long as you want. In fact, in a Roth IRA, you will never be taxed on the investment—not during the accrual period while the

WORST TO FIRST AND ROTH IRAS

The Roth IRA is one of the best investment programs available to investors. Money contributed to a Roth grows tax deferred and is withdrawn tax-free. Thus, if your Roth IRA grows to $2 million (by skillful use of the worst-to-first strategies), you will never pay a dime in taxes when you start to make withdrawals. This is a big advantage over a traditional IRA and your company's 401(k) plan. In order to withdraw your money tax-free, your account has to have been open at least 5 years and your withdrawal occurs either after you reach age 59½, or due to disability, death, or if the money is used for expenses under the first-time home buyer rule.

Anyone is eligible to contribute to a Roth IRA as long as they meet certain income requirements. Individuals with an adjusted gross income of up to $95,000 ($150,000 for couples filing jointly) can make a full $3,000 contribution to a Roth IRA. Partial contributions are allowed for individuals whose adjusted gross income is between $95,000 and $110,000 ($150,000 and $160,000 for couples filing jointly). As mentioned, the maximum contribution to a Roth in 2004 is $3,000. That contribution ceiling jumps to $4,000 in 2005. You can contribute to a Roth IRA even if you contribute to a 401(k) plan.

Unlike the traditional IRA, you can make contributions to a Roth IRA after age 70½ as long as you have earned income. And, unlike the traditional IRA, you are not required to make withdrawals beginning at age 70½. In fact, you are never required to withdraw the money. If you leave your Roth IRA to your heirs, your beneficiaries do not have to pay taxes on the money, either. The ability to leave tax-free income to your heirs makes the Roth an interesting estate-planning tool. You can set up a Roth IRA at virtually any brokerage firm or mutual fund family.

The biggest downside to a Roth IRA is that the contribution is never tax-deductible. Also, if you withdraw your money before your account is 5 years old, your earnings may be subject to federal income taxes plus a 10 percent penalty.

> If you are eligible for a Roth IRA but have yet to fund one, my worst-to-first strategies give you a great reason to start one today.

funds are in the Roth, nor when funds are removed from the Roth IRA (since no taxes are paid on Roth IRA withdrawals).

Where do I come down on taxable versus tax-exempt accounts? I find the argument for tax-exempt accounts, especially a Roth IRA, more compelling. Indeed, the ability to shelter gains over a long period of time and to withdraw those profits without paying taxes adds tremendous leverage to your investment results.

Of course, not every investor is eligible to invest in a Roth IRA. Furthermore, some investors, for a variety of reasons, may only have the option of including worst-to-first portfolios in a taxable account. That's okay. Again, you can limit the tax bite by making sure you hold your investments for 1 year and 1 day in order to pay a maximum 15 percent taxes on long-term capital gains. And for individuals in the two lowest tax brackets (10 percent and 15 percent), the tax issue is relatively minor. Indeed, the long-term capital gains tax rate for investors in the lowest two tax brackets is just 5 percent through 2007 and drops to 0 percent in 2008.

Conclusion

As much as I like my worst-to-first strategies, I also know that prudent portfolio diversification makes it imperative that whenever possible worst-to-first strategies are only one piece of a broader portfolio. I realize it is a lot easier to diversify if you have lots of money. And for some people, investing in worst-to-first strategies and nothing else is the reality of their checkbooks. For those people, I would still recommend my worst-to-first approaches if it means getting them off square one. After all, you have to start somewhere, and I would rather you start investing in this strategy than not investing at all.

Still, as your investment funds grow, you should endeavor to balance out your worst-to-first strategies with investments in other asset classes and investment strategies.

Part V

The Competition—
Dogs Versus Underdogs

8

Worst to First Versus Dogs of the Dow

In 1990, *Beating the Dow* was published. The book, written by Michael O'Higgins with John Downes, showed investors how to beat the Dow by buying the highest-yielding Dow stocks. O'Higgins's and Downes's strategies were so persuasive that the book launched a new movement of Dow-based investing, with billions of dollars finding their way into various Dogs of the Dow strategies.

Many of you who are familiar with the Dogs of the Dow strategies will see similarities between my worst-to-first approaches and the Dow-based investing strategies put forth by O'Higgins and Downes:

- Both strategies focus exclusively on the stocks in the Dow Jones Industrial Average.

- Both strategies limit the portfolios to a maximum of 10 stocks.

- Both strategies require approximately 1-year holding periods.

- Both strategies are based on the notion that buying depressed Dow stocks offers the best way to achieve Dow-beating returns.

Obviously, the strategies differ in the criteria with which stocks are chosen. While the Dogs of the Dow focus exclusively on dividend yield, my various worst-to-first strategies focus on either annual price change or the stock price's relationship to its 200-day moving average.

Which is better? Before I answer that question—and you can probably guess what my answer will be—let's review the basic Dogs of the Dow strategies.

- *Ten highest-yielding stock portfolio.* Investors following this strategy purchase the 10 highest-yielding Dow stocks on the date the portfolio is implemented. (A stock's dividend yield is determined by taking the latest quarterly dividend, multiplying by 4 to get the annual indicated dividend, and dividing by the stock price. For example, a $20 stock paying an indicated annual dividend of $1 per share has a yield of 5 percent: $1 divided by $20.) An investor holds equal-weighted positions in each of the 10 stocks for 12 months and rebalances.

- *Five high-yield/lowest-priced stock portfolio.* This variation of the basic Dogs of the Dow strategy calls for buying the five lowest-priced Dow stocks among the 10 highest yielders. You buy equal dollar positions, hold for 12 months, and rebalance.

- *Penultimate profit prospect.* This strategy calls for buying a single stock—the second lowest-priced Dow stock among the 10 highest yielders.

In many respects, I'm a fan of the Dogs of the Dow strategy, for it meets many of the criteria I lay out in Chapter 1 for validating investment strategies.

- *Consistency of performance over various time frames.* Although performance has slumped over the last decade or so, owning the Dow's highest-yielding stocks has generally provided Dow-beating returns over the last 20 and 30 years.

- *Simplicity.* The Dogs of the Dow strategies are simple to implement. You just buy the highest-yielding Dow stocks, hold for a year, and rebalance.

- *Affordability.* You can implement this Dow yield strategy with $5,000 or less in investment capital.

- *Tax-friendly*. The Dogs of the Dow strategies can be employed in taxable and nontaxable accounts. And because capital gains taxes can be minimized by holding investments for 1 year and 1 day, the strategy is friendly in taxable accounts as well.

- *Transaction-friendly*. The most trades you will make in a year employing the Dogs of the Dow strategy is 20.

- *Discipline*. Once you buy into the strategy, you have no decisions to make. There is no ambiguity, no confusion. The strategy goes on autopilot. You buy the stocks, go away, and come back in 12 months.

- *Risk-friendly*. The basic Dogs of the Dow strategy of buying the 10 highest-yielding Dow stocks has provided Dow-beating returns over the last 30 years at a lower overall risk level (as measured by standard deviation of returns) than the Dow.

- *Easy to keep score*. Since there is no frequent trading and because you are not providing cash infusions during the year, tallying up your performance is rather easy with the Dogs of the Dow strategy. And benchmarking those results is easy, too. Since you have only Dow stocks from which to choose, the Dow Jones Industrial Average provides a clear-cut benchmark by which to judge the strategy's performance.

- *Flexibility*. Investors can implement the strategy anytime during the year, provided they hold the investments for 12 months.

- *Sell discipline*. The Dogs of the Dow strategy makes the sell decisions for you. At the end of 12 months, you dump the stocks that no longer are among the highest-yielding Dow issues.

- *Stock-centric*. You are only buying stocks with the Dogs of the Dow strategies.

DIVIDEND YIELD AS PROXY FOR VALUE

Where the Dogs of the Dow strategy comes up a bit short, in my opinion, is in the logic supporting the whole strategy—that a stock's dividend yield represents a good proxy for value. To be sure, I have no problem including dividend-paying stocks in a portfolio. The regular compounding of dividends can provide a powerful boost to a portfolio's return over time. And with the new tax law giving dividend income preferential treatment (dividends are now taxed at a maximum 15 percent rate), having a dividend component to your investment program makes sense. Having said that, component changes to the Dow over the last decade make dividend yield a much less effective tool for making value comparisons across all Dow stocks.

Remember that the Dogs of the Dow and my worst-to-first strategies use Dow components to beat the index. Thus, the success of both strategies depends on how well the primary selection tool (dividend yield for the Dogs, annual price change for my Underdogs) discerns rebound opportunities across *all* Dow stocks. Indeed, you don't want a strategy whose major selection tool applies to only a limited number of Dow components. You want a measuring stick that has relevance to all Dow stocks, not just some.

O'Higgins and Downes argue that a high yield is a contrarian indicator, a way to identify bargains, because a high yield signals that the investing public has doubts about the stock. The authors make a big deal about the contrarian aspects of their strategy. The problem is that a stock's yield can be a reflection of lots of stuff, not just a stock's value.

Remember that a stock's yield depends on two components: stock price and dividend. Yield levels change as a result of two things: (1) changes in stock price—a rising stock price depresses the yield, whereas a falling stock price boosts the yield; and (2) changes in dividends—a dividend increase will increase the yield (assuming the stock price stays constant), whereas a dividend decrease or omission will reduce or eliminate the yield.

To be sure, companies have no direct control over their stock price. (That's one reason I like my worst-to-first strategies. Price movements cannot be manipulated.) They do, however, have lots of control over the level of dividends they pay. For example, for much of the 1990s and early 2000—when growth stocks were all the rage and dividends didn't matter to investors—what were companies doing with their excess cash? What they *weren't* doing was boosting their dividends. Indeed, *payout* ratios—that is, the percentage of corporate earnings paid out to shareholders in the form of dividends—fell sharply in recent decades.

In a nutshell, companies were choosing other ways to spend their cash flow, such as acquisitions and stock buybacks, rather than boosting dividends. Thus, for the past decade, a stock's yield was more a reflection of a company's dividend policies—policies that reflected what investors wanted at the time—than it was a useful yardstick for a stock's value.

Not surprisingly, the performances of the yield-driven Dogs of the Dow strategies over the past 10 years have been mediocre relative to the Dow. As the following table indicates, none of the Dogs of the Dow strategies—not the 10 highest yielders, not the 5 lowest-priced/highest yields, and especially not the penultimate profit strategy—beat the Dow over the 10-year time frame. The penultimate profit prospect turned in especially dismal results, turning a $1,000 investment into just $1,194. (The Dow over the same time period turned a $1,000 investment into $3,392.)

Interestingly, over the same time period, all of my basic worst-to-first strategies (worst performer, 3 worst performers, 5 worst performers, 10 worst performers), along with two of my worst-to-first strategies based on the relationship between a stock's price and its 200-day moving average, handily outpaced the Dow.

One problem with the Dogs of the Dow's yield approach is that comparing yields across Dow stocks is akin to comparing apples to oranges. O'Higgins and Downes are right. A high yield can be a contrarian indicator, but you need to compare apples to apples—that is, yield works best as a proxy for value when you compare yields of companies *within* the same industry group.

Suppose you are considering two utility stocks. And you are a contrarian investor, so you are trying to buy damaged goods at cheap prices. You can make some interesting value judgments between two utilities if one is yielding 5 percent and the other is yielding 10 percent. Obviously, the utility with the 10 percent yield is one in which investors have a low opinion of the utility and its ability to continue to pay the dividend. That a stock is yielding twice its peer speaks volumes as to the relative popularity of the two stocks.

But what value judgments can be made by comparing the yield on, say, the Dow component Intel (0.4 percent yield at midyear 2003) to the yield on another Dow component, Exxon Mobil (2.8 percent)? The companies are in very different industries. The industries have

1994 to Present

	Value of $1,000 Invested Worst Performer (Price Change)				Value of $1,000 Invested Worst Performer (200-Day Moving Average)				Value of $1,000 Invested			
	1 Stock ($)	3 Stocks ($)	5 Stocks ($)	10 Stocks ($)	1 Stock ($)	3 Stocks ($)	5 Stocks ($)	10 Stocks ($)	Dow Return	Dogs	PPP	5 Low Price/High Yield
1994	1000	1000	1000	1000	1000	1000	1000	1000	1000	1000	1000	1000
1995	1092	953	1044	1040	981	827	868	984	1050	1041	626	1086
1996	955	1125	1348	1348	1261	978	1007	1276	1433	1423	762	1417
1997	611	1286	1624	1717	2134	1307	1292	1624	1842	1820	976	1786
1998	598	1531	2001	2007	2089	1328	1421	1794	2298	2219	1481	2152
1999	729	1455	1901	2207	2545	1433	1461	1891	2712	2454	1806	2416
2000	938	1586	2100	2613	3278	1572	1541	2170	3445	2552	1029	2300
2001	1925	2174	2581	2739	6726	2364	1888	2344	3284	2715	1071	2572
2002	2642	2667	2819	2863	9230	2428	2035	2462	3106	2582	1081	2495
2002	2286	2539	2506	2506	11595	2362	1942	2049	2644	2352	746	2230
2003	3406	4337	3827	3561	18181	4034	3140	3131	3392	3028	1194	2752

Over the last 5-year period, the performance of my worst-to-first strategies, relative to the various Dogs of the Dow strategies, has been even more impressive. Indeed, all of my worst-to-first strategies not only beat the Dow for the 5-year period but also beat every Dogs of the Dow strategy over the same time period:

1999 to Present

	Value of $1,000 Invested Worst Performer (Price Change)				Value of $1,000 Invested Worst Performer (200-Day Moving Average)				Value of $1,000 Invested			5 Low Price/
	1 Stock ($)	3 Stocks ($)	5 Stocks ($)	10 Stocks ($)	1 Stock ($)	3 Stocks ($)	5 Stocks ($)	10 Stocks ($)	Dow Return	Dogs	PPP	High Yield
	1000	1000	1000	1000	1000	1000	1000	1000	1000	1000	1000	1000
1999	1288	1090	1105	1184	1288	1097	1055	1148	1271	1040	570	952
2000	2643	1494	1358	1241	2643	1649	1292	1240	1211	1107	593	1064
2001	3626	1833	1483	1297	3626	1694	1393	1302	1145	1052	599	1032
2002	3138	1745	1318	1136	4555	1648	1329	1084	975	959	413	923
2003	4676	2980	2013	1614	7142	2814	2149	1656	1251	1234	661	1139

very different capital requirements. They have very different growth prospects. And, most importantly for discussion here, the industries have very different dividend policies. Oil companies tend to pay higher dividends than technology companies.

But just because Exxon Mobil has a higher yield, does it always follow that Exxon Mobil is a better value than Intel? Of course not. In fact, Exxon could increase from its current price of $37 to $150 in 12 months and still have a higher yield than Intel (assuming Intel's dividend and stock price remained unchanged). It would be awfully hard to say that Exxon Mobil was undervalued at $150 (relative to Intel) simply because Exxon Mobil had a higher yield. Yet that is the very argument made by the Dogs of the Dow strategy.

And problems with using yield as the main determinant of value among Dow stocks will only worsen as the complexion of the Dow continues to change. Look at the component changes that have occurred in the Dow since 1997.

1997:

In—Hewlett-Packard, Johnson & Johnson, Travelers (now operating under the name Citigroup), Wal-Mart Stores

Out—CBS (Westinghouse), Bethlehem Steel, Texaco, Woolworth

1999:

In—Intel, Microsoft, Home Depot, SBC Communications

Out—Chevron, Goodyear, Sears, Union Carbide

2004:

In—American International Group, Pfizer, Verizon

Out—AT&T, Eastmen Kodak, International Paper

Since 1997, there have been 11 changes to the Dow, or a turnover of approximately one out of every three components. Note that the stocks added to the Dow have much different growth profiles (and yield characteristics) than the stocks that were booted. Indeed, the addition of technology (Intel, Microsoft, Hewlett-Packard), health care (Johnson & Johnson), and "new" retailing (Home Depot, Wal-Mart Stores) stocks has skewed the typical Dow stocks' yield profile significantly.

These changes have had a major impact on the Dogs of the Dow strategy. In the 1970s and even the 1980s, it could be argued that Dow stocks tended to migrate toward the value camp. A greater homogeneity existed among the stocks in the Dow. And using dividend yield as a tool to assess the relative value of homogeneous Dow stocks made perfect sense.

As the complexion of the Dow changes, however, yields become less relevant as a tool for assessing relative values across all Dow stocks. The upshot is that the changing face of the Dow is creating a big dichotomy in the types of yields that are offered by Dow stocks. The current Dow stocks ranked by their yields follow:

Stock	Yield (%)
SBC Communications	5.1
Altria Group	4.9
General Motors	4.3
Verizon Communications	4.1
Merck	3.3
J.P. Morgan Chase	3.3
DuPont	3.2
Citigroup	3.1
General Electric	2.5
Exxon Mobil	2.4
Honeywell International	2.2
Coca-Cola	2.0
Pfizer	1.9
Johnson & Johnson	1.9
Procter & Gamble	1.9
Caterpillar	1.8
Alcoa	1.8

3M	1.7
Boeing	1.6
United Technologies	1.6
Hewlett-Packard	1.4
McDonald's	1.4
Wal-Mart Stores	0.9
Disney	0.8
Home Depot	0.8
American Express	0.8
IBM	0.7
Microsoft	0.6
Intel	0.6
American International Group	0.3

What should jump out immediately is the spread between the highest-yielding stocks and the lowest-yielding stocks. For example, the 10 highest-yielding Dow stocks have an average yield of 3.6 percent. The 10 lowest-yielding Dow stocks, many of which have been added to the Dow since 1997, have an average yield of less than 1 percent. For Dogs of the Dow investors, this spread is very important. It means that if you base investment selection in the Dow strictly on dividend yield, you are relegating yourself to picking among the same 15 to 17 stocks each and every year.

Look at the following lists of Dogs of the Dow components since 1996. (The Dogs listed for 1996, for example, were the 10 highest-yielding Dow stocks at the end of 1995. The stocks are listed in order beginning with the highest yielding.) There is very little change from year to year.

1996

Philip Morris	DuPont
Texaco	Minnesota Mining & Manufacturing
J.P. Morgan	International Paper
Chevron	General Electric
Exxon	Eastman Kodak

1997

Philip Morris

J.P. Morgan

Texaco

Chevron

Exxon

AT&T

General Motors

International Paper

DuPont

Minnesota Mining & Manufacturing

1998

Philip Morris

J.P. Morgan

General Motors

Chevron

Eastman Kodak

Exxon

Minnesota Mining & Manufacturing

International Paper

AT&T

DuPont

1999

J.P. Morgan

Philip Morris

Minnesota Mining &
  Manufacturing

Chevron

General Motors

DuPont

Caterpillar

Eastman Kodak

Goodyear

Exxon

2000

Philip Morris

J.P. Morgan

Caterpillar

General Motors

Eastman Kodak

Minnesota Mining & Manufacturing

Exxon Mobil

DuPont

SBC Communications

International Paper

2001

Philip Morris

Eastman Kodak

General Motors

DuPont

Caterpillar

J.P. Morgan Chase

International Paper

SBC Communications

Exxon Mobil

Minnesota Mining & Manufacturing

2002

Eastman Kodak	Caterpillar
Philip Morris	SBC Communications
General Motors	International Paper
J.P. Morgan Chase	Merck
DuPont	Exxon Mobil

2003

Altria Group (formerly Philip Morris)	DuPont
	Honeywell
J.P. Morgan	General Electric
General Motors	Caterpillar
Eastman Kodak	AT&T
SBC Communications	

2004

Altria (formerly Philip Morris)	Merck
	DuPont
SBC Communications	Citigroup
AT&T	General Electric
General Motors	Exxon Mobil
J.P. Morgan	

- In 1997, there were only two changes from the prior year (AT&T and GM were in, GE and Eastman Kodak were out).

- In 1998, there was only one change to the 10 highest-yielding Dow stocks (Eastman Kodak returned, and Texaco left).

- In 1999, there were two changes (Goodyear and Caterpillar in, International Paper and AT&T out).

- In 2000, there were two changes (International Paper and SBC Communications in, Chevron and Goodyear out). The changes were facilitated by both Chevron and Goodyear being booted from the Dow in 1999.

- In 2001, there were no changes—that is, the 10 highest-yielding stocks at the end of 1999 were also the 10 highest-yielding stocks at the end of 2000.

- In 2002, there was one change (Merck was in, 3M was out).

- In 2003, there were three changes (AT&T, GE, and Honeywell International in, International Paper, Merck, and Exxon Mobil out).

- In 2004, there were three changes (Merck, Citigroup, and Exxon Mobil in, Honeywell International, Caterpillar, and Eastman Kodak out).

In fact, since the end of 1995, only 18 of the 41 Dow stocks (remember, there have been 11 changes in that time) were Dogs of the Dow selections:

AT&T	Goodyear
Caterpillar	Honeywell International
Chevron	International Paper
Citigroup	J.P. Morgan
DuPont	Merck
Eastman Kodak	Minnesota Mining & Manufacturing
Exxon Mobil	Philip Morris (Altria)
General Electric	SBC Communications
General Motors	Texaco

And only two of the Dow stocks that were added to the index since 1997 (SBC Communications and Citigroup) have been among the 10 highest yielders in a given year.

Thus, in the last 9 years, the Dogs of the Dow strategy has basically ignored more than half of all Dow stocks in the selection process. Little wonder its performance has tailed off dramatically. The Dogs of the Dow is not really a Dow-based strategy anymore. Rather, it is a process that winnows a universe of 15 to 17 possibilities down to 10.

Compare the lack of turnover among the 10 Dow Dogs to the turnover of my 10 worst-to-first stocks over the same time period (1996 to 2004). Stocks are listed in order beginning with the worst performer:

1996

Bethlehem Steel	Alcoa
Woolworth	IBM
International Paper	Minnesota Mining & Manufacturing
Caterpillar	DuPont
Chevron	General Motors

1997

Bethlehem Steel
AT&T
McDonald's
General Motors
International Paper

Union Carbide
Goodyear
Sears
Walt Disney
Eastman Kodak

1998

Eastman Kodak
Boeing
Sears
Minnesota Mining &
  Manufacturing
Union Carbide

McDonald's
International Paper
United Technologies
Alcoa
J.P. Morgan

1999

Boeing
Goodyear
Minnesota Mining &
  Manufacturing
DuPont
Walt Disney

Citigroup
J.P. Morgan
Sears
Caterpillar
Union Carbide

2000

Philip Morris
Coca-Cola
SBC Communications
Merck
Eastman Kodak

Walt Disney
AT&T
Caterpillar
McDonald's
Exxon Mobil

2001

AT&T
Microsoft
Eastman Kodak
Home Depot
Hewlett-Packard

General Motors
Procter & Gamble
International Paper
Intel
DuPont

2002

Boeing	Walt Disney
Merck	Eastman Kodak
American Express	Coca-Cola
Hewlett-Packard	McDonald's
Honeywell International	J.P. Morgan

2003

Home Depot	Alcoa
Intel	J.P. Morgan
McDonald's	SBC Communications
General Electric	Honeywell International
IBM	AT&T

2004

Eastman Kodak	Wal-Mart
AT&T	Microsoft
Merck	DuPont
SBC Communications	Coca-Cola
Johnson & Johnson	Procter & Gamble

As you can see, there's been a lot of turnover of the worst-to-first portfolios in the last 9 years.

- In 1997, there were seven changes (new stocks were AT&T, McDonald's, Union Carbide, Goodyear, Sears, Disney, Eastman Kodak).

- In 1998, five changes (Boeing, 3M, United Technologies, Alcoa, J.P. Morgan).

- In 1999, five changes (Goodyear, DuPont, Disney, Citigroup, Caterpillar).

- In 2000, eight changes (Philip Morris, Coca-Cola, SBC Communications, Merck, Eastman Kodak, AT&T, McDonald's, Exxon Mobil).

- In 2001, eight changes (Microsoft, Home Depot, Hewlett-

Packard, General Motors, Procter & Gamble, International Paper, Intel, DuPont).

- In 2002, eight changes (Boeing, Merck, American Express, Honeywell International, Disney, Coca-Cola, McDonald's, J.P. Morgan).

- In 2003, seven changes (Home Depot, Intel, General Electric, IBM, Alcoa, SBC Communications, AT&T).

- In 2004, eight changes (Estman Kodak, Merck, Johnson & Johnson, Wal-Mart, DuPont, Microsoft, Coca-Cola, Procter & Gamble)

Overall, since the end of 1995, 36 of the 41 Dow stocks appeared in worst-to-first portfolios:

Alcoa	IBM
American Express	Intel
AT&T	International Paper
Bethlehem Steel	J.P. Morgan
Boeing	Johnson & Johnson
Caterpillar	McDonald's
Chevron	Merck
Citigroup	Microsoft
Coca-Cola	Minnesota Mining & Manufacturing
DuPont	Philip Morris
Eastman Kodak	Procter & Gamble
Exxon Mobil	SBC Communications
General Electric	Sears
General Motors	Union Carbide
Goodyear	United Technologies
Hewlett-Packard	Wal-Mart
Home Depot	Walt Disney
Honeywell International	Woolworth

This list is in comparison to just 18 over the same time frame for the 10 Dow Dogs strategy. Furthermore, nearly all of the stocks added to the Dow since 1997 have made an appearance in my worst-to-first portfolios.

The upshot is that my worst-to-first strategies take into account many more Dow stocks than the Dogs of the Dow, and that's important. Indeed, any strategy that tries to beat an index by selecting stocks from that index should have selection criteria that are relevant to *all* the stocks in the index, not just a handful.

The Dogs of the Dow believers might say that little or no turnover in the portfolios from year to year is a good thing. After all, turnover means buying and selling, which means higher trading commissions and potential tax liabilities. While there is some truth to this point, keep in mind that there's plenty of potential buying and selling in the Dogs of the Dow portfolios even without stock changes from one year to the next. Why? Remember that Dogs of the Dow portfolios are equal weighted—that is, equal dollar amounts are invested in each of the stocks. Let's assume that you have chosen 10 high-yielding stocks to hold for 1 year. At the end of the year, the same 10 stocks are still the highest-yielding issues. But it is unlikely that all of the stocks performed exactly the same. You might have some stocks that showed big gains, whereas others tanked. In order to invest equal dollar amounts in each of the 10 stocks, you will have to rebalance the portfolio selling shares in the winners and buying more shares in the losers. In fact, depending on the price movements of the 10 Dogs, it is quite possible that you may have to make trades in each of the stocks in order to create a portfolio for the next 12 months that is reasonably equal weighted.

Bottom line: Three factors drive buying and selling in both the worst-to-first and Dogs of the Dow strategies: (1) changes to the stocks in the portfolio; (2) price changes in the various portfolio components; and (3) investing equal dollar amounts in the stocks. Just because you don't change the stocks in the portfolio doesn't mean that you still won't have to buy and sell stocks.

PRICE EFFECT?

Two of the Dogs of the Dow strategies—the five low-price/high yielders and the penultimate profit prospect—rely not only on dividend yield but also stock price for their selection criteria. The logic underlying selection by stock price has a distant relationship to the small firm effect. The small firm effect shows that smaller-capitalization stocks tend to outperform large-capitalization stocks over time. And the historical numbers back this up. According to researcher Ibbotson Associates, small-cap stocks have beaten large-cap stocks by around 2 percentage points per year since 1926.

A problem with ascribing the small firm effect to low-priced Dow stocks is that small cap and small price aren't necessarily the same thing. The small stock effect is a result of small-*cap* companies doing well. Following are the 30 Dow stocks with their current prices, market caps, and annual revenue:

Company	Price ($)	Market Cap ($)	Annual Revenue (Millions $)
3M	83.62	65567.9	18,232
Alcoa	34.26	29754.5	21,504
Altria	55.61	113292.2	60,704
American Express	52.26	67101.8	26,578
American International Group	76.77	200250.5	81,303
Boeing	42.15	33731.9	50,485
Caterpillar	83.75	28790.1	22,763
Citigroup	52.06	268470.8	94,713
Coca-Cola	50.85	124151.9	21,044
Disney	25.70	51741.8	27,061
DuPont	44.06	43940.3	27,137
Exxon Mobil	43.11	283146.5	213,199
General Electric	31.62	318195.9	133,585
General Motors	46.77	26284.6	183,244
Hewlett-Packard	22.63	69066.8	73,061
Home Depot	36.46	82873.6	64,816
Honeywell International	35.01	30190.2	23,103
Intel	27.60	179041.2	30,141
IBM	93.74	158843.3	89,131
J.P. Morgan Chase	41.56	84891.3	44,363
Johnson & Johnson	51.20	151960.2	41,862
McDonald's	29.02	36620.3	17,141

Merck	44.89	99735.0	22,486
Microsoft	25.61	276306.3	32,187
Pfizer	35.67	272126.4	45,188
Procter & Gamble	107.12	138441.9	43,373
SBC Communications	24.47	80879.1	40,843
United Technologies	89.19	45849.2	31,059
Verizon Communications	37.57	103984.7	67,752
Wal-Mart Stores	57.34	248154.8	257,157
Average		123779.5	63,507

Notice two important things:

1. The smallest Dow stock in terms of market capitalization is General Motors, with a market cap of less than $27 billion. That market cap is much higher than the typical market cap of a stock that enjoys the small stock effect.
2. The lowest-priced Dow stocks have some of the biggest market caps. The best example is Microsoft, the software giant. Microsoft's market cap is nearly $280 billion. That is the third-largest market cap of any stock in the Dow (behind GE and Exxon). However, Microsoft's stock price is just $26, putting it among the lowest-priced Dow stocks. Of course, no one would make the argument that Microsoft benefits from any small stock effect simply because its stock price is one of the lowest in the Dow.

What O'Higgins and Downes do argue is that less expensive stocks are prone to greater percentage moves. I will not argue whether absolute stock price and percentage price movement are related. I'll leave that argument to the academics. What I will argue is that O'Higgins and Downes may be confusing correlation with cause and effect. Do low-priced stocks have big price swings simply because they are low-priced stocks? Or do the swings occur because traditional low-priced stocks tend to be small companies whose businesses are volatile, their earnings streams uneven, their finances shaky, and their pedigrees limited? What about low-priced Dow stocks?

Here is where I have a bit of a problem implying low-priced Dow stocks will tend to show greater percentage price movement simply because they are lower priced. Two of every three Dow companies have been around for more than 100 years. The market cap of the average Dow stock is $123 billion. The average Dow stock has annual revenue of more than $63 billion. The average Dow stock is not lacking for pedigree, seasoning, and so on. Thus, the average Dow stock, even the ones with the lowest prices, are not even remotely similar to the typical low-priced stock. And for that reason, I wouldn't expect low-priced Dow stocks to always behave with the type of volatility that you might see in other low-priced stocks.

Keep in mind that a stock's absolute price can be impacted by stock splits, spin-offs, and other corporate actions. Microsoft split its stock in February 2003. That stock split reduced the stock price from the high $40s to the $20s. Because the absolute stock price is now half of what it was, should we expect Microsoft's percentage price gains to become more dramatic?

Following is a comparison between O'Higgins's penultimate profit prospect (remember—it is the second lowest-priced stock among the 10 highest yielders) and what I consider to be the penultimate profit prospects for my worst-to-first portfolios: (1) the worst-performing Dow stock and (2) the Dow stock trading the greatest percentage below its 200-day moving average. I looked at these penultimate profit prospects over the last 1, 3, 5, 10, and 20 years. The performance differences are rather staggering.

	Price (%)	Close Ratio (%)	Penultimate Profit Prospect (%)
1984	−9.2	19.9	−2.8
1985	106.9	106.9	26.4
1986	31.7	31.7	29.6
1987	168.0	168.0	3.3
1988	26.0	26.0	19.5
1989	−11.8	−11.8	12.9
1990	−41.9	−41.9	−17.4
1991	187.2	16.7	185.6
1992	−22.3	−22.3	69.1
1993	15.6	15.6	39.1

1994	9.2	−1.9	−37.4
1995	−12.5	28.5	21.7
1996	−36.0	69.2	28.1
1997	−2.1	−2.1	51.8
1998	21.8	21.8	21.9
1999	28.8	28.8	−43.0
2000	105.2	105.2	4.0
2001	37.2	37.2	1.0
2002	−13.5	25.6	−31.0
2003	49.0	56.8	60.1

Annualized Returns

	Single Worst Stock		Penultimate Profit
Years	Price (%)	Close Ratio (%)	Prospect (%)
1	49.0	56.8	60.1
3	20.9	39.3	3.7
5	36.1	48.2	−7.9
10	13.0	33.6	1.8
20	19.9	26.4	14.4

As you can see, my 1-stock worst-to-first portfolios have outpaced the Dogs of the Dow penultimate profit performer fairly consistently over the last 20 years.

So Why Does Price Matter?

Actually, stock prices *do* matter in the Dow but not always for the reasons espoused in O'Higgins's book. Remember that the stocks having the greatest weight in the Dow are the highest-priced issues. Low-priced stocks carry very little weight in the Dow. Thus, a $20 Dow stock that rises 10 percent doesn't have nearly the impact on the Dow than a $125 stock that rises 10 percent. The 10 percent rise in the $20 stock contributes just 15 points to the Dow (based on the current divisor); the 10 percent rise in the $125 stock contributes 92 points to the Dow.

Because low-priced Dow stocks don't matter much to the Dow, any strategy that picks low-priced Dow stocks that do well relative to the average Dow stock will beat the average most of the time. Why? Our worst-to-first portfolio is equal weighted. A 10 percent increase in a low-priced stock in our portfolio will have the same impact on the portfolio's return as a 10 percent move in the highest-priced stock in the portfolio. That's not the case with the Dow. Thus, low-priced stocks matter to Dow-based investment strategies not just because low-priced stocks have greater percentage price movements. Low-priced stocks matter because of their minimal weighting in the Dow versus their equal weighting in worst-to-first or Dogs of the Dow portfolios.

Simply stated, a useful strategy for beating the Dow does a good job of (1) selecting low-priced Dow stocks that perform well and (2) equal weighting the stocks. The Dogs of the Dow strategy tries to pick these stocks using dividend yield, a tool that really has limited relevancy for comparing Dow stocks. My worst-to-first portfolios use either price change or the price relative to the 200-day moving average as the selection tool. Of course, I'm biased. But I think my tools are a better way to go. And that has certainly been the case over the last two decades and especially in recent years.

CONCLUSION

This chapter is not an attempt to tear down the Dogs of the Dow. Indeed, depending on where you draw the start and finish lines, time periods exist when the Dogs outperformed my worst-to-first strategies, especially during the 1980s. And it is possible that the new tax law, which reduces taxes on dividends, could spark a rebound in the strategy's performance as companies increase their dividends and dividend payout ratios.

Nevertheless, investors have only so many dollars to devote to investment strategies. I believe my worst-to-first approaches merit the bulk of dollars focused on Dow-based investment strategies. My worst-to-first strategies are better suited for making judgments concerning all of the stocks in the Dow index. Furthermore, my strategies make more sense going forward in light of the likelihood of more changes to Dow components over the next few years.

Part VI

The Naysayers— Point/Counterpoint

9

WORST TO FIRST—ADDRESSING THE CRITICS

Trust me—once this book is published, Wall Street "experts" will be falling over themselves to debunk the strategies discussed here. Why? Remember that it is not in anyone's interest on Wall Street to show easy, simple tools for beating the market. Wall Street institutions survive because they are masters at perpetuating the "big secret" of investing.

Wall Street wants you to believe that investing is so complicated and so difficult for you to do on your own that you need a trained professional to manage your money for you. I am a trained professional money manager, so I believe there is a benefit for individuals who have their money managed by professionals. That benefit is usually threefold:

1. Professional money managers help investors better diversify and allocate their resources across stocks, bonds, and cash. Individual investors are frequently weak in diversifying, which is their biggest mistake.
2. Professional money managers make the tough decisions that individuals are usually reluctant to make. Individuals often bring a lot of emotional baggage to the investment process. Consequently, making the tough decisions—such as selling an investment—can become extremely difficult. Professional money managers don't have such emotional ties to investments. Pros can pull the trigger more easily and timely than individuals.

3. Professional money managers bring a consistent and disciplined approach to an investment program.

However, one thing professional money managers *don't* have is a monopoly on the best investment strategies to make money. That's what makes the worst-to-first strategy so, well, *dangerous* to the investment community. Here is an easy, simple tool that anyone can implement, a strategy that has shown an impressive record of making money for investors, a strategy based on the same principles and logic that the pros *truly believe*. And that makes this book very dangerous, indeed. Thus, I expect a full-frontal assault on the worst-to-first strategy, with the following arguments, opinions, and questions fueling the debate:

Chuck, for every academic study you cite favoring reversion to the mean in investing, I can cite you five that say it doesn't exist. How do you respond?

Academics once said that the world was flat. Academics once said that the sun revolved around the earth. Well, guess what. The world isn't flat. The sun doesn't revolve around the earth.

In part, progress is about debunking what was once considered gospel. What causes us to reconsider our view of the world? Better technology. More information. Improved ways to measure results. That is exactly what is happening in the investment research field. What practitioners have today to perform stock research—powerful computers, tons of data, reams of research—was not available 20 or 30 years ago. Heck, it wasn't available 5 or 10 years ago.

Yes, I'm well aware of the research—much of it rather dated, I might add—that shows that mean reversion doesn't exist in stock prices. For example, a 1970 study by noted researcher and efficient-market pioneer Eugene Fama found no economically significant evidence of serial correlation in stock returns. However, I can show you recent research that says mean reversion *does* exist. In Chapter 2, I cite a 2001 study by Jonathan Lewellen at MIT showing that mean reversion in stock prices is stronger than commonly believed. Another recent work looking at mean reversion was authored by Kent

Daniel ("The Power and Size of Mean Reversion Test") of Northwestern University's Kellogg School of Management.

Investment research is and always will be a work in progress. By clinging to conventional wisdom, investors may miss opportunities going forward. To put an exclamation point on this topic, I'll quote Jay Ritter, a finance professor at University of Florida and a thought leader in the field, about what we know today versus what we'll know tomorrow: "Twenty years from now, I expect that my former doctoral students will be saying that a lot of what they learned in graduate school was wrong. I just wish that I knew now which things that I'm teaching are wrong, rather than having to wait twenty years to find out."

As more work is done on the concept of mean reversion and stock prices, especially as it applies to Dow components, I believe the research will continue to support mean-reversion patterns in Dow stocks.

There are a lot of theories that seem good on paper—theories derived from going through reams of data to develop a system that worked in the past. Oftentimes, however, these theories fail to work going forward. Why should I believe the worst-to-first strategy is any different?

Yes, when advancing a new investment approach, the temptation is always great to "data mine"—that is, sift through data to create a *historically* foolproof investment strategy that supports your thesis. The point is that I didn't have to data mine. *The story told itself.* Indeed, the data were so compelling that the story didn't need to be contrived or manipulated to fit some agenda.

To be sure, I think it would have been intellectually dishonest to simply look at the last 5 or 10 years when evaluating my worst-to-first strategies. That's why I went back to 1930 to see how this system worked. And the results hold up very well.

I think one reason the story holds up is that there is truly an underlying logic to the worst-to-first strategy, a true cause and effect that is lacking in many other investment strategies. This underlying logic, of course, is reversion to the mean. I also believe that this strategy works because it forces you to buy depressed stocks.

Of course, only time will tell whether this strategy works as well going forward as it does on paper. I'm betting it will. One reason is that the performance of the worst-to-first strategies, judging from the big gains over the last 5 years, is gaining momentum.

Why is annual price change a good tool for picking contrarian Dow stocks? It seems to me that a stock's 12-month price movement, relative to other stocks, is unrelated and not necessarily reflective of whether a stock offers good value.

An investment system built on mean reversion is trying to find stocks that have moved to extremes. Although certainly not perfect, a dramatic move in a stock's price in a 12-month period usually signals that the stock has probably moved out of its equilibrium range.

Keep in mind the word *dramatic*. Mean reversion is not saying that a stock that goes down 12 percent in one year has necessarily moved to extreme levels and is ready to rebound the next year. The strategy is trying to exploit big price changes—declines of 30 percent or more in a particular year.

Look at the last 5 years—a period when the worst-to-first strategies have been knocking the cover off the ball relative to the Dow. You have seen pretty significant price changes in the worst-to-first stocks. In 2002, the worst-performing stock, Home Depot, declined 53 percent. The second and third worst performers, Intel and McDonald's, were down 50 percent and 39 percent, respectively. In 2001, Boeing, the worst performer among the Dow stocks, declined more than 41 percent, followed by Merck (down 37 percent). In 2000, AT&T declined a whopping 66 percent. The second worst performer, Microsoft, fell 63 percent. These are all what I would consider dramatic price declines and thus declines that had pushed the stock prices to unsustainable extremes.

Remember that one of my worst-to-first strategies examined a stock's price to its 200-day moving average price. Using a moving average as a baseline equilibrium range, rather than simply price change, was an attempt to address the question about the validity of just using price change. I discovered that in most years the Dow stocks showing the biggest price declines usually were the Dow stocks trading the greatest percentage below their 200-day moving average price. For example, Home Depot, Intel, and McDonald's were the three worst performers in 2002. These three stocks were also the three Dow stocks trading the greatest percentage below their 200-day moving average prices. You can see how closely annual price change and ratio change correlate each year in the annual results shown in the Appendix.

To be sure, you may have instances when a stock rises 80 percent in one year only to decline 50 percent the next. Does the 50 percent decline represent a significant move out of an equilibrium range (in which case you would expect a big price rebound the following year), or does the 50 percent decline merely restore the stock to its equilibrium range following the 80 percent gain in the previous year? Actually, this is a good question to ask and answer when looking at prospective worst-to-first stocks. Indeed, a great argument could be made that 12-month price change isn't long enough; that to get a better handle on whether a stock has truly bolted from its equilibrium range, you should be looking at 2-year price changes or even 3-year price changes.

Actually, a worthy research effort would be to examine 24-month price change as a better tool for picking worst-to-first stocks. Likewise, perhaps comparing a stock's price to its 400-day moving average price would yield better results.

At the end of the day, however, an investment strategy has to be reasonably practical from an implementation side. The inputs that go into deciding the stock picks have to be easily obtained and computed. I opted on the side of simplicity by looking at 12-month price change, 200-day moving average price, and 12-month holding periods as the basis for my worst-to-first strategies. These numbers are easily found in the newspaper or online. The more exotic you get in terms of the criteria you use to make your selections, the more difficult it is to actually put the strategy into practice. As the results show, I don't believe we're leaving too much money on the table by taking the simple approach.

And as for whether annual price change is a relevant yardstick for assessing value across Dow stocks, consider this: If one Dow stock goes down 50 percent and another goes up 20 percent, can't you legitimately gain insight into which stock has been more popular with investors? The worst-to-first strategies are contrarian strategies. These strategies are trying to avoid popular stocks and buy unpopular stocks in the Dow. Annual percentage change does provide a useful score-card for judging popularity among the Dow stocks over the preceding 12-month period. It's an easier indicator to grasp than trying to deter-mine relative popularity of Dow stocks by looking at things like price/earnings ratios (remember—earnings have been known to be manipulated by a company or two via shady accounting, etc.) or divi-dend yields. Comparing annual price change may not be perfect, but I challenge you to come up with a different metric for assessing popular-ity across all Dow stocks, regardless of their industry, that is as easy to obtain, easy to understand, and free from the type of manipulation and shenanigans that can distort other metrics.

Even if the worst-to-first strategy works, it will eventually fall victim to its own success. Indeed, as more and more investors adopt the strategy, it will become less and less effective.

Of course, if *everyone* adopted the worst-to-first strategy, its effective-ness would diminish. However, as much as I hope that would happen (think of the book sales!), I don't believe it will occur.

The strategy is employed using the biggest and most liquid stocks in the market. This is significant. If I were selling you a strategy that used very small stocks to generate big returns, it would be difficult for a lot of investors to implement the strategy. Market liquidity (i.e., the ability to buy and sell stocks easily, cheaply, and with little disturbance to the actual price) would constrain the participants and eventually doom the strategy. That won't happen with the worst-to-first strategies.

But the big reason is that this strategy will have too many skeptics, too many people who simply refuse to believe that money can be made with such an easy formula. There will also be investors who may buy the strategy's logic but simply cannot bring themselves to buy some of the types of stocks that may be the Dow's Underdogs in a given year.

Popularity is often used as the reason the Dogs of the Dow strate-gies have lost their bark over the last decade. Since everyone was fol-lowing the strategy, nobody could win with the strategy. That statement is simply not true. Yes, a lot of money was invested in Dogs of the Dow. At one point, several billions of dollars were invested in Dogs of the Dow unit investment trusts. But while, say, $20 billion may seem like a lot of money, it is a drop in the bucket relative to the dollars sloshing around in the equity markets.

The total market capitalization of just the 30 stocks in the Dow Jones Industrial Average is nearly $3.7 trillion. And that's just 30 stocks. No, it is simply not true that the Dogs' poor performance was due to everyone following the strategy. Everyone wasn't following it. As discussed in Chapter 8, the problems with the Dogs of the Dow strategy were twofold: (1) changes in dividend policies made dividend yield a much less effective tool for selecting rebound stocks in the Dow; and (2) changes in the Dow components altered the complexion of the Dow significantly, thus creating a tiered Dow in terms of dividend yields. This two-tiered Dow in terms of dividend yields (extremely high yields and extremely low yields) made yield a less effective yardstick for measuring value.

The market is too efficient to let such a money-making anomaly exist. You simply cannot make money this easily.

I have an MBA from the University of Chicago, the birthplace of the efficient market theory. So I approach any discussion of market anomalies with a fairly jaundiced eye. My education and more than two decades of experience tell me that free lunches don't exist on Wall Street. My personal belief is that markets are reasonably efficient. Having said that, however, I also believe that market efficiency is not a steady state. Markets are reasonably efficient over time but not by the hour or day or week or month.

It is fair to say that academia is quickly coming around to the idea that markets may not be as efficient as once thought. Indeed, Nobel prizes are being awarded to people who claim that individuals may not always behave rationally. Academics who espoused efficient market theories are opening up investment shops to exploit anomalies or value-added investment strategies that they now claim exist.

Successful investing is about covering the bases. You own large-cap and small-cap stocks because you don't know which stocks will do well from one year to the next. You own both growth and value stocks because you don't know which style will capture investors' fancy from one year to the next. You diversify across bonds and stocks because you want to make sure you are situated in the asset class that performs well in any given year. To follow this train of thought, it makes perfect sense to believe in the power of the efficient market—and, as a result, to own index funds—as well as to place bets on your ability to exploit cracks in the efficient market.

Bottom line: I own index funds. I also play the worst-to-first strategy. Think of it as diversification across investment strategies.

Yes, the results of your worst-to-first strategy are impressive relative to the Dow Jones Industrial Average. But they ought to be impressive. After all, you are assuming a lot more risk in this strategy. And because you are accepting a lot more risk, you should be generating much greater returns.

The risk-return argument is a good one. Risk and return are joined at the hip. You cannot have higher expected returns without assuming a higher level of risk. Interestingly, while my worst-to-first portfolios have carried a higher level of risk (as measured by standard deviation of returns) than the Dow over long periods of time, they have actually been less risky over shorter periods. For example, over the last 10 years, my basic 10-stock worst-to-first portfolio has had a lower standard deviation of returns than the Dow. Thus, over the last 10 years, my basic 10-stock worst-to-first portfolio has not only had much greater returns than the Dow but has achieved those returns by taking on less risk.

A good measure of risk-adjusted returns is the Sharpe ratio. The ratio, developed by Nobel prize winner William Sharpe, looks at the reward per unit of risk. The Sharpe ratio is calculated by using standard deviation and excess return. The higher the Sharpe ratio, the better the investment's historical risk-adjusted performance.

I have provided the standard deviations and Sharpe ratios for my various worst-to-first portfolios, along with the standard deviation and Sharpe ratio of the Dow. Again, notice the impressive numbers for my basic worst-to-first strategies (5-stock and 10-stock portfolios) over the last 10 years and especially the last 5 years.

Years	Prior Year Price Action				Prior Year Close Ratio				
Std. Dev.	1 Stock (%)	3 Stocks (%)	5 Stocks (%)	10 Stocks (%)	1 Stock (%)	3 Stocks (%)	5 Stocks (%)	10 Stocks (%)	Dow (%)
5	42.6	29.0	23.5	20.3	32.8	32.5	26.0	25.3	20.1
10	40.0	23.2	18.3	15.7	32.7	26.7	20.8	19.2	17.8
20	63.5	26.0	20.9	16.0	48.6	31.5	22.9	18.1	15.0
30	66.0	31.2	24.3	19.2	5.1	32.7	28.2	21.9	16.8

Sharpe Ratio	5 Stocks	10 Stocks	5 Stocks	10 Stocks	Dow
5	0.50	0.33	0.51	0.28	-0.06
10	0.56	0.59	0.38	0.41	0.49
20	0.48	0.54	0.29	0.43	0.60
30	0.33	0.38	0.22	0.29	0.37

C'mon, Chuck. Would you really put your mother into this strategy?

You hear this phrase around Wall Street as the acid test for a strategy: Would you put your mom into the strategy? My response is an emphatic yes, with some qualifiers:

- This would not be my mother's only investment strategy. Again, within a diversified portfolio, you can incorporate fairly risky investment approaches and still maintain an appropriate risk level for a given investment time horizon.

- I would be inclined to control the downside risk by implementing stops or stop-loss orders, especially if I were starting a 1-stock worst-to-first portfolio. As I've discussed in previous chapters, you can take a pretty big hit from the worst-to-first strategy if you are focusing on 1-stock portfolios. For example, in 1996, the 1-stock worst-to-first portfolio declined 36 percent. That's the sort of hit from which it is tough to come back if you have a limited investment time horizon. Therefore, a prudent approach for implementing this strategy would be to protect yourself from the one big wipeout that could happen in a given year. You do that by automatically selling the stock if it declines some percentage amount, perhaps 15 percent or so.

No system works every year, and this one will not be any different.

You are absolutely right. No investment strategy is infallible. The worst-to-first strategy has not made money or beaten the Dow every year. And if you followed the strategy for only a few years during one of its dry spells—such as the 1990s—you would have trailed the Dow.

Remember, this strategy depends to a large extent on extreme price movements among the Dow stocks. It should not be surprising as the greater the stocks are from their means, the more vigorous will be the reversion to those means. However, plenty of years exist when market volatility has been modest and the spread between the best-performing and worst-performing Dow stocks has been fairly modest. You would not expect the system to work well in such an environment.

Also, it is possible that you can get submarined by a Dow stock that becomes financially distressed. For example, in 1990, the strategy didn't work well relative to the Dow partly because Navistar had two dreadful years in 1989 and 1990.

My point, however, is that this strategy has worked well enough over many different time periods to merit being another weapon in your investment arsenal, another tool to use to broaden your portfolio's ability to capture stock market profits.

When you account for trading commissions and taxes, your tremendous results disappear.

This is the most effective argument against the worst-to-first strategy. Yes, when you take into account taxes and trading costs, the performance gap between the worst-to-first strategy and the Dow narrows. Since 1931, the average annual return of my 5-stock and 10-stock worst-to-first portfolios has been around 11 percent, roughly 1 percent better than the return of the Dow over that time frame. Although 1 percent doesn't seem like much, the effect of beating the Dow by 1 percent per year over 74 years means your investment returns are double those of the Dow.

But what if that 1 percent gets chewed up in trading commissions each year? Actually, that was very possible before the 1990s and the advent of deep discounters. However, today you should be able to keep your trading commissions at 1 percent or below, regardless of the size of your investment portfolio.

You can limit the impact of taxes on your results by doing one of two things:

1. *House your worst-to-first portfolios in a tax-exempt account, preferably a Roth IRA.* In a Roth, you won't pay taxes on the investment gains, nor will you pay taxes when the money is withdrawn.
2. *Make sure you hold your investments for at least 12 months and 1 day in order to receive favorable capital gains tax treatment.* Because of the new tax law, long-term capital gains and dividends are taxed at maximum 15 percent rates. For investors in the top tax brackets, holding investments long enough to gain the favorable capital

gains tax treatment makes a lot of sense. And for investors in the 10 percent or 15 percent tax bracket, the long-term capital gains rate falls to just 5 percent through 2007 and 0 percent in 2008.

Aren't your worst-to-first strategies simply a slant on the January effect?

Under the January effect, stocks that are beaten up in one year tend to rebound sharply the following January. One reason given for the January effect is that stocks that do poorly during the year are hit with tax-loss selling toward year-end, driving their prices down even more. Once the new year begins, however, the selling pressure subsides and the stocks rise sharply on any buying support.

The January effect is a play on mean reversion. It relies on stocks that show extreme price moves below their equilibrium ranges to rebound. Since the January effect and my worst-to-first strategies both rely on mean reversion, it would follow that the January effect does work hand-in-hand with my worst-to-first strategies.

I don't see the fact that the January effect and my worst-to-first strategies have common ground as a negative, however. In fact, I view the link as further validation of my strategies and the logic underlying them. Having said that, I do believe that my strategies don't rely exclusively on gains in January to be effective. The January effect is usually associated with small-cap stocks, not the large-cap stocks that frequent the Dow. Thus, although I wouldn't be surprised to see abnormal January returns for my worst-to-first stocks, I don't believe all of my strategies' outperformance versus the Dow is a result of one good month per year.

I see dividend stocks getting a big boost from the new tax plan. Your strategy doesn't take into account dividends or yield. Don't you think that is a mistake going forward?

I am a big fan of reducing taxes on dividends. Dividends have been taxed twice in our tax system—at the corporate level in the form of profits and at the individual level in the form of dividends—for too long. I would have preferred that taxes be eliminated on dividends altogether, but the reduction in the tax rate on dividends to a maximum 15 percent was a good consolation prize.

Dividends have clearly been the most talked about aspect of the new tax law. But it is significant that taxes on long-term capital gains were also reduced under the new law to a maximum 15 percent. Many experts claim that the best way to capitalize on the new tax plan is to focus on high-yielding stocks. I disagree. I think investors should be focusing on stocks with decent appreciation potential (to take advantage of lower capital gains tax rates), reasonable yields (to take advantage of lower taxes on dividends), and healthy dividend growth (to exploit the power of compounding dividends, especially now that dividends are taxed at lower rates).

Fortunately, many of the stocks in the Dow fit this description nicely. Many Dow stocks have yields in the 1 percent to 3 percent range. They have decent appreciation potential. And I would expect many Dow stocks to raise their dividends by at least 5 percent annually over the next decade.

One reason my worst-to-strategies don't focus on yield (other than that I don't believe yield is a good tool for assessing values across all Dow stocks) is that my strategies *don't have to focus on yield* in order to get yield into the portfolios. By virtue of buying Dow stocks, my worst-to-first portfolios usually have a nice yield component, a dividend growth component, and a capital gains component. And to my way of thinking, that's the best way to maximize the opportunities presented by the new tax plan.

PART VII

CONCLUSION

10

WORST TO FIRST—THE FUTURE

The only constant in life is change. When I got into this business in 1982, the Dow Jones Industrial Average was under 800. Today, the Dow is trading around 10,000. When I first got into this business, nobody ever heard of Microsoft. You couldn't even buy the stock (the company was still private). Today, Microsoft dominates the software market and is neck and neck with General Electric as the most valuable company in corporate America (as measured by market capitalization). When I first got into this business, you couldn't use your computer to buy and sell stocks. Today, trading over the Internet is as common as calling your broker.

In a changing world, many things get left behind: 5¼-inch floppy disks (remember those?). Betamax. Kmart. Will my worst-to-first strategies be left behind, victims of changing market conditions?

I suppose anything is possible. We've seen the deterioration of the Dogs of the Dow strategy partly as a result of the changing face of the Dow Jones Industrial Average. I cannot assure you that something similar won't happen to my worst-to-first strategies.

One point my worst-to-first strategies have in their favor is a timeless and universal yardstick that will not change despite what happens to the Dow over the near and long term. Indeed, using a stock's annual percentage price change as a popularity index should hold up well regardless of what Dow components are added/deleted over the next several years.

My sense is that my worst-to-first strategies will become even more potent as time progresses. Already we've seen a ramp-up in their effectiveness over the last decade and especially over the last 5 years as more changes have occurred to the Dow components. Those changes brought Dow stocks on board that tend to exhibit higher growth potential but also potentially more volatile price action. Fortunately, volatility is truly a friend to mean-reversion strategies such as my worst-to-first portfolios.

If you go back through history, there doesn't seem to be a consistent timetable for Dow changes. Periods existed, especially in the early 1930s, when changes were made nearly every year. There have also been long periods—from June 1959 through August 1976, for example—when no changes were made.

Is the Dow on the cusp of advancing its makeover of recent years? Only John Prestbo, the current keeper of the Dow, knows for sure. Given the changes made in April 2004, it could be a few years before another round of changes occurs.

History says that the major catalysts for changes in the Dow are takeovers and financial distress. On the latter score, no Dow stock is currently feeling the sort of heat financially that would cause its membership in the index to be in doubt.

As for takeovers, anything is possible. At the time of this writing, merger and acquisition activity in corporate America, though way down from the late 1990s, is perking up. And certain areas of the economy—telecom, technology, health care—continue to scream out for further consolidation. Still, I don't view the Dow stocks—perhaps with the exception of Honeywell International—to be true acquisition candidates.

Another factor that would cause the Dow keepers to make changes would be if a Dow stock simply became so irrelevant to the economy and the market that its presence in the Dow was keeping a more worthy stock out of the index. On this score, I see a few Dow components that could find their membership rescinded.

Following is the current list of Dow stocks. I've grouped them by what I believe is the likelihood of the stock being in the index a decade from now:

Locks to Stay in Dow

American International Group

Citigroup

Disney

Exxon Mobil

General Electric
General Motors
IBM
Intel
Johnson & Johnson
Microsoft

Pfizer
Procter & Gamble
3M
Verizon
Wal-Mart Stores

Likely to Stay

Altria Group
American Express
Boeing
Caterpillar
Coca-Cola
DuPont

Hewlett-Packard
Home Depot
Merck & Co.
SBC Communications
United Technologies

On the Bubble

Alcoa
Honeywell International

J.P. Morgan Chase
McDonald's

It's worth noting that several of the stocks that I believe could be dumped from the Dow over the next decade tend to be slow- or no-growth issues with decent yields. If history holds, you'll probably see the keepers of the Dow replace these companies with firms from the same or similar industry groups. However, the new firms will likely have a much different growth profile.

The following are stocks that I see as possible Dow additions over the next 10 years:

ALLTEL
Amgen
Anheuser-Busch
Automatic Data Processing
Bank of America
Cisco
Dell Computer
Ebay
Emerson Electric

Gannett
Kraft Foods
Medtronic
Nucor
Sysco
Tribune
Walgreen
Wells Fargo

Bottom line: The Dow will continue to skew more toward growth, less toward value and dividend yield. That spells good news for my worst-to-first strategies.

APPLYING MEAN-REVERSION STRATEGIES TO OTHER INDEXES

This book has focused on the Dow Jones Industrial Average as the universe for implementing mean-reversion investment approaches. And, as we have seen, these strategies work exceedingly well with the Dow Industrials. The success of my worst-to-first strategies in the Dow begs the question: If mean reversion is so powerful, why couldn't you apply the worst-to-first approach to other indexes?

Actually, you probably can apply them to non-Dow stocks but with the following caveats:

- Mean reversion seems to be most effective with larger, seasoned companies that have demonstrated the ability to weather market and economic cycles.

- Mean reversion requires companies with strong financial positions.

If you can find stocks that meet these criteria, you probably have found stocks well suited for worst-to-first strategies.

One area for future research would be to examine worst-to-first strategies using other old-line indexes. Two indexes that come quickly to mind are the Dow Jones Utility Average and the Dow Jones Transportation Average.

Dow Jones Utility Average

AES Corp. (AES)
American Electric Power (AEP)
CenterPoint Energy (CNP)
Consolidated Edison (ED)
Dominion Resources (D)
Duke Energy (DUK)
Edison International (EIX)
Exelon (EXC)
FirstEnergy (FE)
Nisource (NI)
PG&E (PCG)
Public Service Enterprise (PEG)
Southern Co. (SO)
TXU Corp (TXU)
Williams Companies (WMB)

Dow Jones Transportation Average

Alexander & Baldwin (ALEX) GATX (GMT)
AMR (AMR) J.B. Hunt Transport (JBHT)
Burlington Northern Santa Fe (BNI) Norfolk Southern (NSC)
C.H. Robinson Worldwide (CHRW) Northwest Air (NWAC)
CNF (CNF) Ryder System (R)
Continental Airlines (CAL) Southwest Airlines (LUV)
CSX (CSX) Union Pacific (UNP)
Delta Air Lines (DAL) United Parcel Services (UPS)
Expeditors Int'l (EXPD) USF (USFC)
FedEx (FDX) Yellow Corp. (YELL)

These two indexes would provide worthwhile laboratories for exploring the power of mean-reversion strategies in specific industry sectors. Interestingly, had you bought the five worst-performing stocks in 2002 in each of these two indexes (that weren't in bankruptcy) . . .

Dow Transports (2002 price change)
Continental Air: −72.3 percent
AMR: −70.4 percent
Delta: −58.6 percent
Northwest Air: −53.2 percent
GATX: −29.8 percent

Dow Utilities (2002 price change)
Williams Companies: −89.4 percent
AES: −81.5 percent
CenterPoint Energy: −62.8 percent
TXU: −60.4 percent
Duke Energy: −50.2 percent

. . . your returns in 2003 would have been the following:

Dow Transports (price change through December 31, 2003)
Continental Air: +124.4 percent
AMR: +96.2 percent
Delta: −2.4 percent

Northwest Air: +72.2 percent
GATX: +22.6 percent
Portfolio return (assuming equal dollar investments):
  +62.6 percent
Price change of Dow Transports (through December 31, 2003):
  +30.2 percent

Dow Utilities (price change through December 31, 2003)
Williams Companies: +263.7 percent
AES: +212.6 percent
CenterPoint Energy: +21.0 percent
TXU: +27.0 percent
Duke Energy: +4.7 percent
Portfolio return (assuming equal dollar investments):
  +105.8 percent
Price change of Dow Utilities (through December 31, 2003):
  +24.0 percent

It is especially noteworthy (aside, of course, from the huge gains of these worst-to-first portfolios for both the Dow Transports and Utilities in 2003) that the two worst-performing stocks in both Dow Transports and Dow Utilities in 2002 registered the most impressive gains in 2003. Of course, one year is way too short a time frame to evaluate any investment strategy. Still, the early results are promising, to say the least.

CONCLUSION

The tendency of most people is to extrapolate near-term trends well into the future. Indeed, in the late 1990s, we all thought 20 percent or 30 percent per year market returns would continue forever. During the bear market of 2000 to 2002, we all thought we'd never see another up year.

If I had to guess about what stocks will do over the next 10 years, my head and my gut tell me that we still need to work off some of the excesses created by the never-before-seen market advance of 1982 through 1999. Thus, I think investors should not expect average annual market returns much above 6 percent to 8 percent.

Although those returns may not sound like much, you can make good money over time if your investments rise, say, 7 percent per year. At 7 percent per year, your money doubles roughly every 10 years. Just squeezing out a percent or two more per year, however, can have an exponential impact on your portfolio performance. For example, if you can generate 9 percent per year on your investments over the next decade, your money will double in roughly 8 years, and double again in another 8 years. Thus, at 9 percent per year over the next 16 years, $50,000 becomes $200,000 without any additional contributions.

Of course, you need a strategy that beats the market by a few percentage points per year, and that's no easy feat. Fortunately, you have in your hands a system for outperforming the market that is both simple and powerful. And in the investment business, simple and powerful can add up to big profits.

PART VIII

THE HISTORY—TRACKING THE DOW COMPONENT PERFORMANCE

Appendix

DOW COMPONENTS AND RETURN DATA—1930 THROUGH 2003

1930

Company Name	Price Chg (%)	Total Return (%)	Rank Price Chg
RADIO CORP AMER	72.7	−72.7	1
NATIONAL CASH REG	−62.9	−57.7	2
HUDSON MTR CAR CO	−59.7	−54.3	3
JOHNS MANVILLE CORP	−57.3	−55.6	4
CHRYSLER CORP	−55.1	−50.9	5
INTERNATIONAL NICKEL CO CDA LTD	−53.5	−51.7	6
UNITED AIRCRAFT & TRANS CORP	−49.2	−49.2	7
MACK TRUCKS INC	−48.6	−43.0	8
SEARS ROEBUCK & CO	−47.4	−45.5	9
BETHLEHEM STEEL CORP	−46.7	−42.9	10
TEXAS CO	−43.9	−40.0	
AMERICAN SMLT & REFNG CO	−43.7	−40.2	
INTERNATIONAL HARVESTER CO	−37.9	−35.6	
WESTINGHOUSE ELECTRIC & MFG CO	−36.9	−34.3	
ALLIED CHEMICAL & DYE CORP	−30.6	−28.9	
STANDARD OIL CO N J	−28.7	−26.5	
GENERAL ELECTRIC CO	−28.3	−26.4	
UNION CARBIDE & CARBON CORP	−27.7	−25.1	
PARAMOUNT PUBLIX CORP	−26.2	−20.5	
GOODYEAR TIRE & RUBR CO	−26.0	−21.5	
STANDARD OIL CO CALIFORNIA	−25.6	−20.8	
WOOLWORTH F W CO	−21.4	−18.4	
UNITED STATES STEEL CORP	−18.6	−15.2	
EASTMAN KODAK CO	−17.1	−13.9	
TEXAS GULF SULPHUR CO	−15.7	−9.8	
GENERAL MOTORS CORP	−12.7	−6.4	
AMERICAN CAN CO	−10.1	−6.5	
LIGGETT & MYERS TOB CO	0.2	5.2	
GENERAL FOODS CORP	2.1	7.9	
BORDEN CO	4.3	11.8	
Average	−33.3	−29.6	

Worst-to-First Performance	1931 (%)
1-stock portfolio	−54.2
3-stock portfolio	−57.4
5-stock portfolio	−49.4
10-stock portfolio	−48.4
Dow Performance	−47.6

1931

Company Name	Price Chg (%)	Total Return (%)	Rank Price Chg
PARAMOUNT PUBLIX CORP	−80.5	−79.5	1
WESTINGHOUSE ELECTRIC & MFG CO	−74.5	−73.4	2
NATIONAL CASH REG	−72.2	−68.3	3
UNITED STATES STEEL CORP	−72.2	−70.5	4
JOHNS MANVILLE CORP	−67.0	−65.0	5
BETHLEHEM STEEL CORP	−62.9	−58.6	6
TEXAS CO	−61.9	−57.1	7
ALLIED CHEMICAL & DYE CORP	−60.8	−58.7	8
MACK TRUCKS INC	−60.4	−56.7	9
GOODYEAR TIRE & RUBR CO	−58.2	−53.9	10
AMERICAN SMLT & REFNG CO	−54.6	−50.9	
RADIO CORP AMER	−54.2	−54.2	
HUDSON MTR CAR CO	−53.7	−49.8	
UNITED AIRCRAFT & TRANS CORP	−53.1	−53.1	
INTERNATIONAL HARVESTER CO	−52.0	−48.2	
TEXAS GULF SULPHUR CO	−50.8	−46.3	
INTERNATIONAL NICKEL CO CDA LTD	−48.8	−46.9	
UNION CARBIDE & CARBON CORP	−45.7	−42.2	
AMERICAN CAN CO	−45.5	−42.7	
BORDEN CO	−45.2	−42.2	
STANDARD OIL CO CALIFORNIA	−45.1	−41.3	
LIGGETT & MYERS TOB CO	−44.2	−40.0	
EASTMAN KODAK CO	−44.0	−40.0	
GENERAL ELECTRIC CO	−42.7	−40.0	
STANDARD OIL CO N J	−40.9	−37.6	
GENERAL MOTORS CORP	−36.0	−30.1	
GENERAL FOODS CORP	−30.6	−26.0	
WOOLWORTH F W CO	−27.9	−22.5	
SEARS ROEBUCK & CO	−25.4	−21.6	
CHRYSLER CORP	−14.5	−9.7	
Average	−50.9	−47.6	

Worst-to-First Performance	1932 (%)
1-stock portfolio	−71.4
3-stock portfolio	−16.8
5-stock portfolio	−13.0
10-stock portfolio	0.7
Dow Performance	−17.1

1932

Company Name	Price Chg (%)	Total Return (%)	Rank Price Chg
SEARS ROEBUCK & CO	−42.0	−38.8	1
GENERAL MOTORS CORP	−42.0	−36.7	2
GENERAL ELECTRIC CO	−39.0	−34.0	3
BORDEN CO	−36.8	−30.7	4
INTERNATIONAL SHOE CO	−36.1	−30.7	5
EASTMAN KODAK CO	−33.4	−28.2	6
AMERICAN SMLT & REFNG CO	−32.9	−32.4	7
DRUG INC	−32.2	−24.0	8
COCA COLA CO	−29.9	−23.6	9
LOEWS INC	−29.0	−19.0	10
UNITED STATES STEEL CORP	−28.8	−28.0	
PROCTER & GAMBLE CO	−26.8	−21.5	
NASH MOTORS CO	−24.3	−14.7	
GENERAL FOODS CORP	−23.9	−17.3	
GOODYEAR TIRE & RUBR CO	−22.4	−21.1	
BETHLEHEM STEEL CORP	−21.3	−18.9	
AMERICAN TOB CO	−20.3	−12.6	
UNION CARBIDE & CARBON CORP	−15.3	−10.3	
INTERNATIONAL BUSINESS MACHS COR	−13.7	−7.4	
INTERNATIONAL HARVESTER CO	−12.0	−4.3	
WOOLWORTH F W CO	−11.3	−5.3	
AMERICAN CAN CO	−8.5	−0.3	
STANDARD OIL CO CALIFORNIA	−2.0	6.9	
INTERNATIONAL NICKEL CO CDA LTD	6.5	6.5	
STANDARD OIL CO N J	8.5	16.5	
JOHNS MANVILLE CORP	13.5	13.5	
CHRYSLER CORP	17.0	28.7	
WESTINGHOUSE ELECTRIC & MFG CO	18.3	22.7	
ALLIED CHEMICAL & DYE CORP	20.2	32.3	
TEXAS CO	20.8	31.3	
Average	−16.0	−10.0	

Worst-to-First Performance	1933 (%)
1-stock portfolio	122.2
3-stock portfolio	113.1
5-stock portfolio	83.3
10-stock portfolio	84.7
Dow Performance	72.4

1933

Company Name	Price Chg (%)	Total Return (%)	Rank Price Chg
BORDEN CO	−16.1	−10.4	1
UNITED AIRCRAFT & TRANS CORP	21.2	21.2	2
WOOLWORTH F W CO	21.8	30.6	3
AMERICAN TOB CO	24.7	33.4	4
GENERAL FOODS CORP	25.6	33.3	5
GENERAL ELECTRIC CO	27.9	30.8	6
COCA COLA CO	28.0	37.2	7
PROCTER & GAMBLE CO	32.8	38.7	8
WESTINGHOUSE ELECTRIC & MFG CO	38.2	47.6	9
CORN PRODUCTS REFINING CO	40.5	49.9	10
EASTMAN KODAK CO	47.9	54.3	
LOEWS INC	49.4	57.4	
STANDARD OIL CO N J	51.2	56.7	
INTERNATIONAL BUSINESS MACHS COR	58.6	66.7	
STANDARD OIL CO CALIFORNIA	67.3	74.9	
TEXAS CO	68.1	76.7	
UNITED STATES STEEL CORP	73.6	73.6	
ALLIED CHEMICAL & DYE CORP	79.7	90.4	
AMERICAN CAN CO	80.4	90.1	
UNION CARBIDE & CARBON CORP	81.0	86.1	
NASH MOTORS CO	88.7	97.3	
INTERNATIONAL HARVESTER CO	89.3	92.9	
SEARS ROEBUCK & CO	122.2	122.2	
GOODYEAR TIRE & RUBR CO	142.4	142.4	
BETHLEHEM STEEL CORP	150.8	150.8	
INTERNATIONAL NICKEL CO CDA LTD	166.7	166.7	
GENERAL MOTORS CORP	170.5	106.4	
JOHNS MANVILLE CORP	202.5	202.5	
CHRYSLER CORP	251.9	259.6	
AMERICAN SMLT & REFNG CO	258.0	258.0	
Average	84.8	90.6	

Worst-to-First Performance	1934 (%)
1-stock portfolio	25.9
3-stock portfolio	7.4
5-stock portfolio	12.1
10-stock portfolio	16.2
Dow Performance	7.8

1934

Company Name	Price Chg (%)	Total Return (%)	Rank Price Chg
GOODYEAR TIRE & RUBR CO	−29.7	−29.7	1
CHRYSLER CORP	−27.8	−25.5	2
NASH MOTORS CO	−26.5	−23.4	3
STANDARD OIL CO CALIFORNIA	−20.7	−18.4	4
UNITED STATES STEEL CORP	−18.3	−18.3	5
TEXAS CO	−13.8	−10.1	6
AMERICAN SMLT & REFNG CO	−13.4	−13.4	7
CORN PRODUCTS REFINING CO	−12.6	−9.6	8
BETHLEHEM STEEL CORP	−12.2	−12.2	9
JOHNS MANVILLE CORP	−10.7	−10.7	10
ALLIED CHEMICAL & DYE CORP	−7.3	−3.1	
SEARS ROEBUCK & CO	−6.8	−6.8	
STANDARD OIL CO N J	−5.5	−2.7	
GENERAL MOTORS CORP	−3.9	0.7	
WESTINGHOUSE ELECTRIC & MFG CO	−1.0	−1.0	
UNION CARBIDE & CARBON CORP	−0.8	2.2	
GENERAL FOODS CORP	3.8	9.6	
INTERNATIONAL HARVESTER CO	5.6	7.4	
NATIONAL DISTILLERS PRODS CORP	8.2	8.2	
INTERNATIONAL NICKEL CO CDA LTD	8.5	10.8	
INTERNATIONAL BUSINESS MACHS COR	9.0	13.6	
PROCTER & GAMBLE CO	12.5	17.7	
GENERAL ELECTRIC CO	14.1	17.5	
AMERICAN CAN CO	15.4	20.2	
BORDEN CO	18.0	25.9	
LOEWS INC	20.0	26.6	
AMERICAN TOB CO	20.7	28.8	
WOOLWORTH F W CO	24.9	30.8	
EASTMAN KODAK CO	38.3	44.5	
COCA COLA CO	68.2	77.3	
Average	1.9	5.2	

Worst-to-First Performance	1935 (%)
1-stock portfolio	−5.5
3-stock portfolio	43.1
5-stock portfolio	36.4
10-stock portfolio	43.5
Dow Performance	42.9

1935

Company Name	Price Chg (%)	Total Return (%)	Rank Price Chg
GOODYEAR TIRE & RUBR CO	−5.5	−5.5	1
NASH MOTORS CO	−1.4	5.4	2
GENERAL FOODS CORP	0.7	6.1	3
WOOLWORTH F W CO	3.2	7.6	4
CORN PRODUCTS REFINING CO	5.7	10.6	5
NATIONAL DISTILLERS PRODS CORP	9.3	17.6	6
PROCTER & GAMBLE CO	10.0	13.9	7
ALLIED CHEMICAL & DYE CORP	14.6	19.3	8
AMERICAN CAN CO	18.2	23.0	9
STANDARD OIL CO N J	19.7	24.5	10
AMERICAN TOB CO	19.7	26.4	
INTERNATIONAL BUSINESS MACHS COR	20.5	24.7	
UNITED STATES STEEL CORP	24.4	24.4	
STANDARD OIL CO CALIFORNIA	24.6	28.4	
EASTMAN KODAK CO	39.4	44.7	
TEXAS CO	41.7	48.4	
INTERNATIONAL HARVESTER CO	45.0	47.2	
DU PONT E I DE NEMOURS & CO	45.9	51.5	
NATIONAL STEEL CORP	50.0	54.0	
LOEWS INC	50.7	59.5	
UNION CARBIDE & CARBON CORP	52.3	56.6	
AMERICAN SMLT & REFNG CO	56.1	56.1	
BETHLEHEM STEEL CORP	59.2	59.2	
SEARS ROEBUCK & CO	65.9	72.3	
GENERAL MOTORS CORP	66.7	75.6	
GENERAL ELECTRIC CO	71.9	76.1	
JOHNS MANVILLE CORP	76.4	78.8	
INTERNATIONAL NICKEL CO CDA LTD	90.6	95.4	
CHRYSLER CORP	121.3	129.4	
WESTINGHOUSE ELECTRIC & MFG CO	159.1	172.2	
Average	41.9	46.8	

Worst-to-First Performance	1936 (%)
1-stock portfolio	21.1
3-stock portfolio	14.0
5-stock portfolio	13.3
10-stock portfolio	16.4
Dow Performance	29.7

1936

Company Name	Price Chg (%)	Total Return (%)	Rank Price Chg
AMERICAN CAN CO	−13.7	−9.4	1
NASH MOTORS CO	−8.3	−2.7	2
NATIONAL DISTILLERS PRODS CORP	−8.1	1.1	3
AMERICAN TOB CO	−4.0	1.0	4
NATIONAL STEEL CORP	−3.7	0.7	5
CORN PRODUCTS REFINING CO	−1.3	6.8	6
INTERNATIONAL BUSINESS MACHS COR	5.8	9.4	7
STANDARD OIL CO CALIFORNIA	9.3	12.7	8
GENERAL MOTORS CORP	11.6	19.5	9
EASTMAN KODAK CO	12.1	16.6	10
WOOLWORTH F W CO	13.0	18.0	
PROCTER & GAMBLE CO	16.1	20.9	
GENERAL FOODS CORP	16.5	23.5	
GOODYEAR TIRE & RUBR CO	21.1	21.1	
DU PONT E I DE NEMOURS & CO	24.0	28.9	
CHRYSLER CORP	25.6	39.3	
LOEWS INC	27.4	35.3	
SEARS ROEBUCK & CO	28.8	38.5	
STANDARD OIL CO N J	32.9	37.1	
INTERNATIONAL NICKEL CO CDA LTD	39.8	43.2	
GENERAL ELECTRIC CO	43.1	48.0	
ALLIED CHEMICAL & DYE CORP	43.7	48.2	
UNION CARBIDE & CARBON CORP	44.6	48.7	
BETHLEHEM STEEL CORP	45.9	48.8	
WESTINGHOUSE ELECTRIC & MFG CO	51.3	57.6	
AMERICAN SMLT & REFNG CO	54.1	61.3	
JOHNS MANVILLE CORP	58.5	63.3	
UNITED STATES STEEL CORP	60.8	60.8	
INTERNATIONAL HARVESTER CO	72.2	77.8	
TEXAS CO	84.0	91.0	
Average	26.8	32.2	

Worst-to-First Performance	1937 (%)
1-stock portfolio	−37.3
3-stock portfolio	−30.9
5-stock portfolio	−27.3
10-stock portfolio	−25.0
Dow Performance	−27.9

1937

Company Name	Price Chg (%)	Total Return (%)	Rank Price Chg
CHRYSLER CORP	−58.9	−54.0	1
GENERAL MOTORS CORP	−52.8	−48.8	2
AMERICAN SMLT & REFNG CO	−48.3	−44.1	3
JOHNS MANVILLE CORP	−47.5	−44.9	4
WOOLWORTH F W CO	−42.1	−39.0	5
INTERNATIONAL HARVESTER CO	−41.2	−38.6	6
NASH KELVINATOR CORP	−39.8	−36.5	7
AMERICAN CAN CO	−39.7	−37.3	8
GOODYEAR TIRE & RUBR CO	−39.1	−33.5	9
DU PONT E I DE NEMOURS & CO	−35.3	−32.3	10
SEARS ROEBUCK & CO	−35.2	−29.6	
STANDARD OIL CO CALIFORNIA	−34.5	−30.9	
STANDARD OIL CO N J	−34.2	−31.1	
AMERICAN TOB CO	−34.0	−29.8	
WESTINGHOUSE ELECTRIC & MFG CO	−32.5	−29.1	
LOEWS INC	−32.1	−24.3	
UNITED STATES STEEL CORP	−30.8	−29.5	
INTERNATIONAL NICKEL CO CDA LTD	−30.3	−27.3	
UNION CARBIDE & CARBON CORP	−29.2	−26.6	
ALLIED CHEMICAL & DYE CORP	−28.3	−25.5	
NATIONAL DISTILLERS PRODS CORP	−27.0	−18.8	
TEXAS CO	−25.2	−21.2	
GENERAL ELECTRIC CO	−24.9	−21.3	
INTERNATIONAL BUSINESS MACHS COR	−23.9	−20.8	
GENERAL FOODS CORP	−23.0	−18.9	
BETHLEHEM STEEL CORP	−22.5	−16.9	
NATIONAL STEEL CORP	−18.2	−14.1	
PROCTER & GAMBLE CO	−17.9	−14.0	
CORN PRODUCTS REFINING CO	−13.4	−9.0	
EASTMAN KODAK CO	−8.3	−3.8	
Average	−32.3	−28.4	

Worst-to-First Performance	1938 (%)
1-stock portfolio	79.9
3-stock portfolio	57.0
5-stock portfolio	50.7
10-stock portfolio	45.0
Dow Performance	32.2

1938

Company Name	Price Chg (%)	Total Return (%)	Rank Price Chg
NASH KELVINATOR CORP	−13.8	−12.6	1
INTERNATIONAL HARVESTER CO	−2.8	0.4	2
STANDARD OIL CO CALIFORNIA	−1.3	3.6	3
GENERAL ELECTRIC CO	5.8	8.5	4
AMERICAN SMLT & REFNG CO	12.5	18.3	5
CORN PRODUCTS REFINING CO	12.7	18.0	6
EASTMAN KODAK CO	15.1	19.5	7
ALLIED CHEMICAL & DYE CORP	18.8	23.2	8
STANDARD OIL CO N J	19.2	23.0	9
WESTINGHOUSE ELECTRIC & MFG CO	20.1	23.3	10
LOEWS INC	20.3	28.1	
UNION CARBIDE & CARBON CORP	21.9	25.4	
PROCTER & GAMBLE CO	22.0	26.8	
TEXAS CO	22.3	28.3	
INTERNATIONAL NICKEL CO CDA LTD	26.5	31.8	
UNITED STATES STEEL CORP	28.0	28.0	
GENERAL FOODS CORP	29.9	38.2	
BETHLEHEM STEEL CORP	34.7	34.7	
SEARS ROEBUCK & CO	35.6	42.2	
NATIONAL DISTILLERS PRODS CORP	35.8	48.2	
NATIONAL STEEL CORP	37.0	39.3	
WOOLWORTH F W CO	37.0	44.4	
JOHNS MANVILLE CORP	37.3	37.9	
DU PONT E DE NEMOURS & CO	37.9	41.5	
AMERICAN TOB CO	39.8	49.3	
INTERNATIONAL BUSINESS MACHS COR	42.0	47.6	
AMERICAN CAN CO	43.4	49.9	
GENERAL MOTORS CORP	66.7	72.9	
CHRYSLER CORP	74.3	79.9	
GOODYEAR TIRE & RUBR CO	115.0	117.4	
Average	29.8	34.6	

Worst-to-First Performance	1939 (%)
1-stock portfolio	−23.2
3-stock portfolio	−9.5
5-stock portfolio	−5.5
10-stock portfolio	−4.6
Dow Performance	1.0

1939

Company Name	Price Chg (%)	Total Return (%)	Rank Price Chg
GOODYEAR TIRE & RUBR CO	–38.9	–36.6	1
INTERNATIONAL NICKEL CO CDA LTD	–34.7	–31.8	2
LOEWS INC	–34.2	–29.6	3
JOHNS MANVILLE CORP	–31.2	–28.6	4
WOOLWORTH F W CO	–23.5	–19.2	5
STANDARD OIL CO N J	–15.3	–13.0	6
NATIONAL DISTILLERS PRODS CORP	–13.8	–6.6	7
STANDARD OIL CO CALIFORNIA	–13.1	–9.4	8
NATIONAL STEEL CORP	–10.8	–8.4	9
ALLIED CHEMICAL & DYE CORP	–8.5	–3.7	10
EASTMAN KODAK CO	–8.5	–5.1	
TEXAS CO	–7.3	–2.7	
GENERAL ELECTRIC CO	–7.2	–3.6	
UNITED STATES STEEL CORP	–4.3	–4.3	
UNION CARBIDE & CARBON CORP	–3.2	–0.8	
CORN PRODUCTS REFINING CO	–2.6	2.2	
WESTINGHOUSE ELECTRIC & MFG CO	–2.3	0.9	
AMERICAN TOB CO	–2.3	3.8	
AMERICAN SMLT & REFNG CO	–1.9	4.5	
INTERNATIONAL HARVESTER CO	1.2	4.0	
BETHLEHEM STEEL CORP	2.9	5.1	
CHRYSLER CORP	7.8	14.9	
GENERAL MOTORS CORP	9.0	17.1	
UNITED AIRCRAFT CORP	9.4	14.8	
AMERICAN CAN CO	12.9	17.6	
AMERICAN TELEPHONE & TELEG CO	13.9	20.4	
SEARS ROEBUCK & CO	16.2	22.7	
DU PONT E I DE NEMOURS & CO	17.8	23.0	
PROCTER & GAMBLE CO	19.2	23.7	
GENERAL FOODS CORP	21.1	27.6	
Average	–4.4	0.0	

Worst-to-First Performance	1940 (%)
1-stock portfolio	–11.0
3-stock portfolio	–12.7
5-stock portfolio	–11.9
10-stock portfolio	–10.2
Dow Performance	–8.0

1940

Company Name	Price Chg (%)	Total Return (%)	Rank Price Chg
INTERNATIONAL NICKEL CO CDA LTD	–33.8	–28.6	1
CORN PRODUCTS REFINING CO	–29.3	–26.2	2
STANDARD OIL CO CALIFORNIA	–25.6	–21.7	3
AMERICAN CAN CO	–22.2	–19.2	4
STANDARD OIL CO N J	–21.7	–17.3	5
GENERAL FOODS CORP	–20.3	–16.5	6
UNION CARBIDE & CARBON CORP	–19.7	–16.9	7
CHRYSLER CORP	–19.6	–13.3	8
GENERAL ELECTRIC CO	–18.0	–13.4	9
AMERICAN TOB CO	–17.9	–12.3	10
INTERNATIONAL HARVESTER CO	–17.4	–13.4	
GOODYEAR TIRE & RUBR CO	–16.8	–11.0	
EASTMAN KODAK CO	–16.7	–12.9	
JOHNS MANVILLE CORP	–16.6	–12.8	
AMERICAN SMLT & REFNG CO	–16.3	–10.6	
WOOLWORTH F W CO	–14.7	–8.9	
PROCTER & GAMBLE CO	–13.1	–9.4	
GENERAL MOTORS CORP	–11.9	–4.7	
UNITED AIRCRAFT CORP	–11.0	–3.7	
WESTINGHOUSE ELECTRIC & MFG CO	–10.5	–6.2	
DU PONT E I DE NEMOURS & CO	–10.2	–6.3	
TEXAS CO	–10.1	–5.4	
ALLIED CHEMICAL & DYE CORP	–8.5	–3.9	
SEARS ROEBUCK & CO	–8.2	–3.0	
LOEWS INC	–8.1	1.5	
NATIONAL STEEL CORP	–7.0	–3.3	
NATIONAL DISTILLERS PRODS CORP	–5.2	3.6	
AMERICAN TELEPHONE & TELEG CO	–1.8	3.6	
UNITED STATES STEEL CORP	5.3	10.6	
BETHLEHEM STEEL CORP	7.0	13.9	
Average	–14.0	–8.9	

Worst-to-First Performance	1941 (%)
1-stock portfolio	19.9
3-stock portfolio	18.8
5-stock portfolio	11.3
10-stock portfolio	–0.1
Dow Performance	–9.6

1941

Company Name	Price Chg (%)	Total Return (%)	Rank Price Chg
GOODYEAR TIRE & RUBR CO	−47.1	−42.8	1
CHRYSLER CORP	−37.0	−30.1	2
GENERAL MOTORS CORP	−35.9	−29.4	3
AMERICAN TOB CO	−35.1	−30.4	4
SEARS ROEBUCK & CO	−33.3	−29.0	5
AMERICAN CAN CO	−32.2	−28.9	6
NATIONAL STEEL CORP	−26.7	−22.0	7
WESTINGHOUSE ELECTRIC & MFG CO	−25.2	−20.7	8
WOOLWORTH F W CO	−24.9	−19.5	9
BETHLEHEM STEEL CORP	−24.9	−18.0	10
UNITED STATES STEEL CORP	−23.3	−17.6	
AMERICAN TELEPHONE & TELEG CO	−22.5	−17.7	
GENERAL ELECTRIC CO	−19.6	−14.8	
UNITED AIRCRAFT CORP	−15.0	−5.4	
DU PONT E I DE NEMOURS & CO	−12.5	−8.3	
ALLIED CHEMICAL & DYE CORP	−10.5	−5.7	
NATIONAL DISTILLERS PRODS CORP	−10.4	−1.7	
PROCTER & GAMBLE CO	−10.0	−5.0	
INTERNATIONAL HARVESTER CO	−8.4	−2.4	
JOHNS MANVILLE CORP	−7.1	−2.5	
AMERICAN SMLT & REFNG CO	−2.6	6.0	
TEXAS CO	−1.3	4.9	
EASTMAN KODAK CO	−0.7	4.4	
GENERAL FOODS CORP	1.3	6.8	
STANDARD OIL CO CALIFORNIA	2.0	9.1	
UNION CARBIDE & CARBON CORP	6.3	10.8	
INTERNATIONAL NICKEL CO CDA LTD	10.8	19.9	
LOEWS INC	11.5	21.5	
CORN PRODUCTS REFINING CO	10.0	27.3	
STANDARD OIL CO N J	21.5	29.0	
Average	−13.2	7.1	

Worst-to-First Performance	1942 (%)
1-stock portfolio	175.7
3-stock portfolio	95.6
5-stock portfolio	62.9
10-stock portfolio	39.7
Dow Performance	13.4

1942

Company Name	Price Chg (%)	Total Return (%)	Rank Price Chg
UNITED AIRCRAFT CORP	−27.2	−18.1	1
BETHLEHEM STEEL CORP	−13.5	−3.5	2
UNITED STATES STEEL CORP	−11.5	−3.8	3
AMERICAN SMLT & REFNG CO	−10.6	−3.2	4
DU PONT E I DE NEMOURS & CO	−9.1	−5.7	5
GENERAL FOODS CORP	−8.1	−3.0	6
AMERICAN TOB CO	−7.0	0.0	7
PROCTER & GAMBLE CO	−5.1	−1.1	8
AMERICAN TELEPHONE & TELEG CO	−1.2	6.6	9
ALLIED CHEMICAL & DYE CORP	0.3	5.7	10
CORN PRODUCTS REFINING CO	3.0	8.9	
TEXAS CO	5.1	11.1	
WESTINGHOUSE ELECTRIC & MFG CO	6.0	11.9	
NATIONAL STEEL CORP	6.7	13.3	
INTERNATIONAL NICKEL CO CDA LTD	7.9	16.0	
EASTMAN KODAK CO	8.3	13.0	
UNION CARBIDE & CARBON CORP	9.5	14.3	
STANDARD OIL CO N J	10.5	16.3	
GENERAL ELECTRIC CORP	14.5	20.7	
SEARS ROEBUCK & CO	18.7	27.9	
AMERICAN CAN CO	19.6	26.4	
NATIONAL DISTILLERS PRODS CORP	25.6	37.8	
WOOLWORTH F W CO	26.0	33.9	
LOEWS INC	26.0	36.4	
JOHNS MANVILLE CORP	29.0	34.0	
INTERNATIONAL HARVESTER CO	29.3	36.1	
GENERAL MOTORS CORP	44.3	52.2	
CHRYSLER CORP	49.6	58.9	
STANDARD OIL CO CALIFORNIA	55.0	65.5	
GOODYEAR TIRE & RUBR CO	155.6	175.7	
Average	15.2	22.8	

Worst-to-First Performance	1943 (%)
1-stock portfolio	16.6
3-stock portfolio	14.5
5-stock portfolio	11.8
10-stock portfolio	17.8
Dow Performance	19.1

1943

Company Name	Price Chg (%)	Total Return (%)	Rank Price Chg
INTERNATIONAL NICKEL CO CDA LTD	−7.3	−1.1	1
UNION CARBIDE & CARBON CORP	−1.5	2.1	2
AMERICAN SMLT & REFNG CO	−1.4	5.1	3
BETHLEHEM STEEL CORP	0.0	10.4	4
CORN PRODUCTS REFINING CO	0.7	5.3	5
ALLIED CHEMICAL & DYE CORP	2.1	6.1	6
UNITED AIRCRAFT CORP	5.9	16.6	7
DU PONT E I DE NEMOURS & CO	7.3	10.5	8
UNITED STATES STEEL CORP	7.9	16.4	9
EASTMAN KODAK CO	8.4	11.7	10
NATIONAL STEEL CORP	11.1	16.8	
WESTINGHOUSE ELECTRIC & MFG CO	15.3	20.5	
GENERAL FOODS CORP	15.4	20.2	
PROCTER & GAMBLE CO	15.6	19.9	
TEXAS CO	15.7	20.4	
AMERICAN CAN CO	16.4	20.7	
JOHNS MANVILLE CORP	16.6	19.7	
WOOLWORTH F W CO	18.2	23.6	
GENERAL MOTORS CORP	18.3	23.1	
CHRYSLER CORP	19.9	24.7	
INTERNATIONAL HARVESTER CO	20.8	25.1	
GENERAL ELECTRIC CO	20.9	25.4	
AMERICAN TELEPHONE & TELEG CO	22.7	30.1	
STANDARD OIL CO N J	24.2	28.8	
NATIONAL DISTILLERS PRODS CORP	27.2	35.8	
STANDARD OIL CO CALIFORNIA	27.4	34.5	
LOEWS INC	27.7	36.6	
AMERICAN TOB CO	34.6	42.6	
SEARS ROEBUCK & CO	43.8	51.9	
GOODYEAR TIRE & RUBR CO	48.3	57.0	
Average	16.1	22.0	

Worst-to-First Performance	1944 (%)
1-stock portfolio	14.3
3-stock portfolio	11.6
5-stock portfolio	14.4
10-stock portfolio	15.9
Dow Performance	16.9

1944

Company Name	Price Chg (%)	Total Return (%)	Rank Price Chg
UNION CARBIDE & CARBON CORP	−0.2	3.7	1
GENERAL FOODS CORP	0.9	4.9	2
PROCTER & GAMBLE CO	1.9	6.1	3
TEXAS CO	2.1	7.5	4
STANDARD OIL CO CALIFORNIA	2.3	8.0	5
ALLIED CHEMICAL & DYE CORP	2.7	6.9	6
STANDARD OIL CO N J	3.0	7.7	7
AMERICAN TELEPHONE & TELEG CO	4.7	10.7	8
CORN PRODUCTS REFINING CO	5.1	8.8	9
GENERAL ELECTRIC CO	7.1	11.2	10
AMERICAN CAN CO	7.8	11.5	
INTERNATIONAL NICKEL CO CDA LTD	7.9	14.3	
EASTMAN KODAK CO	9.9	13.6	
AMERICAN SMLT & REFNG CO	10.3	16.8	
INTERNATIONAL HARVESTER CO	11.5	15.8	
DU PONT E I DE NEMOURS & CO	11.7	15.7	
UNITED AIRCRAFT CORP	12.0	24.1	
NATIONAL DISTILLERS PRODS CORP	12.6	19.6	
AMERICAN TOB CO	13.6	19.4	
WOOLWORTH F W CO	15.1	19.7	
BETHLEHEM STEEL CORP	16.4	28.5	
CHRYSLER CORP	17.1	21.1	
SEARS ROEBUCK & CO	18.0	23.3	
UNITED STATES STEEL CORP	18.1	27.0	
NATIONAL STEEL CORP	19.7	25.4	
JOHNS MANVILLE CORP	21.1	24.6	
GENERAL MOTORS CORP	21.9	28.1	
WESTINGHOUSE ELECTRIC & MFG CO	31.0	36.3	
GOODYEAR TIRE & RUBR CO	34.5	40.5	
LOEWS INC	36.0	43.7	
Average	12.5	18.1	

Worst-to-First Performance	1945 (%)
1-stock portfolio	31.3
3-stock portfolio	26.5
5-stock portfolio	28.1
10-stock portfolio	25.9
Dow Performance	31.0

1945

Company Name	Price Chg (%)	Total Return (%)	Rank Price Chg
AMERICAN CAN CO	11.7	15.2	1
PROCTER & GAMBLE CO	14.4	18.3	2
UNITED AIRCRAFT CORP	14.9	22.6	3
WESTINGHOUSE ELECTRIC CORP	15.0	18.3	4
CORN PRODUCTS REFINING CO	15.9	20.8	5
GOODYEAR TIRE & RUBR CO	16.2	20.3	6
AMERICAN TELEPHONE & TELEG CO	16.7	22.8	7
NATIONAL STEEL CORP	17.9	22.8	8
GENERAL MOTORS CORP	18.0	23.1	9
INTERNATIONAL HARVESTER CO	18.4	22.5	10
STANDARD OIL CO N J	18.7	23.3	
DU PONT E I DE NEMOURS & CO	19.5	23.2	
GENERAL ELECTRIC CO	20.9	25.3	
ALLIED CHEMICAL & DYE CORP	22.4	26.8	
TEXAS CO	24.5	30.3	
STANDARD OIL CO CALIFORNIA	24.6	30.5	
GENERAL FOODS CORP	25.3	29.9	
WOOLWORTH F W CO	27.1	31.5	
UNION CARBIDE & CARBON CORP	27.2	31.3	
EASTMAN KODAK CO	27.2	31.8	
LOEWS INC	28.2	34.6	
INTERNATIONAL NICKEL CO CDA LTD	29.3	35.3	
UNITED STATES STEEL CORP	34.6	42.5	
AMERICAN TOB CO	35.4	40.9	
CHRYSLER CORP	37.7	41.2	
SEARS ROEBUCK & CO	38.1	42.7	
JOHNS MANVILLE CORP	42.5	46.2	
BETHLEHEM STEEL CORP	46.6	57.7	
AMERICAN SMLT & REFNG CO	59.0	66.4	
NATIONAL DISTILLERS PRODS CORP	100.0	109.2	
Average	28.3	33.6	

Worst-to-First Performance	1946 (%)
1-stock portfolio	−6.0
3-stock portfolio	−18.1
5-stock portfolio	−13.4
10-stock portfolio	−11.4
Dow Performance	−4.3

1946

Company Name	Price Chg (%)	Total Return (%)	Rank Price Chg
UNITED AIRCRAFT CORP	−48.9	−46.6	1
GENERAL MOTORS CORP	−30.5	−28.0	2
CHRYSLER CORP	−30.2	−28.3	3
WESTINGHOUSE ELECTRIC CORP	−29.9	−27.6	4
LOEWS INC	−24.9	−21.2	5
GENERAL ELECTRIC CO	−24.9	−22.0	6
INTERNATIONAL HARVESTER CO	−24.2	−21.4	7
GENERAL FOODS CORP	−16.8	−13.5	8
WOOLWORTH F W CO	−12.9	−9.4	9
UNITED STATES STEEL CORP	−11.6	−7.1	10
AMERICAN TELEPHONE & TELEG CO	−9.2	−4.6	
AMERICAN CAN CO	−9.0	−6.0	
AMERICAN SMLT & REFNG CO	−8.8	−4.0	
NATIONAL DISTILLERS PRODS CORP	8.7	−3.7	
GOODYEAR TIRE & RUBR CO	−8.5	−2.2	
ALLIED CHEMICAL & DYE CORP	−8.1	−3.9	
AMERICAN TOB CO	−7.7	−4.3	
INTERNATIONAL NICKEL CO CDA LTD	−5.3	−1.0	
BETHLEHEM STEEL CORP	−5.2	0.6	
PROCTER & GAMBLE CO	−4.5	−1.6	
UNION CARBIDE & CARBON CORP	−4.4	−1.6	
JOHNS MANVILLE CORP	−3.3	−0.8	
TEXAS CO	−2.0	3.0	
EASTMAN KODAK CO	−0.9	2.2	
DU PONT E I DE NEMOURS & CO	2.4	6.2	
STANDARD OIL CO N J	3.7	6.7	
NATIONAL STEEL CORP	4.9	8.9	
SEARS ROEBUCK & CO	7.2	12.1	
CORN PRODUCTS REFINING CO	9.2	14.6	
STANDARD OIL CO CALIFORNIA	21.6	27.0	
Average	−9.7	−5.9	

Worst-to-First Performance	1947 (%)
1-stock portfolio	41.2
3-stock portfolio	34.9
5-stock portfolio	21.8
10-stock portfolio	13.0
Dow Performance	7.4

1947

Company Name	Price Chg (%)	Total Return (%)	Rank Price Chg
LOEWS INC	−28.3	−22.9	1
INTERNATIONAL NICKEL CO CDA LTD	−24.6	−19.4	2
GOODYEAR TIRE & RUBR CO	−20.7	−13.7	3
GENERAL FOODS CORP	−17.3	−13.2	4
CORN PRODUCTS REFINING CO	−14.8	−10.6	5
AMERICAN TOB CO	−14.1	−9.8	6
AMERICAN CAN CO	−12.4	−9.5	7
JOHNS MANVILLE CORP	−11.7	−8.8	8
AMERICAN TELEPHONE & TELEG CO	−10.6	−5.4	9
NATIONAL DISTILLERS PRODS CORP	−5.1	4.4	10
SEARS ROEBUCK & CO	−2.6	2.1	
DU PONT E I DE NEMOURS & CO	−2.0	2.3	
WOOLWORTH F W CO	−1.1	4.3	
GENERAL ELECTRIC CO	−0.4	4.2	
EASTMAN KODAK CO	−0.3	3.2	
TEXAS CO	4.5	8.5	
NATIONAL STEEL CORP	6.4	11.6	
UNION CARBIDE & CARBON CORP	6.5	10.7	
STANDARD OIL CO CALIFORNIA	8.9	15.1	
UNITED STATES STEEL CORP	8.9	16.7	
PROCTER & GAMBLE CO	10.3	17.4	
ALLIED CHEMICAL & DYE CORP	10.8	16.3	
GENERAL MOTORS CORP	11.0	16.8	
BETHLEHEM STEEL CORP	13.2	21.0	
STANDARD OIL CO N J	14.6	21.0	
AMERICAN SMLT & REFNG CO	15.6	25.2	
WESTINGHOUSE ELECTRIC CORP	21.6	27.3	
INTERNATIONAL HARVESTER CO	23.6	30.8	
UNITED AIRCRAFT CORP	33.1	41.2	
CHRYSLER CORP	39.3	46.7	
Average	2.1	7.8	

Worst-to-First Performance	1948 (%)
1-stock portfolio	−15.1
3-stock portfolio	4.3
5-stock portfolio	5.5
10-stock portfolio	3.2
Dow Performance	4.2

1948

Company Name	Price Chg (%)	Total Return (%)	Rank Price Chg
LOEWS INC	−22.4	−15.1	1
CHRYSLER CORP	−18.2	−12.3	2
WESTINGHOUSE ELECTRIC CORP	−16.9	−13.0	3
NATIONAL DISTILLERS PRODS CORP	−13.2	−3.7	4
AMERICAN TOB CO	−10.9	−5.4	5
UNITED STATES STEEL CORP	−10.6	−4.4	6
INTERNATIONAL HARVESTER CO	−9.8	−4.4	7
TEXAS CO	−9.0	−4.2	8
CORN PRODUCTS REFINING CO	−8.3	−2.8	9
PROCTER & GAMBLE CO	−6.5	−0.8	10
BETHLEHEM STEEL CORP	−5.7	1.3	
STANDARD OIL CO N J	−4.5	−2.2	
ALLIED CHEMICAL & DYE CORP	−4.5	0.3	
JOHNS MANVILLE CORP	−4.3	0.9	
AMERICAN SMLT & REFNG CO	−4.0	5.9	
WOOLWORTH F W CO	−1.9	3.7	
UNITED AIRCRAFT CORP	−1.6	6.3	
GOODYEAR TIRE & RUBR CO	−1.4	8.0	
DU PONT E I DE NEMOURS & CO	−1.3	4.5	
AMERICAN TELEPHONE & TELEG CO	−0.7	5.3	
GENERAL MOTORS CORP	0.9	8.9	
AMERICAN CAN CO	1.9	7.0	
EASTMAN KODAK CO	2.9	6.8	
SEARS ROEBUCK & CO	3.3	9.5	
GENERAL ELECTRIC CO	8.7	13.9	
NATIONAL STEEL CORP	8.8	15.0	
GENERAL FOODS CORP	11.5	17.5	
INTERNATIONAL NICKEL CO CDA LTD	12.1	20.0	
STANDARD OIL CO CALIFORNIA	12.3	19.6	
UNION CARBIDE & CARBON CORP	19.8	25.5	
Average	−2.5	3.7	

Worst-to-First Performance	1949 (%)
1-stock portfolio	30.2
3-stock portfolio	36.6
5-stock portfolio	35.9
10-stock portfolio	30.6
Dow Performance	20.1

1949

Company Name	Price Chg (%)	Total Return (%)	Rank Price Chg
INTERNATIONAL NICKEL CO CDA LTD	-6.3	0.8	1
STANDARD OIL CO N J	-5.6	0.0	2
AMERICAN TELEPHONE & TELEG CO	-1.7	4.6	3
BETHLEHEM STEEL CORP	-1.2	7.6	4
STANDARD OIL CO CALIFORNIA	1.5	8.1	5
AMERICAN SMLT & REFNG CO	2.3	13.5	6
NATIONAL STEEL CORP	2.8	9.9	7
INTERNATIONAL HARVESTER CO	3.7	11.0	8
GOODYEAR TIRE & RUBR CO	4.4	15.1	9
WOOLWORTH F W CO	8.0	14.0	10
GENERAL ELECTRIC CO	8.4	15.5	
UNION CARBIDE & CARBON CORP	8.5	14.3	
EASTMAN KODAK CO	11.9	16.2	
SEARS ROEBUCK & CO	12.8	19.4	
TEXAS CO	13.1	21.2	
ALLIED CHEMICAL & DYE CORP	13.3	19.3	
UNITED AIRCRAFT CORP	14.0	24.3	
UNITED STATES STEEL CORP	14.3	25.8	
LOEWS INC	19.3	30.2	
GENERAL FOODS CORP	21.6	28.2	
GENERAL MOTORS CORP	21.9	38.3	
AMERICAN TOB CO	22.1	29.4	
CORN PRODUCTS REFINING CO	23.6	29.1	
NATIONAL DISTILLERS PRODS CORP	26.2	40.2	
CHRYSLER CORP	29.0	42.2	
JOHNS MANVILLE CORP	29.5	38.0	
WESTINGHOUSE ELECTRIC CORP	29.9	37.3	
AMERICAN CAN CO	30.5	36.1	
PROCTER & GAMBLE CO	31.0	39.1	
DU PONT E I DE NEMOURS & CO	33.6	42.6	
Average	14.1	22.4	

Worst-to-First Performance	1950 (%)
1-stock portfolio	37.2
3-stock portfolio	31.0
5-stock portfolio	42.4
10-stock portfolio	41.3
Dow Performance	25.7

1950

Company Name	Price Chg (%)	Total Return (%)	Rank Price Chg
AMERICAN TOB CO	-13.3	-8.1	1
AMERICAN CAN CO	-12.4	-8.0	2
WOOLWORTH F W CO	-9.2	-4.3	3
LOEWS INC	-8.1	0.9	4
GENERAL FOODS CORP	-5.9	-1.0	5
CORN PRODUCTS REFINING CO	-5.0	0.2	6
JOHNS MANVILLE CORP	-4.3	3.3	7
CHRYSLER CORP	2.2	17.4	8
AMERICAN TELEPHONE & TELEG CO	3.1	9.3	9
WESTINGHOUSE ELECTRIC CORP	5.7	12.3	10
EASTMAN KODAK CO	8.5	12.8	
ALLIED CHEMICAL & DYE CORP	15.1	21.2	
INTERNATIONAL HARVESTER CO	16.2	24.3	
GENERAL ELECTRIC CO	18.1	26.8	
SEARS ROEBUCK & CO	19.0	26.0	
NATIONAL DISTILLERS PRODS CORP	20.8	31.5	
UNION CARBIDE & CARBON CORP	23.5	30.1	
PROCTER & GAMBLE CO	24.7	32.0	
INTERNATIONAL NICKEL CO CDA LTD	28.9	37.2	
GENERAL MOTORS CORP	29.1	47.4	
AMERICAN SMLT & REFNG CO	32.6	45.7	
UNITED AIRCRAFT CORP	33.5	42.3	
TEXAS CO	36.2	47.0	
DU PONT E I DE NEMOURS & CO	36.3	46.2	
STANDARD OIL CO N J	37.5	46.5	
STANDARD OIL CO CALIFORNIA	41.3	51.4	
GOODYEAR TIRE & RUBR CO	47.5	61.1	
BETHLEHEM STEEL CORP	51.6	67.5	
UNITED STATES STEEL CORP	58.2	74.0	
NATIONAL STEEL CORP	63.8	74.9	
Average	19.8	28.9	

Worst-to-First Performance	1951 (%)
1-stock portfolio	2.6
3-stock portfolio	10.5
5-stock portfolio	11.3
10-stock portfolio	16.8
Dow Performance	21.3

1951

Company Name	Price Chg (%)	Total Return (%)	Rank Price Chg
PROCTER & GAMBLE CO	-6.0	-1.9	1
UNITED STATES STEEL CORP	-5.3	1.6	2
WOOLWORTH F W CO	-4.2	1.3	3
AMERICAN TOB CO	-3.7	2.6	4
GENERAL FOODS CORP	-1.6	3.9	5
CHRYSLER CORP	1.8	12.7	6
AMERICAN TELEPHONE & TELEG CO	4.7	10.9	7
NATIONAL STEEL CORP	5.2	11.6	8
BETHLEHEM STEEL CORP	6.2	14.5	9
SEARS ROEBUCK & CO	6.7	12.1	10
UNITED AIRCRAFT CORP	7.3	14.5	
CORN PRODUCTS REFINING CO	8.3	13.8	
INTERNATIONAL HARVESTER CO	8.5	15.1	
DU PONT E I DE NEMOURS & CO	9.5	13.8	
EASTMAN KODAK CO	9.7	14.1	
LOEWS INC	10.4	20.8	
STANDARD OIL CO CALIFORNIA	10.7	16.0	
GENERAL MOTORS CORP	12.4	21.7	
UNION CARBIDE & CARBON CORP	15.4	19.4	
WESTINGHOUSE ELECTRIC CORP	15.6	21.8	
INTERNATIONAL NICKEL CO CDA LTD	16.6	24.6	
GENERAL ELECTRIC CO	19.6	26.0	
AMERICAN CAN CO	22.0	27.8	
NATIONAL DISTILLERS PRODS CORP	23.5	31.8	
ALLIED CHEMICAL & DYE CORP	28.0	33.4	
AMERICAN SMLT & REFNG CO	30.0	40.6	
GOODYEAR TIRE & RUBR CO	33.3	41.9	
TEXAS CO	36.5	44.8	
JOHNS MANVILLE CORP	42.4	52.5	
STANDARD OIL CO N J	65.1	76.2	
Average	14.3	21.3	

Worst-to-First Performance	1952 (%)
1-stock portfolio	5.6
3-stock portfolio	10.9
5-stock portfolio	14.4
10-stock portfolio	16.1
Dow Performance	14.2

1952

Company Name	Price Chg (%)	Total Return (%)	Rank Price Chg
NATIONAL DISTILLERS PRODS CORP	-34.1	-29.6	1
LOEWS INC	-26.1	-20.8	2
AMERICAN SMLT & REFNG CO	-10.0	-3.5	3
INTERNATIONAL HARVESTER CO	-6.4	-0.6	4
NATIONAL STEEL CORP	-4.0	2.4	5
EASTMAN KODAK CO	-2.7	1.3	6
CORN PRODUCTS REFINING CO	-1.4	5.2	7
PROCTER & GAMBLE CO	1.5	5.6	8
ALLIED CHEMICAL & DYE CORP	1.8	6.0	9
STANDARD OIL CO N J	2.6	8.5	10
TEXAS CO	2.9	8.6	
AMERICAN TELEPHONE & TELEG CO	3.6	9.7	
DU PONT E I DE NEMOURS & CO	5.0	9.3	
WOOLWORTH F W CO	6.2	12.5	
UNITED STATES STEEL CORP	6.3	14.6	
AMERICAN TOB CO	6.8	14.1	
SEARS ROEBUCK & CO	7.1	12.5	
BETHLEHEM STEEL CORP	7.3	16.1	
JOHNS MANVILLE CORP	8.8	15.4	
INTERNATIONAL NICKEL CO CDA LTD	9.8	16.4	
UNION CARBIDE & CARBON CORP	12.6	17.0	
STANDARD OIL CO CALIFORNIA	16.5	22.9	
GENERAL FOODS CORP	18.9	25.2	
WESTINGHOUSE ELECTRIC CORP	19.7	25.9	
UNITED AIRCRAFT CORP	20.2	27.6	
GENERAL ELECTRIC CO	22.3	28.1	
AMERICAN CAN CO	26.9	32.0	
GOODYEAR TIRE & RUBR CO	30.1	39.1	
GENERAL MOTORS CORP	32.5	42.0	
CHRYSLER CORP	37.1	48.1	
Average	7.4	13.7	

Worst-to-First Performance	1953 (%)
1-stock portfolio	-13.4
3-stock portfolio	-11.5
5-stock portfolio	-9.6
10-stock portfolio	-1.7
Dow Performance	1.8

1953

Company Name	Price Chg (%)	Total Return (%)	Rank Price Chg
CHRYSLER CORP	-38.2	-32.8	1
AMERICAN SMLT & REFNG CO	-34.7	-29.8	2
INTERNATIONAL NICKEL CO CDA LTD	-24.5	-19.9	3
NATIONAL DISTILLERS PRODS CORP	-17.8	-13.4	4
INTERNATIONAL HARVESTER CO	-17.6	-11.4	5
GENERAL MOTORS CORP	-13.4	-7.6	6
JOHNS MANVILLE CORP	-11.3	-5.2	7
STANDARD OIL CO CALIFORNIA	-10.8	-5.6	8
BETHLEHEM STEEL CORP	-9.5	-2.2	9
NATIONAL STEEL CORP	-9.1	-2.3	10
STANDARD OIL CO N J	-7.4	-1.4	
UNITED STATES STEEL CORP	-6.8	0.7	
AMERICAN TOB CO	-5.7	-0.3	
ALLIED CHEMICAL & DYE CORP	-4.6	-0.4	
WOOLWORTH F W CO	-3.9	1.6	
AMERICAN TELEPHONE & TELEG CO	-0.5	5.4	
TEXAS CO	-0.2	6.3	
GOODYEAR TIRE & RUBR CO	1.8	7.9	
LOEWS INC	2.0	8.8	
PROCTER & GAMBLE CO	2.2	6.4	
SEARS ROEBUCK & CO	3.3	8.2	
UNION CARBIDE & CARBON CORP	3.7	7.5	
CORN PRODUCTS REFINING CO	5.9	11.8	
WESTINGHOUSE ELECTRIC CORP	6.5	11.3	
AMERICAN CAN CO	10.5	14.8	
EASTMAN KODAK CO	10.6	15.2	
DU PONT E I DE NEMOURS & CO	11.1	15.4	
GENERAL FOODS CORP	12.2	17.7	
GENERAL ELECTRIC CO	20.3	27.0	
UNITED AIRCRAFT CORP	22.7	31.6	
Average	-3.4	2.2	

Worst-to-First Performance	1954 (%)
1-stock portfolio	28.8
3-stock portfolio	59.3
5-stock portfolio	52.3
10-stock portfolio	62.5
Dow Performance	50.2

1954

Company Name	Price Chg (%)	Total Return (%)	Rank Price Chg
AMERICAN TOB CO	6.5	14.5	1
AMERICAN TELEPHONE & TELEG CO	12.1	18.2	2
AMERICAN CAN CO	13.3	17.7	3
CORN PRODUCTS REFINING CO	15.1	20.8	4
UNION CARBIDE & CARBON CORP	16.2	19.9	5
WOOLWORTH F W CO	19.7	26.5	6
CHRYSLER CORP	19.8	28.8	7
SEARS ROEBUCK & CO	24.6	30.1	8
GENERAL FOODS CORP	27.3	32.6	9
NATIONAL DISTILLERS PRODS CORP	28.4	35.1	10
JOHNS MANVILLE CORP	34.5	42.0	
INTERNATIONAL HARVESTER CO	39.8	48.5	
ALLIED CHEMICAL & DYE CORP	39.9	44.7	
NATIONAL STEEL CORP	41.2	49.6	
PROCTER & GAMBLE CO	41.7	47.9	
TEXAS CO	49.2	56.8	
STANDARD OIL CO CALIFORNIA	52.2	59.4	
EASTMAN KODAK CO	53.0	58.2	
STANDARD OIL CO N J	53.6	61.5	
DU PONT E I DE NEMOURS & CO	56.0	62.3	
WESTINGHOUSE ELECTRIC CORP	58.2	64.2	
GENERAL ELECTRIC CO	60.3	66.1	
AMERICAN SMLT & REFNG CO	61.2	70.5	
GENERAL MOTORS CORP	64.2	75.0	
LOEWS INC	66.3	75.4	
INTERNATIONAL NICKEL CO CDA LTD	68.2	78.6	
UNITED STATES STEEL CORP	86.4	97.7	
UNITED AIRCRAFT CORP	93.0	104.3	
GOODYEAR TIRE & RUBR CO	101.6	110.9	
BETHLEHEM STEEL CORP	118.3	137.3	
Average	47.4	55.2	

Worst-to-First Performance	1955 (%)
1-stock portfolio	32.0
3-stock portfolio	17.2
5-stock portfolio	17.7
10-stock portfolio	18.1
Dow Performance	26.1

1955

Company Name	Price Chg (%)	Total Return (%)	Rank Price Chg
WESTINGHOUSE ELECTRIC CORP	–25.5	–23.2	1
LOEWS INC	–11.0	–6.5	2
NATIONAL DISTILLERS PRODS CORP	–8.4	–4.0	3
WOOLWORTH F W CO	–8.2	–3.5	4
INTERNATIONAL HARVESTER CO	–3.3	2.0	5
JOHNS MANVILLE CORP	0.0	5.0	6
CORN PRODUCTS REFINING CO	0.4	5.6	7
PROCTER & GAMBLE CO	2.3	6.0	8
AMERICAN TELEPHONE & TELEG CO	4.9	10.3	9
AMERICAN CAN CO	5.3	9.3	10
NATIONAL STEEL CORP	9.5	14.9	
AMERICAN SMLT & REFNG CO	11.1	17.5	
EASTMAN KODAK CO	17.9	21.5	
ALLIED CHEMICAL & DYE CORP	18.2	21.4	
CHRYSLER CORP	21.6	27.5	
GOODYEAR TIRE & RUBR CO	21.7	25.8	
GENERAL FOODS CORP	23.3	28.0	
GENERAL ELECTRIC CO	23.5	27.6	
AMERICAN TOB CO	24.0	32.0	
STANDARD OIL CO CALIFORNIA	24.7	29.2	
UNION CARBIDE & CARBON CORP	27.7	31.6	
UNITED AIRCRAFT CORP	37.8	44.6	
DU PONT E I DE NEMOURS & CO	37.9	42.6	
STANDARD OIL CO N J	38.0	43.8	
INTERNATIONAL NICKEL CO CDA LTD	39.9	46.9	
SEARS ROEBUCK & CO	41.2	44.6	
TEXAS CO	41.3	47.1	
GENERAL MOTORS CORP	43.4	51.2	
BETHLEHEM STEEL CORP	52.9	60.9	
UNITED STATES STEEL CORP	57.6	64.7	
Average	19.0	24.1	

Worst-to-First Performance	1956 (%)
1-stock portfolio	–0.6
3-stock portfolio	8.1
5-stock portfolio	6.5
10-stock portfolio	6.1
Dow Performance	7.0

1956

Company Name	Price Chg (%)	Total Return (%)	Rank Price Chg
SEARS ROEBUCK & CO	–19.7	–17.1	1
CHRYSLER CORP	–19.1	–15.4	2
DU PONT E I DE NEMOURS & CO	–16.6	–13.8	3
ALLIED CHEMICAL & DYE CORP	–13.4	–10.9	4
AMERICAN CAN CO	–12.2	–8.1	5
AMERICAN TOB CO	–9.7	–3.6	6
WOOLWORTH F W CO	–8.2	–3.1	7
INTERNATIONAL PAPER CO	–7.7	–2.5	8
GENERAL FOODS CORP	–7.4	–3.8	9
GENERAL MOTORS CORP	–4.9	–0.5	10
WESTINGHOUSE ELECTRIC CORP	–4.2	–0.6	
TEXAS CO	–1.4	2.6	
AMERICAN TELEPHONE & TELEG CO	–1.2	3.9	
PROCTER & GAMBLE CO	1.5	5.4	
GENERAL ELECTRIC CO	4.3	7.8	
CORN PRODUCTS REFINING CO	4.4	9.5	
UNION CARBIDE & CARBON CORP	5.1	8.0	
INTERNATIONAL HARVESTER CO	5.5	11.4	
STANDARD OIL CO CALIFORNIA	8.2	12.0	
NATIONAL STEEL CORP	8.4	14.7	
JOHNS MANVILLE CORP	11.9	17.2	
EASTMAN KODAK CO	13.7	17.2	
AMERICAN SMLT & REFNG CO	14.7	22.6	
STANDARD OIL CO N J	15.5	19.2	
BETHLEHEM STEEL CORP	21.3	28.0	
NATIONAL DISTILLERS PRODS CORP	25.4	30.6	
UNITED AIRCRAFT CORP	26.3	31.4	
UNITED STATES STEEL CORP	26.7	32.2	
INTERNATIONAL NICKEL CO CDA LTD	28.4	33.6	
GOODYEAR TIRE & RUBR CO	30.8	35.3	
Average	4.2	8.8	

Worst-to-First Performance	1957 (%)
1-stock portfolio	–8.0
3-stock portfolio	–11.2
5-stock portfolio	–10.3
10-stock portfolio	–8.6
Dow Performance	–8.4

1957

Company Name	Price Chg (%)	Total Return (%)	Rank Price Chg
AMERICAN SMLT & REFNG CO	-38.3	-34.5	1
INTERNATIONAL NICKEL CO CDA LTD	-33.6	-30.6	2
NATIONAL STEEL CORP	-32.2	-27.9	3
INTERNATIONAL HARVESTER CO	-30.8	-26.4	4
UNITED STATES STEEL CORP	-30.1	-26.6	5
UNITED AIRCRAFT CORP	-29.5	-26.4	6
BETHLEHEM STEEL CORP	-26.7	-22.6	7
ALLIED CHEMICAL & DYE CORP	-25.5	-22.8	8
CHRYSLER CORP	-24.6	-20.4	9
GENERAL MOTORS CORP	-23.9	-20.0	10
JOHNS MANVILLE CORP	-22.7	-19.0	
NATIONAL DISTILLERS & CHEM CORP	-21.4	-18.1	
UNION CARBIDE CORP	-17.9	-15.2	
WOOLWORTH F W CO	-17.2	-12.0	
INTERNATIONAL PAPER CO	-15.4	-12.8	
STANDARD OIL CO N J	-14.8	-11.5	
SEARS ROEBUCK & CO	-11.0	-8.0	
DU PONT E I DE NEMOURS & CO	-8.5	-5.2	
STANDARD OIL CO CALIFORNIA	-6.6	-3.0	
AMERICAN TELEPHONE & TELEG CO	-2.3	3.0	
AMERICAN CAN CO	0.0	4.8	
GENERAL ELECTRIC CO	2.1	5.4	
GOODYEAR TIRE & RUBR CO	2.9	5.9	
AMERICAN TOB CO	4.8	12.1	
TEXAS CO	6.3	10.0	
WESTINGHOUSE ELECTRIC CORP	10.4	14.2	
PROCTER & GAMBLE CO	11.6	16.2	
EASTMAN KODAK CO	12.7	15.9	
GENERAL FOODS CORP	15.5	20.5	
CORN PRODUCTS REFINING CO	15.6	21.4	
Average	-11.7	-7.8	

Worst-to-First Performance	1958 (%)
1-stock portfolio	40.7
3-stock portfolio	40.6
5-stock portfolio	56.6
10-stock portfolio	44.7
Dow Performance	38.6

1958

Company Name	Price Chg (%)	Total Return (%)	Rank Price Chg
CHRYSLER CORP	-2.8	0.1	1
UNITED AIRCRAFT CORP	14.5	20.2	2
WESTINGHOUSE ELECTRIC CORP	15.2	18.9	3
STANDARD OIL CO N J	15.5	20.4	4
DU PONT E I DE NEMOURS & CO	21.2	25.2	5
AMERICAN CAN CO	21.5	26.8	6
AMERICAN TOB CO	24.4	32.1	7
INTERNATIONAL NICKEL CO CDA LTD	25.6	29.8	8
GENERAL ELECTRIC CO	27.4	31.4	9
ALLIED CHEMICAL CORP	29.4	34.2	10
STANDARD OIL CO CALIFORNIA	29.9	35.1	
PROCTER & GAMBLE CO	31.1	35.3	
UNION CARBIDE CORP	32.8	37.8	
AMERICAN SMLT & REFNG CO	35.9	40.7	
AMERICAN TELEPHONE & TELEG CO	36.6	43.2	
TEXAS CO	37.5	42.1	
JOHNS MANVILLE CORP	38.6	45.4	
INTERNATIONAL PAPER CO	39.1	43.3	
NATIONAL STEEL CORP	43.6	51.2	
NATIONAL DISTILLERS & CHEM CORP	43.6	49.5	
BETHLEHEM STEEL CORP	45.4	53.6	
EASTMAN KODAK CO	46.1	49.6	
GOODYEAR TIRE & RUBR CO	46.7	50.9	
WOOLWORTH F W CO	47.1	55.4	
GENERAL MOTORS CORP	47.8	55.2	
GENERAL FOODS CORP	50.2	55.5	
INTERNATIONAL HARVESTER CO	56.8	66.0	
SEARS ROEBUCK & CO	57.4	63.5	
CORN PRODUCTS CO	59.1	65.7	
UNITED STATES STEEL CORP	87.3	95.6	
Average	36.8	42.4	

Worst-to-First Performance	1959 (%)
1-stock portfolio	35.0
3-stock portfolio	19.1
5-stock portfolio	14.9
10-stock portfolio	16.6
Dow Performance	20.0

1959

Company Name	Price Chg (%)	Total Return (%)	Rank Price Chg
UNITED AIRCRAFT CORP	−34.0	−30.6	1
STANDARD OIL CO CALIFORNIA	−15.9	−12.6	2
AMERICAN CAN CO	−13.9	−10.0	3
STANDARD OIL CO N J	−13.9	−10.0	4
JOHNS MANVILLE CORP	−6.0	−2.4	5
TEXACO INC	1.9	5.2	6
UNITED STATES STEEL CORP	2.5	5.6	7
BETHLEHEM STEEL CORP	3.1	7.7	8
ANACONDA CO	6.0	10.2	9
AMERICAN TELEPHONE & TELEG CO	6.3	10.7	10
GENERAL MOTORS CORP	10.1	14.4	
AMERICAN TOB CO	11.5	17.2	
GOODYEAR TIRE & RUBR CO	14.0	16.2	
ALUMINUM COMPANY AMER	14.1	15.1	
UNION CARBIDE CORP	16.6	19.6	
INTERNATIONAL PAPER CO	17.7	20.5	
INTERNATIONAL HARVESTER CO	18.3	23.5	
OWENS ILLINOIS GLASS CO	19.4	22.6	
PROCTER & GAMBLE CO	21.0	24.4	
ALLIED CHEMICAL CORP	23.1	26.5	
DU PONT E I DE NEMOURS & CO	23.5	27.0	
INTERNATIONAL NICKEL CO CDA LTD	24.9	28.8	
WOOLWORTH F W CO	25.4	31.1	
GENERAL ELECTRIC CO	26.5	29.5	
SEARS ROEBUCK & CO	27.4	31.2	
SWIFT & CO	30.0	35.0	
CHRYSLER CORP	32.9	35.0	
GENERAL FOODS CORP	38.4	42.2	
EASTMAN KODAK CO	48.8	51.4	
WESTINGHOUSE ELECTRIC CORP	49.6	53.0	
Average	14.3	17.9	

Worst-to-First Performance	1960 (%)
1-stock portfolio	−1.0
3-stock portfolio	−4.8
5-stock portfolio	−1.3
10-stock portfolio	−3.4
Dow Performance	−6.2

1960

Company Name	Price Chg (%)	Total Return (%)	Rank Price Chg
CHRYSLER CORP	−43.7	−41.6	1
ALUMINUM COMPANY AMER	−35.4	−34.4	2
ANACONDA CO	−32.0	−28.4	3
INTERNATIONAL PAPER CO	−29.3	−27.5	4
DU PONT E I DE NEMOURS & CO	−29.1	−26.7	5
BETHLEHEM STEEL CORP	−27.3	−23.2	6
GENERAL MOTORS CORP	−25.5	−22.0	7
GENERAL ELECTRIC CO	−24.8	−23.0	8
UNITED STATES STEEL CORP	−23.4	−20.5	9
GOODYEAR TIRE & RUBR CO	−22.9	−21.1	10
UNION CARBIDE CORP	−19.1	−16.7	
AMERICAN CAN CO	−18.2	−13.8	
STANDARD OIL CO N J	−16.9	−12.2	
INTERNATIONAL HARVESTER CO	−13.7	−8.7	
OWENS ILLINOIS GLASS CO	−11.0	−8.7	
WESTINGHOUSE ELECTRIC CORP	−9.7	−7.7	
UNITED AIRCRAFT CORP	−6.0	−1.0	
ALLIED CHEMICAL CORP	−5.6	−2.4	
STANDARD OIL CO CALIFORNIA	−4.2	0.3	
SWIFT & CO	−2.9	1.2	
TEXACO INC	1.7	5.6	
WOOLWORTH F W CO	3.9	8.1	
EASTMAN KODAK CO	4.0	5.9	
INTERNATIONAL NICKEL CO CDA LTD	6.8	9.8	
SEARS ROEBUCK & CO	11.9	14.8	
JOHNS MANVILLE CORP	15.9	20.2	
AMERICAN TOB CO	22.4	28.4	
AMERICAN TELEPHONE & TELEG CO	34.3	39.1	
GENERAL FOODS CORP	35.6	38.7	
PROCTER & GAMBLE CO	52.7	56.6	
Average	−7.1	−3.7	

Worst-to-First Performance	1961 (%)
1-stock portfolio	29.2
3-stock portfolio	14.3
5-stock portfolio	20.3
10-stock portfolio	20.8
Dow Performance	22.4

1961

Company Name	Price Chg (%)	Total Return (%)	Rank Price Chg
WESTINGHOUSE ELECTRIC CORP	-21.5	-19.3	1
SWIFT & CO	-5.7	-1.7	2
ALUMINUM COMPANY AMER	-5.1	-3.4	3
JOHNS MANVILLE CORP	-0.4	2.7	4
EASTMAN KODAK CO	-0.3	1.8	5
GENERAL ELECTRIC CO	1.0	4.0	6
UNION CARBIDE CORP	2.1	4.9	7
ALLIED CHEMICAL CORP	2.3	5.5	8
OWENS ILLINOIS GLASS CO	2.9	5.7	9
UNITED STATES STEEL CORP	4.0	7.7	10
BETHLEHEM STEEL CORP	7.6	13.6	
ANACONDA CO	11.8	17.1	
UNITED AIRCRAFT CORP	12.3	17.5	
STANDARD OIL CO CALIFORNIA	19.5	24.2	
INTERNATIONAL PAPER CO	20.7	24.4	
INTERNATIONAL HARVESTER CO	21.7	27.5	
STANDARD OIL CO N J	23.0	29.3	
CHRYSLER CORP	26.4	29.2	
AMERICAN TELEPHONE & TELEG CO	28.7	32.5	
DU PONT E I DE NEMOURS & CO	30.0	34.4	
GOODYEAR TIRE & RUBR CO	30.6	33.4	
AMERICAN CAN CO	31.1	37.6	
WOOLWORTH F W CO	33.6	38.2	
PROCTER & GAMBLE CO	33.7	35.9	
TEXACO INC	34.4	38.5	
GENERAL FOODS CORP	36.0	38.4	
GENERAL MOTORS CORP	40.3	47.6	
INTERNATIONAL NICKEL CO CDA LTD	45.0	48.1	
AMERICAN TOB CO	54.0	59.0	
SEARS ROEBUCK & CO	57.8	61.2	
Average	19.2	23.2	

Worst-to-First Performance	1962 (%)
1-stock portfolio	-14.2
3-stock portfolio	-10.1
5-stock portfolio	-10.3
10-stock portfolio	-14.0
Dow Performance	-7.6

1962

Company Name	Price Chg (%)	Total Return (%)	Rank Price Chg
UNITED STATES STEEL CORP	-44.4	-41.5	1
AMERICAN TOB CO	-41.5	-39.0	2
BETHLEHEM STEEL CORP	-32.8	-28.5	3
WOOLWORTH F W CO	-31.4	-28.9	4
INTERNATIONAL NICKEL CO CDA LTD	-26.8	-24.7	5
GOODYEAR TIRE & RUBR CO	-26.7	-24.7	6
INTERNATIONAL PAPER CO	-26.2	-23.5	7
JOHNS MANVILLE CORP	-24.6	-21.3	8
OWENS ILLINOIS GLASS CO	-23.4	-21.0	9
PROCTER & GAMBLE CO	-22.3	-20.7	10
ALLIED CHEMICAL CORP	-20.4	-17.1	
GENERAL FOODS CORP	-18.5	-16.6	
WESTINGHOUSE ELECTRIC CORP	-17.4	-14.2	
UNION CARBIDE CORP	-16.9	-13.9	
ANACONDA CO	-16.7	-11.8	
ALUMINUM COMPANY AMER	-16.3	-14.5	
AMERICAN TELEPHONE & TELEG CO	-14.2	-11.6	
SEARS ROEBUCK & CO	-13.8	-11.9	
SWIFT & CO	-5.5	-1.7	
INTERNATIONAL HARVESTER CO	-4.1	0.7	
EASTMAN KODAK CO	-2.2	0.1	
DU PONT E I DE NEMOURS & CO	-1.6	15.8	
AMERICAN CAN CO	-1.3	3.2	
GENERAL MOTORS CORP	2.0	7.7	
GENERAL ELECTRIC CO	2.0	5.0	
TEXACO INC	7.8	11.6	
STANDARD OIL CO N J	17.2	22.8	
STANDARD OIL CO CALIFORNIA	20.8	25.1	
UNITED AIRCRAFT CORP	23.1	28.4	
CHRYSLER CORP	51.3	54.0	
Average	-10.8	-7.1	

Worst-to-First Performance	1963 (%)
1-stock portfolio	26.7
3-stock portfolio	13.9
5-stock portfolio	15.2
10-stock portfolio	18.5
Dow Performance	20.6

1963

Company Name	Close Ratio	Price Chg (%)	Total Return (%)	Rank Close Ratio	Rank Price Chg
UNITED AIRCRAFT CORP	0.94	−16.7	−13.1	3	1
STANDARD OIL CO CALIFORNIA	0.92	−5.6	−2.5	1	2
AMERICAN CAN CO	0.97	−4.6	−0.3	5	3
AMERICAN TOB CO	0.98	−3.0	2.2	6	4
WESTINGHOUSE ELECTRIC CORP	0.94	5.9	9.5	2	5
SWIFT & CO	1.06	7.1	11.2		6
BETHLEHEM STEEL CORP	0.98	7.4	12.7	7	7
INTERNATIONAL NICKEL CO CDA LTD	1.09	9.8	13.8		8
EASTMAN KODAK CO	1.08	11.6	14.2		9
PROCTER & GAMBLE CO	1.03	12.1	14.5		10
DU PONT E I DE NEMOURS & CO	1.08	12.4	15.9		
TEXACO INC	1.02	13.1	16.7	10	
JOHNS MANVILLE CORP	1.01	13.4	18.2	9	
GENERAL ELECTRIC CO	1.09	13.5	16.5		
GENERAL FOODS CORP	1.07	14.5	17.2		
ANACONDA CO	0.97	15.4	21.6	4	
WOOLWORTH F W CO	1.01	16.1	20.7	8	
OWENS ILLINOIS GLASS CO	1.02	16.7	20.3		
AMERICAN TELEPHONE & TELEG CO	1.10	19.3	22.7		
UNION CARBIDE CORP	1.10	19.5	23.5		
INTERNATIONAL HARVESTER CO	1.03	20.6	25.7		
UNITED STATES STEEL CORP	1.05	21.8	26.7		
INTERNATIONAL PAPER CO	1.03	21.9	26.1		
ALLIED CHEMICAL CORP	1.08	23.7	28.3		
ALUMINUM COMPANY AMER	1.09	25.9	28.3		
GOODYEAR TIRE & RUBR CO	1.10	26.8	30.3		
SEARS ROEBUCK & CO	1.07	27.1	29.6		
STANDARD OIL CO N J	1.10	27.7	33.0		
GENERAL MOTORS CORP	1.07	35.3	42.7		
CHRYSLER CORP	1.20	126.9	129.9		
Average	1.04	17.9	21.9		

Worst-to-First Performance

Price Change	1964 (%)	Close Ratio	1964 (%)
1-stock portfolio	59.3	1-stock portfolio	33.6
3-stock portfolio	32.0	3-stock portfolio	40.9
5-stock portfolio	29.6	5-stock portfolio	28.7
10-stock portfolio	25.7	10-stock portfolio	25.0
Dow	18.7		

1964

Company Name	Close Ratio	Price Chg (%)	Total Return (%)	Rank Close Ratio	Rank Price Chg
ALUMINUM COMPANY AMER	0.89	−10.5	−9.0	2	1
GENERAL FOODS CORP	0.92	−10.3	−8.2	3	2
ALLIED CHEMICAL CORP	0.96	−5.7	−2.5	7	3
UNITED STATES STEEL CORP	0.89	−4.0	−0.5	1	4
AMERICAN CAN CO	0.98	−1.4	3.2	10	5
AMERICAN TELEPHONE & TELEG CO	0.98	−0.4	2.6		6
INTERNATIONAL PAPER CO	0.97	1.9	5.7	9	7
PROCTER & GAMBLE CO	0.98	2.0	4.2		8
UNION CARBIDE CORP	1.02	5.4	8.5		9
GENERAL ELECTRIC CO	1.09	7.0	9.8		10
GOODYEAR TIRE & RUBR CO	1.02	9.4	12.2		
JOHNS MANVILLE CORP	0.95	9.7	13.7	5	
ANACONDA CO	1.08	11.8	17.5		
WOOLWORTH F W CO	0.98	12.4	16.4		
BETHLEHEM STEEL CORP	0.93	14.2	19.1	4	
AMERICAN TOB CO	0.97	16.2	22.0	8	
STANDARD OIL CO N J	1.03	18.6	22.8		
EASTMAN KODAK CO	1.05	19.7	22.4		
DU PONT E I DE NEMOURS & CO	1.10	21.5	24.9		
OWENS ILLINOIS GLASS CO	1.03	21.9	24.9		
INTERNATIONAL NICKEL CO CDA LTD	1.04	22.4	26.7		
GENERAL MOTORS CORP	1.06	24.5	30.7		
WESTINGHOUSE ELECTRIC CORP	1.15	25.5	29.7		
INTERNATIONAL HARVESTER CO	0.96	26.0	30.7	6	
STANDARD OIL CO CALIFORNIA	1.13	29.5	33.6		
TEXACO INC	1.11	31.4	35.2		
SEARS ROEBUCK & CO	1.09	32.1	34.3		
SWIFT & CO	1.11	32.4	37.0		
CHRYSLER CORP	1.16	52.4	55.4		
UNITED AIRCRAFT CORP	1.25	53.2	59.3		
Average	1.03	15.6	19.4		

Worst-to-First Performance

Price Change	1965 (%)	Close Ratio	1965 (%)
1-stock portfolio	27.1	1-stock portfolio	6.6
3-stock portfolio	10.9	3-stock portfolio	12.8
5-stock portfolio	14.8	5-stock portfolio	13.1
10-stock portfolio	9.1	10-stock portfolio	14.6
Dow	14.2		

1965

Company Name	Close Ratio	Price Chg (%)	Total Return (%)	Rank Close Ratio	Rank Price Chg
PROCTER & GAMBLE CO	0.96	−14.9	−12.7	3	1
AMERICAN TELEPHONE & TELEG CO	0.91	−11.0	−8.2	1	2
CHRYSLER CORP	1.05	−10.9	−8.7		3
STANDARD OIL CO N J	1.02	−10.8	−7.2		4
TEXACO INC	1.02	−8.3	−5.4		5
INTERNATIONAL PAPER CO	0.98	−6.1	−2.3	4	6
SWIFT & CO	1.08	−5.2	−1.5		7
ALLIED CHEMICAL CORP	0.98	−2.9	0.7	5	8
DU PONT E I DE NEMOURS & CO	1.00	−0.7	1.8	9	9
SEARS ROEBUCK & CO	0.99	2.1	3.9	8	10
GENERAL FOODS CORP	0.99	2.3	4.8	7	
UNITED STATES STEEL CORP	1.04	2.5	6.6		
JOHNS MANVILLE CORP	0.99	3.5	7.3	6	
GOODYEAR TIRE & RUBR CO	0.95	5.0	7.6	2	
GENERAL MOTORS CORP	1.01	5.7	11.3		
INTERNATIONAL NICKEL CO CDA LTD	1.02	7.4	11.2		
UNION CARBIDE CORP	1.04	7.9	11.2		
STANDARD OIL CO CALIFORNIA	1.09	8.9	12.2		
WOOLWORTH F W CO	1.09	14.5	18.6		
BETHLEHEM STEEL CORP	1.08	14.9	19.7		
AMERICAN TOB CO	1.01	16.6	21.8	10	
OWENS ILLINOIS INC	1.11	20.6	23.4		
INTERNATIONAL HARVESTER CO	1.20	21.3	26.0		
ALUMINUM COMPANY AMER	1.09	24.6	27.1		
GENERAL ELECTRIC CO	1.10	26.5	29.4		
AMERICAN CAN CO	1.09	29.4	34.7		
WESTINGHOUSE ELECTRIC CORP	1.16	46.5	49.9		
ANACONDA CO	1.16	54.3	62.9		
EASTMAN KODAK CO	1.28	69.5	72.9		
UNITED AIRCRAFT CORP	1.40	88.1	92.8		
Average	1.06	13.4	17.1		

Worst-to-First Performance

Price Change	1966 (%)	Close Ratio	1966 (%)
1-stock portfolio	8.4	1-stock portfolio	−5.8
3-stock portfolio	−12.3	3-stock portfolio	−2.5
5-stock portfolio	−12.4	5-stock portfolio	−9.8
10-stock portfolio	−18.8	10-stock portfolio	−15.3
Dow	−15.6		

1966

Company Name	Close Ratio	Price Chg (%)	Total Return (%)	Rank Close Ratio	Rank Price Chg
CHRYSLER CORP	0.79	−42.4	−39.4	1	1
DU PONT E I DE NEMOURS & CO	0.80	−40.0	−38.0	2	2
WOOLWORTH F W CO	0.88	−37.9	−35.3	9	3
GENERAL MOTORS CORP	0.83	−36.4	−32.5	4	4
SEARS ROEBUCK & CO	0.84	−32.4	−30.8	5	5
ALLIED CHEMICAL CORP	0.87	−31.5	−28.0	8	6
UNION CARBIDE CORP	0.85	−31.0	−28.5	6	7
UNITED STATES STEEL CORP	0.89	−29.4	−25.8		8
BETHLEHEM STEEL CORP	0.93	−27.6	−23.3		9
GENERAL ELECTRIC CO	0.89	−25.0	−23.0		10
INTERNATIONAL HARVESTER CO	0.82	−24.8	−21.4	3	
WESTINGHOUSE ELECTRIC CORP	0.91	−23.9	−21.9		
STANDARD OIL CO N J	0.92	−21.3	−17.5		
STANDARD OIL CO CALIFORNIA	0.97	−21.0	−17.9		
AMERICAN TOB CO	0.94	−20.1	−15.6		
SWIFT & CO	0.97	−18.9	−15.4		
INTERNATIONAL PAPER CO	0.93	−17.5	−13.7		
AMERICAN CAN CO	0.92	−15.5	−11.9		
OWENS ILLINOIS INC	0.88	−13.9	−12.0	10	
GENERAL FOODS CORP	1.00	−13.2	−10.5		
JOHNS MANVILLE CORP	0.95	−13.1	−9.3		
GOODYEAR TIRE & RUBR CO	0.86	−12.6	−10.1	7	
TEXACO INC	1.01	−11.0	−7.9		
AMERICAN TELEPHONE & TELEG CO	1.01	−9.5	−5.8		
INTERNATIONAL NICKEL CO CDA LTD	1.03	−1.4	1.9		
ANACONDA CO	0.98	−0.8	5.7		
UNITED AIRCRAFT CORP	1.04	−0.1	2.0		
ALUMINUM COMPANY AMER	0.97	2.3	4.3		
PROCTER & GAMBLE CO	1.07	5.2	8.4		
EASTMAN KODAK CO	1.02	8.8	10.7		
Average	0.92	−18.5	−15.4		

Worst-to-First Performance

Price Change	1967 (%)	Close Ratio	1967 (%)
1-stock portfolio	91.4	1-stock portfolio	91.4
3-stock portfolio	46.4	3-stock portfolio	37.8
5-stock portfolio	40.2	5-stock portfolio	35.1
10-stock portfolio	28.3	10-stock portfolio	29.0
Dow	19.0		

1967

Company Name	Close Ratio	Price Chg (%)	Total Return (%)	Rank Close Ratio	Rank Price Chg
AMERICAN TELEPHONE & TELEG CO	0.93	-8.4	-4.5	3	1
GENERAL FOODS CORP	0.94	-2.8	0.5	7	2
UNITED AIRCRAFT CORP	0.89	0.2	2.0	1	3
ALUMINUM COMPANY AMER	0.95	2.7	4.9	10	4
INTERNATIONAL HARVESTER CO	0.96	2.9	8.0		5
UNION CARBIDE CORP	0.95	3.7	7.8	8	6
AMERICAN TOB CO	0.96	4.0	10.0		7
STANDARD OIL CO CALIFORNIA	1.06	4.4	8.9		8
OWENS ILLINOIS INC	1.03	6.0	8.6		9
STANDARD OIL CO N J	1.05	6.7	12.7		10
GENERAL ELECTRIC CO	0.97	8.5	11.5		
AMERICAN CAN CO	0.93	9.6	14.3	5	
DU PONT E I DE NEMOURS & CO	1.01	10.5	14.1		
UNITED STATES STEEL CORP	0.91	10.5	16.8	2	
BETHLEHEM STEEL CORP	0.93	11.5	16.5	4	
JOHNS MANVILLE CORP	0.95	13.2	17.7	9	
TEXACO INC	1.09	16.1	20.3		
EASTMAN KODAK CO	1.08	16.6	18.4		
ANACONDA CO	1.02	18.4	24.7		
INTERNATIONAL PAPER CO	1.08	21.2	27.3		
ALLIED CHEMICAL CORP	0.99	23.6	29.6		
GENERAL MOTORS CORP	1.00	24.5	30.6		
PROCTER & GAMBLE CO	1.03	26.4	29.6		
SEARS ROEBUCK & CO	1.02	28.6	31.4		
WOOLWORTH F W CO	0.93	28.7	33.7	6	
GOODYEAR TIRE & RUBR CO	1.18	31.0	35.1		
INTERNATIONAL NICKEL CO CDA LTD	1.16	31.7	35.9		
SWIFT & CO	1.16	47.0	53.2		
WESTINGHOUSE ELECTRIC CORP	1.10	47.8	51.7		
CHRYSLER CORP	1.18	82.9	91.4		
Average	1.02	17.6	22.1		

Worst-to-First Performance

Price Change	1968 (%)	Close Ratio	1968 (%)
1-stock portfolio	10.2	1-stock portfolio	-17.1
3-stock portfolio	4.5	3-stock portfolio	1.6
5-stock portfolio	3.4	5-stock portfolio	4.5
10-stock portfolio	10.7	10-stock portfolio	13.3
Dow	7.7		

1968

Company Name	Close Ratio	Price Chg (%)	Total Return (%)	Rank Close Ratio	Rank Price Chg
UNITED AIRCRAFT CORP	0.97	-19.2	-17.1	7	1
INTERNATIONAL NICKEL CO CDA LTD	0.96	-16.8	-14.2	6	2
ALLIED CHEMICAL CORP	1.00	-10.0	-5.7	10	3
ALUMINUM COMPANY AMER	1.03	-9.3	-7.0		4
SWIFT & CO	1.09	-8.8	-6.3		5
UNION CARBIDE CORP	1.03	-7.7	-3.3		6
PROCTER & GAMBLE CO	0.95	-6.2	-3.7	3	7
BETHLEHEM STEEL CORP	1.04	-3.8	1.4		8
GENERAL MOTORS CORP	0.98	-3.5	1.8	8	9
WESTINGHOUSE ELECTRIC CORP	0.95	-2.5	0.0	4	10
GENERAL ELECTRIC CO	1.05	-2.2	0.7		
EASTMAN KODAK CO	0.96	-1.7	-0.2	5	
CHRYSLER CORP	0.89	-0.4	2.9	1	
TEXACO INC	1.04	0.3	3.9		
GOODYEAR TIRE & RUBR CO	1.02	3.0	5.7		
DU PONT E I DE NEMOURS & CO	1.02	4.1	7.7		
INTERNATIONAL HARVESTER CO	1.10	4.9	10.6		
AMERICAN TELEPHONE & TELEG CO	1.02	5.2	10.2		
UNITED STATES STEEL CORP	1.06	5.2	11.6		
SEARS ROEBUCK & CO	0.94	8.5	10.7	2	
AMERICAN CAN CO	1.12	11.2	16.2		
STANDARD OIL CO CALIFORNIA	1.12	14.9	19.9		
STANDARD OIL CO N J	1.06	16.5	22.3		
GENERAL FOODS CORP	0.99	17.1	20.5	9	
AMERICAN TOB CO	1.12	17.5	24.4		
INTERNATIONAL PAPER CO	1.16	22.4	27.7		
OWENS ILLINOIS INC	1.19	24.3	27.1		
WOOLWORTH F W CO	1.18	30.2	35.3		
ANACONDA CO	1.34	36.1	42.5		
JOHNS MANVILLE CORP	1.26	60.1	65.2		
Average	1.05	6.3	10.4		

Worst-to-First Performance

Price Change	1969 (%)	Close Ratio	1969 (%)
1-stock portfolio	-38.4	1-stock portfolio	-35.8
3-stock portfolio	-17.6	3-stock portfolio	1.9
5-stock portfolio	-9.1	5-stock portfolio	1.6
10-stock portfolio	-5.7	10-stock portfolio	-4.6
Dow	-11.6		

1969

Company Name	Close Ratio	Price Chg (%)	Total Return (%)	Rank Close Ratio	Rank Price Chg
ANACONDA CO	0.84	−53.3	−50.2	7	1
UNITED AIRCRAFT CORP	0.70	−40.4	−38.4	1	2
CHRYSLER CORP	0.81	−38.6	−35.8	2	3
DU PONT E I DE NEMOURS & CO	0.82	−36.4	−33.7	3	4
INTERNATIONAL HARVESTER CO	0.85	−33.6	−29.2	9	5
ALLIED CHEMICAL CORP	0.84	−32.3	−29.5	8	6
JOHNS MANVILLE CORP	0.86	−31.2	−28.9		7
AMERICAN CAN CO	0.83	−28.6	−25.5	4	8
TEXACO INC	0.86	−26.4	−23.2		9
STANDARD OIL CO CALIFORNIA	0.83	−25.6	−22.2	5	10
STANDARD OIL CO N J	0.85	−21.5	−17.3	10	
UNITED STATES STEEL CORP	0.84	−21.3	−16.6	6	
UNION CARBIDE CORP	0.89	−18.2	−14.3		
GENERAL ELECTRIC CO	0.89	−17.4	−14.9		
WESTINGHOUSE ELECTRIC CORP	0.97	−14.8	−12.3		
BETHLEHEM STEEL CORP	0.87	−13.5	−8.6		
OWENS ILLINOIS INC	0.91	−13.3	−11.6		
GENERAL MOTORS CORP	0.91	−12.6	−6.1		
AMERICAN TELEPHONE & TELEG CO	0.92	−8.3	−4.0		
AMERICAN BRANDS INC	1.00	−5.3	0.0		
ALUMINUM COMPANY AMER	0.97	−2.4	0.0		
INTERNATIONAL PAPER CO	0.93	−1.3	2.5		
GENERAL FOODS CORP	1.04	2.0	5.4		
SWIFT & CO	1.13	5.0	7.2		
SEARS ROEBUCK & CO	0.99	9.2	11.4		
GOODYEAR TIRE & RUBR CO	1.05	9.8	13.0		
INTERNATIONAL NICKEL CO CDA LTD	1.15	11.5	15.1		
EASTMAN KODAK CO	1.09	12.5	14.3		
WOOLWORTH F W CO	1.04	14.8	18.7		
PROCTER & GAMBLE CO	1.14	26.6	30.2		
Average	0.93	−13.5	−10.2		

Worst-to-First Performance

Price Change	1970 (%)	Close Ratio	1970 (%)
1-stock portfolio	−24.5	1-stock portfolio	−9.3
3-stock portfolio	−16.8	3-stock portfolio	2.3
5-stock portfolio	0.3	5-stock portfolio	4.5
10-stock portfolio	8.3	10-stock portfolio	5.3
Dow	8.8		

1970

Company Name	Close Ratio	Price Chg (%)	Total Return (%)	Rank Close Ratio	Rank Price Chg
ANACONDA CO	0.89	−30.3	−24.5	1	1
ALUMINUM COMPANY AMER	1.04	−19.6	−17.1	6	2
CHRYSLER CORP	1.17	−18.5	−16.6		3
BETHLEHEM STEEL CORP	0.98	−15.7	−9.1	2	4
UNITED AIRCRAFT CORP	1.06	−14.0	−9.3	8	5
EASTMAN KODAK CO	1.12	−8.2	−6.4		6
OWENS ILLINOIS INC	1.22	−8.1	−5.4		7
INTERNATIONAL PAPER CO	1.04	−5.1	−0.8	7	8
SWIFT & CO	1.12	−3.6	−1.4		9
UNITED STATES STEEL CORP	1.02	−3.3	3.9	4	10
WOOLWORTH F W CO	1.12	−3.3	0.3		
AMERICAN CAN CO	1.00	−2.8	2.8	3	
ALLIED CHEMICAL CORP	1.24	−1.0	4.8		
AMERICAN TELEPHONE & TELEG CO	1.07	1.9	7.7	9	
GOODYEAR TIRE & RUBR CO	1.20	3.3	6.6		
INTERNATIONAL NICKEL CO CDA LTD	1.08	4.3	7.7	10	
GENERAL FOODS CORP	1.12	5.3	8.8		
PROCTER & GAMBLE CO	1.10	5.9	8.7		
STANDARD OIL CO CALIFORNIA	1.21	6.6	13.1		
UNION CARBIDE CORP	1.10	7.8	13.9		
INTERNATIONAL HARVESTER CO	1.11	11.1	19.2		
SEARS ROEBUCK & CO	1.17	12.1	14.4		
TEXACO INC	1.18	13.9	20.6		
WESTINGHOUSE ELECTRIC CORP	1.03	14.8	18.1	5	
GENERAL MOTORS CORP	1.14	16.5	22.1		
STANDARD OIL CO N J	1.18	19.3	26.7		
GENERAL ELECTRIC CO	1.21	21.1	25.2		
AMERICAN BRANDS INC	1.19	26.2	33.5		
DU PONT E I DE NEMOURS & CO	1.14	27.0	32.7		
JOHNS MANVILLE CORP	1.20	35.0	39.9		
Average	1.12	3.3	8.0		

Worst-to-First Performance

Price Change	1971 (%)	Close Ratio	1971 (%)
1-stock portfolio	−24.4	1-stock portfolio	−24.4
3-stock portfolio	−13.7	3-stock portfolio	−0.7
5-stock portfolio	−3.2	5-stock portfolio	7.4
10-stock portfolio	2.2	10-stock portfolio	−1.8
Dow	9.8		

1971

Company Name	Close Ratio	Price Chg (%)	Total Return (%)	Rank Close Ratio	Rank Price Chg
INTERNATIONAL NICKEL CO CDA LTD	0.94	−29.2	−26.6	9	1
ANACONDA CO	0.87	−26.2	−24.4	4	2
ALUMINUM COMPANY AMER	0.81	−23.8	−21.2	1	3
OWENS ILLINOIS INC	0.86	−18.4	−16.4	2	4
GENERAL FOODS CORP	0.98	−18.0	−14.8		5
AMERICAN CAN CO	0.93	−16.0	−10.9	8	6
UNITED AIRCRAFT CORP	0.86	−13.0	−8.1	3	7
AMERICAN TELEPHONE & TELEG CO	1.00	−7.8	−2.3		8
UNITED STATES STEEL CORP	0.98	−7.3	−1.2		9
AMERICAN BRANDS INC	0.96	−7.2	−2.5	10	10
TEXACO INC	1.00	−1.4	3.4		
INTERNATIONAL PAPER CO	1.01	−0.7	3.6		
GENERAL MOTORS CORP	0.99	0.0	4.3		
GOODYEAR TIRE & RUBR CO	1.00	0.4	3.2		
STANDARD OIL CO N J	0.99	0.5	5.9		
JOHNS MANVILLE CORP	1.00	0.6	3.7		
CHRYSLER CORP	1.00	2.2	4.4		
STANDARD OIL CO CALIFORNIA	1.02	5.3	10.8		
UNION CARBIDE CORP	0.93	6.0	10.8	7	
INTERNATIONAL HARVESTER CO	1.08	8.6	14.5		
DU PONT E I DE NEMOURS & CO	1.00	8.7	12.6		
SWIFT & CO	0.92	19.5	21.6	6	
ALLIED CHEMICAL CORP	0.96	20.7	25.7		
WOOLWORTH F W CO	0.91	23.6	26.9	5	
BETHLEHEM STEEL CORP	1.20	26.8	33.3		
EASTMAN KODAK CO	1.17	28.6	30.7		
GENERAL ELECTRIC CO	1.05	33.4	36.5		
SEARS ROEBUCK & CO	1.13	34.4	36.7		
PROCTER & GAMBLE CO	1.15	35.3	38.4		
WESTINGHOUSE ELECTRIC CORP	1.03	37.5	40.3		
Average	0.99	4.1	8.0		

Worst-to-First Performance

Price Change	1972 (%)	Close Ratio	1972 (%)
1-stock portfolio	2.2	1-stock portfolio	26.1
3-stock portfolio	18.3	3-stock portfolio	25.8
5-stock portfolio	6.2	5-stock portfolio	15.1
10-stock portfolio	11.8	10-stock portfolio	12.0
Dow	18.2		

1972

Company Name	Close Ratio	Price Chg (%)	Total Return (%)	Rank Close Ratio	Rank Price Chg
WOOLWORTH F W CO	0.85	−30.7	−28.5	1	1
JOHNS MANVILLE CORP	0.95	−23.3	−20.6	5	2
GENERAL FOODS CORP	1.06	−20.6	−16.5		3
OWENS ILLINOIS INC	0.91	−10.2	−7.4	2	4
WESTINGHOUSE ELECTRIC CORP	0.93	−6.3	−4.3	3	5
AMERICAN CAN CO	1.02	−5.2	1.5		6
GOODYEAR TIRE & RUBR CO	1.06	−1.2	1.7		7
INTERNATIONAL NICKEL CO CDA LTD	0.97	−0.8	2.2	7	8
ALLIED CHEMICAL CORP	0.97	−0.4	3.6	6	9
AMERICAN BRANDS INC	0.95	0.6	5.9	4	10
GENERAL MOTORS CORP	1.04	0.8	6.6		
UNITED STATES STEEL CORP	1.00	0.8	6.2	9	
BETHLEHEM STEEL CORP	0.98	1.3	5.4	8	
TEXACO INC	1.11	9.1	14.4		
SWIFT & CO	1.16	9.4	11.6		
SEARS ROEBUCK & CO	1.04	13.2	14.8		
GENERAL ELECTRIC CO	1.10	16.4	18.9		
AMERICAN TELEPHONE & TELEG CO	1.16	17.9	25.1		
UNION CARBIDE CORP	1.05	18.3	23.6		
EXXON CORP	1.12	18.6	24.4		
INTERNATIONAL PAPER CO	1.12	19.6	24.5		
ALUMINUM COMPANY AMER	1.02	21.8	26.1	10	
DU PONT E I DE NEMOURS & CO	1.04	22.4	26.3		
ANACONDA CO	1.04	25.8	26.6		
INTERNATIONAL HARVESTER CO	1.12	28.5	34.3		
STANDARD OIL CO CALIFORNIA	1.22	38.8	45.0		
PROCTER & GAMBLE CO	1.14	42.0	44.4		
CHRYSLER CORP	1.24	43.2	47.3		
UNITED AIRCRAFT CORP	1.11	51.5	58.6		
EASTMAN KODAK CO	1.13	52.6	54.2		
Average	1.05	11.8	15.9		

Worst-to-First Performance

Price Change	1973 (%)	Close Ratio	1973 (%)
1-stock portfolio	−38.0	1-stock portfolio	−38.0
3-stock portfolio	−31.3	3-stock portfolio	−33.5
5-stock portfolio	−31.3	5-stock portfolio	−32.6
10-stock portfolio	−14.5	10-stock portfolio	1.7
Dow	−13.1		

1973

Company Name	Close Ratio	Price Chg (%)	Total Return (%)	Rank Close Ratio	Rank Price Chg
CHRYSLER CORP	0.62	-61.9	-59.7	1	1
GOODYEAR TIRE & RUBR CO	0.68	-51.6	-49.4	2	2
JOHNS MANVILLE CORP	0.78	-47.2	-44.0	6	3
UNITED AIRCRAFT CORP	0.77	-46.6	-43.4	5	4
GENERAL MOTORS CORP	0.72	-43.1	-37.8	3	5
WOOLWORTH F W CO	0.86	-41.2	-38.0	8	6
WESTINGHOUSE ELECTRIC CORP	0.75	-41.0	-39.3	4	7
ESMARK INC	1.00	-36.8	-34.8		8
INTERNATIONAL HARVESTER CO	0.86	-32.9	-29.3	10	9
UNION CARBIDE CORP	0.90	-31.7	-28.3		10
SEARS ROEBUCK & CO	0.84	-30.8	-29.5	7	
OWENS ILLINOIS INC	0.90	-26.0	-23.1		
AMERICAN BRANDS INC	0.86	-23.4	-18.3	9	
EASTMAN KODAK CO	0.88	-21.8	-20.7		
TEXACO INC	0.89	-21.7	-17.6		
PROCTER & GAMBLE CO	0.92	-17.5	-16.2		
AMERICAN CAN CO	0.87	-17.0	-10.9		
GENERAL FOODS CORP	0.93	-16.7	-11.9		
GENERAL ELECTRIC CO	1.03	-13.6	-11.5		
STANDARD OIL CO CALIFORNIA	0.98	-12.1	-8.0		
DU PONT E I DE NEMOURS & CO	0.94	-10.4	-7.2		
AMERICAN TELEPHONE & TELEG CO	1.00	-5.0	0.7		
EXXON CORP	1.01	7.6	12.7		
INTERNATIONAL NICKEL CO CDA LTD	1.10	10.6	14.7		
BETHLEHEM STEEL CORP	1.12	12.3	19.1		
UNITED STATES STEEL CORP	1.18	23.4	29.8		
INTERNATIONAL PAPER CO	1.25	24.2	29.7		
ANACONDA CO	1.18	34.0	37.0		
ALUMINUM COMPANY AMER	1.12	36.9	41.1		
ALLIED CHEMICAL CORP	1.30	69.0	75.0		
Average	0.94	-14.4	-10.6		

Worst-to-First Performance

Price Change	1974 (%)	Close Ratio	1974 (%)
1-stock portfolio	-48.2	1-stock portfolio	-48.2
3-stock portfolio	-10.4	3-stock portfolio	-28.5
5-stock portfolio	-2.3	5-stock portfolio	-19.1
10-stock portfolio	-8.7	10-stock portfolio	-16.8
Dow	-23.1		

1974

Company Name	Close Ratio	Price Chg (%)	Total Return (%)	Rank Close Ratio	Rank Price Chg
WESTINGHOUSE ELECTRIC CORP	0.77	-60.8	-57.7	9	1
CHRYSLER CORP	0.53	-53.6	-48.2	1	2
WOOLWORTH F W CO	0.71	-49.0	-44.5	4	3
ANACONDA CO	0.66	-48.3	-45.5	2	4
GENERAL ELECTRIC CO	0.78	-47.0	-44.9	10	5
EASTMAN KODAK CO	0.72	-45.8	-44.4	5	6
ALLIED CHEMICAL CORP	0.79	-42.1	-39.7		7
DU PONT E I DE NEMOURS & CO	0.68	-42.0	-39.3	3	8
SEARS ROEBUCK & CO	0.72	-39.9	-38.1	6	9
INTERNATIONAL NICKEL CO CDA LTD	0.81	-39.0	-35.5		10
ALUMINUM COMPANY AMER	0.72	-38.4	-36.3	7	
STANDARD OIL CO CALIFORNIA	0.87	-36.4	-31.3		
GENERAL MOTORS CORP	0.74	-33.3	-27.6	8	
EXXON CORP	0.92	-31.3	-26.3		
INTERNATIONAL PAPER CO	0.82	-31.3	-28.3		
TEXACO INC	0.86	-28.9	-22.7		
GENERAL FOODS CORP	0.84	-24.7	-19.7		
BETHLEHEM STEEL CORP	0.85	-24.6	-18.6		
INTERNATIONAL HARVESTER CO	0.87	-23.3	-17.7		
GOODYEAR TIRE & RUBR CO	0.84	-15.6	-9.7		
PROCTER & GAMBLE CO	0.92	-11.4	-9.6		
AMERICAN TELEPHONE & TELEG CO	0.99	-11.0	-4.5		
AMERICAN BRANDS INC	0.92	-6.2	1.3		
UNITED STATES STEEL CORP	0.90	1.0	6.5		
OWENS ILLINOIS INC	0.95	9.3	14.2		
AMERICAN CAN CO	1.09	10.5	19.9		
ESMARK INC	1.01	12.1	16.6		
JOHNS MANVILLE CORP	1.13	18.2	26.6		
UNION CARBIDE CORP	1.03	21.2	28.1		
UNITED AIRCRAFT CORP	1.19	37.4	47.5		
Average	0.86	-22.5	-17.6		

Worst-to-First Performance

Price Change	1975 (%)	Close Ratio	1975 (%)
1-stock portfolio	42.9	1-stock portfolio	39.7
3-stock portfolio	78.7	3-stock portfolio	38.2
5-stock portfolio	62.4	5-stock portfolio	68.1
10-stock portfolio	51.2	10-stock portfolio	59.5
Dow	44.4		

1975

Company Name	Close Ratio	Price Chg (%)	Total Return (%)	Rank Close Ratio	Rank Price Chg
AMERICAN CAN CO	1.03	8.2	17.2		1
PROCTER & GAMBLE CO	0.97	9.2	11.6		2
TEXACO INC	0.95	12.0	21.3	8	3
INTERNATIONAL HARVESTER CO	0.88	13.3	21.3	1	4
AMERICAN TELEPHONE & TELEG CO	1.04	14.0	22.1		5
ALLIED CHEMICAL CORP	0.94	17.2	23.3	7	6
INTERNATIONAL NICKEL CO CDA LTD	0.97	17.4	25.2	10	7
JOHNS MANVILLE CORP	1.06	19.2	26.0		8
ANACONDA CO	1.01	26.9	32.8		9
AMERICAN BRANDS INC	1.02	27.7	37.0		10
ALUMINUM COMPANY AMER	0.92	29.3	33.7	4	
STANDARD OIL CO CALIFORNIA	1.02	32.0	41.6		
BETHLEHEM STEEL CORP	0.93	32.2	43.7	6	
SEARS ROEBUCK & CO	0.97	33.7	37.4	9	
WESTINGHOUSE ELECTRIC CORP	0.88	33.8	42.9	2	
DU PONT E I DE NEMOURS & CO	1.04	37.1	42.2		
EXXON CORP	1.03	37.3	45.7		
GENERAL ELECTRIC CO	0.99	38.2	43.0		
CHRYSLER CORP	0.93	39.7	39.7	5	
ESMARK INC	1.18	41.8	48.6		
UNITED TECHNOLOGIES CORP	0.91	42.1	48.4	3	
UNION CARBIDE CORP	1.03	47.7	54.0		
OWENS ILLINOIS INC	1.19	53.7	60.0		
GENERAL FOODS CORP	1.10	54.5	63.2		
INTERNATIONAL PAPER CO	1.10	61.5	68.1		
EASTMAN KODAK CO	1.07	68.8	72.3		
GOODYEAR TIRE & RUBR CO	1.13	68.9	79.2		
UNITED STATES STEEL CORP	1.05	71.1	79.5		
GENERAL MOTORS CORP	1.17	87.4	97.3		
WOOLWORTH F W CO	1.30	134.7	153.5		
Average	1.03	40.4	47.7		

Worst-to-First Performance

Price Change	1976 (%)	Close Ratio	1976 (%)
1-stock portfolio	32.7	1-stock portfolio	56.3
3-stock portfolio	22.8	3-stock portfolio	38.2
5-stock portfolio	31.6	5-stock portfolio	54.2
10-stock portfolio	37.7	10-stock portfolio	39.9
Dow	22.7		

1976

Company Name	Close Ratio	Price Chg (%)	Total Return (%)	Rank Close Ratio	Rank Price Chg
EASTMAN KODAK CO	0.89	−19.0	−17.2	1	1
UNION CARBIDE CORP	0.95	1.2	5.1	3	2
MINNESOTA MINING & MFG CO	0.95	2.0	4.6	2	3
PROCTER & GAMBLE CO	1.01	5.2	7.7		4
DU PONT E I DE NEMOURS & CO	0.99	6.8	11.0	8	5
SEARS ROEBUCK & CO	1.02	7.0	9.5		6
OWENS ILLINOIS INC	0.98	8.4	12.1	5	7
GOODYEAR TIRE & RUBR CO	1.06	9.2	14.7		8
GENERAL FOODS CORP	0.99	9.5	15.1	10	9
ESMARK INC	1.03	13.0	18.3		10
UNITED STATES STEEL CORP	0.97	14.8	19.8	4	
WOOLWORTH F W CO	1.11	17.0	23.3		
AMERICAN BRANDS INC	1.11	18.4	26.8		
TEXACO INC	1.03	18.7	28.0		
INTERNATIONAL PAPER CO	0.99	19.3	22.7	7	
ALLIED CHEMICAL CORP	1.05	20.3	26.2		
GENERAL ELECTRIC CO	1.04	20.6	24.4		
EXXON CORP	1.05	20.8	27.6		
BETHLEHEM STEEL CORP	0.99	22.8	29.0	9	
AMERICAN CAN CO	1.11	24.3	32.7		
AMERICAN TELEPHONE & TELEG CO	1.08	24.8	33.2		
INCO LTD	0.98	29.2	35.6	6	
WESTINGHOUSE ELECTRIC CORP	1.07	31.8	40.0		
GENERAL MOTORS CORP	1.12	36.2	47.4		
STANDARD OIL CO CALIFORNIA	1.12	39.6	48.3		
JOHNS MANVILLE CORP	1.10	44.1	50.8		
INTERNATIONAL HARVESTER CO	1.14	47.5	56.3		
ALUMINUM COMPANY AMER	1.05	48.2	52.1		
UNITED TECHNOLOGIES CORP	1.14	67.7	73.9		
CHRYSLER CORP	1.03	101.2	104.4		
Average	1.04	23.7	29.4		

Worst-to-First Performance

Price Change	1977 (%)	Close Ratio	1977 (%)
1-stock portfolio	−38.4	1-stock portfolio	−38.4
3-stock portfolio	−26.5	3-stock portfolio	−26.5
5-stock portfolio	−18.3	5-stock portfolio	−24.8
10-stock portfolio	−14.3	10-stock portfolio	−24.4
Dow	−12.7		

1977

Company Name	Close Ratio	Price Chg (%)	Total Return (%)	Rank Close Ratio	Rank Price Chg
BETHLEHEM STEEL CORP	0.80	–47.7	–44.9	3	1
INCO LTD	0.75	–47.5	–44.8	1	2
EASTMAN KODAK CO	0.87	–40.6	–38.4	6	3
CHRYSLER CORP	0.79	–38.0	–34.4	2	4
UNITED STATES STEEL CORP	0.86	–36.7	–32.8	5	5
INTERNATIONAL PAPER CO	0.91	–36.5	–33.8	9	6
UNION CARBIDE CORP	0.86	–33.7	–29.8	4	7
GOODYEAR TIRE & RUBR CO	0.90	–27.4	–22.7	8	8
WOOLWORTH F W CO	0.89	–26.7	–21.9	7	9
GENERAL MOTORS CORP	0.93	–19.9	–11.4	10	10
SEARS ROEBUCK & CO	0.95	–18.8	–15.9		
ALUMINUM COMPANY AMER	0.93	–18.6	–15.7		
ESMARK INC	0.97	–16.1	–11.0		
OWENS ILLINOIS INC	0.94	–15.1	–11.4		
MINNESOTA MINING & MFG CO	0.98	–14.3	–11.4		
DU PONT E I DE NEMOURS & CO	1.02	–10.9	–6.5		
GENERAL ELECTRIC CO	0.95	–10.3	–6.6		
EXXON CORP	0.97	–10.3	–4.7		
INTERNATIONAL HARVESTER CO	0.95	–8.3	–2.6		
PROCTER & GAMBLE CO	1.06	–8.3	–5.3		
UNITED TECHNOLOGIES CORP	0.97	–7.7	–3.5		
AMERICAN BRANDS INC	0.96	–6.0	0.4		
STANDARD OIL CO CALIFORNIA	0.95	–5.2	0.4		
AMERICAN TELEPHONE & TELEG CO	0.98	–4.7	2.0		
JOHNS MANVILLE CORP	0.96	–3.0	1.8		
AMERICAN CAN CO	0.98	–0.6	5.8		
TEXACO INC	1.00	0.0	7.5		
WESTINGHOUSE ELECTRIC CORP	0.94	2.8	8.3		
GENERAL FOODS CORP	0.96	4.1	9.4		
ALLIED CHEMICAL CORP	0.98	10.6	15.0		
Average	0.93	–16.5	–12.0		

Worst-to-First Performance

Price Change	1978 (%)	Close Ratio	1978 (%)
1-stock portfolio	–2.8	1-stock portfolio	–3.8
3-stock portfolio	4.3	3-stock portfolio	–11.0
5-stock portfolio	–8.3	5-stock portfolio	–14.4
10-stock portfolio	–5.9	10-stock portfolio	–5.9
Dow	2.7		

1978

Company Name	Close Ratio	Price Chg (%)	Total Return (%)	Rank Close Ratio	Rank Price Chg
ALLIED CHEMICAL CORP	0.77	–36.2	–32.6	2	1
UNITED STATES STEEL CORP	0.81	–32.5	–28.4	4	2
CHRYSLER CORP	0.78	–31.7	–26.4	3	3
JOHNS MANVILLE CORP	0.76	–30.4	–25.9	1	4
SEARS ROEBUCK & CO	0.86	–29.5	–25.5	7	5
OWENS ILLINOIS INC	0.85	–25.1	–21.1	6	6
ESMARK INC	0.87	–20.0	–14.4	8	7
UNION CARBIDE CORP	0.88	–17.1	–10.9	10	8
INTERNATIONAL PAPER CO	0.88	–16.6	–12.3		9
GENERAL MOTORS CORP	0.88	–14.5	–5.4		10
TEXACO INC	0.96	–14.0	–6.7		
WESTINGHOUSE ELECTRIC CORP	0.82	–8.3	–3.6	5	
INCO LTD	0.96	–0.0	–3.8		
AMERICAN CAN CO	0.91	–7.4	–0.9		
BETHLEHEM STEEL CORP	0.87	–7.1	–2.8	9	
GOODYEAR TIRE & RUBR CO	0.95	–6.5	1.1		
GENERAL ELECTRIC CO	0.92	–5.5	–0.6		
AMERICAN TELEPHONE & TELEG CO	0.99	0.0	7.8		
GENERAL FOODS CORP	1.01	2.0	7.7		
EXXON CORP	1.02	2.1	9.4		
ALUMINUM COMPANY AMER	1.06	2.4	7.0		
WOOLWORTH F W CO	0.98	2.6	10.5		
PROCTER & GAMBLE CO	1.04	3.5	7.1		
DU PONT E I DE NEMOURS & CO	1.05	4.7	11.3		
UNITED TECHNOLOGIES CORP	0.92	8.4	13.9		
EASTMAN KODAK CO	1.03	14.7	19.6		
AMERICAN BRANDS INC	1.02	17.2	26.1		
INTERNATIONAL HARVESTER CO	1.02	19.8	27.6		
STANDARD OIL CO CALIFORNIA	1.08	20.6	28.0		
MINNESOTA MINING & MFG CO	1.11	30.2	35.0		
Average	0.93	–6.1	–0.3		

Worst-to-First Performance

Price Change	1979 (%)	Close Ratio	1979 (%)
1-stock portfolio	84.0	1-stock portfolio	15.1
3-stock portfolio	17.6	3-stock portfolio	26.4
5-stock portfolio	13.0	5-stock portfolio	19.1
10-stock portfolio	15.6	10-stock portfolio	18.9
Dow	10.5		

1979

Company Name	Close Ratio	Price Chg (%)	Total Return (%)	Rank Close Ratio	Rank Price Chg
MINNESOTA MINING & MFG CO	0.93	–20.4	–16.8	8	1
GOODYEAR TIRE & RUBR CO	0.84	–20.2	–13.1	2	2
EASTMAN KODAK CO	0.87	–17.9	–13.4	3	3
UNITED STATES STEEL CORP	0.80	–17.6	–11.3	1	4
PROCTER & GAMBLE CO	0.96	–16.5	–12.9		5
AMERICAN TELEPHONE & TELEG CO	0.92	–13.8	–6.1	7	6
INTERNATIONAL BUSINESS MACHS COR	0.91	–13.7	–9.5	6	7
SEARS ROEBUCK & CO	0.93	–8.9	–2.7	9	8
GENERAL MOTORS CORP	0.87	–7.0	2.3	4	9
DU PONT E I DE NEMOURS & CO	0.95	–3.9	2.6		10
AMERICAN CAN CO	0.95	–0.7	7.0		
INTERNATIONAL PAPER CO	0.87	1.4	6.9	5	
GENERAL FOODS CORP	1.02	4.7	10.9		
JOHNS MANVILLE CORP	0.98	6.6	15.1		
MERCK & CO INC	1.07	6.8	10.0		
GENERAL ELECTRIC CO	1.02	7.4	13.7		
BETHLEHEM STEEL CORP	0.94	7.6	15.3		
INTERNATIONAL HARVESTER CO	0.99	7.9	14.6		
UNITED TECHNOLOGIES CORP	1.09	10.6	17.0		
EXXON CORP	1.01	12.2	20.6		
OWENS ILLINOIS INC	1.00	13.3	20.7		
ALUMINUM COMPANY AMER	1.02	14.9	20.8		
STANDARD OIL CO CALIFORNIA	1.07	20.3	27.4		
TEXACO INC	1.03	20.9	30.9		
WESTINGHOUSE ELECTRIC CORP	1.04	21.1	27.5		
UNION CARBIDE CORP	1.05	23.5	33.1		
WOOLWORTH F W CO	0.94	29.7	37.9	10	
AMERICAN BRANDS INC	1.10	34.7	45.5		
INCO LTD	1.17	50.8	54.6		
ALLIED CHEMICAL CORP	1.28	73.9	84.0		
Average	0.99	7.6	14.4		

Worst-to-First Performance

Price Change	1980 (%)	Close Ratio		1980 (%)
1-stock portfolio	23.5	1-stock portfolio		52.8
3-stock portfolio	37.5	3-stock portfolio		47.3
5-stock portfolio	32.6	5-stock portfolio		31.6
10-stock portfolio	17.4	10-stock portfolio		19.2
Dow	21.4			

1980

Company Name	Close Ratio	Price Chg (%)	Total Return (%)	Rank Close Ratio	Rank Price Chg
INTERNATIONAL HARVESTER CO	0.88	–34.5	–29.4	1	1
SEARS ROEBUCK & CO	0.92	–15.3	–8.0	3	2
AMERICAN CAN CO	0.98	–14.7	–6.7	8	3
INCO LTD	0.91	–14.2	–11.6	2	4
GENERAL FOODS CORP	1.04	–10.0	–3.1		5
GENERAL MOTORS CORP	0.93	–10.0	–4.4	4	6
AMERICAN TELEPHONE & TELEG CO	0.93	–8.2	1.2	5	7
PROCTER & GAMBLE CO	0.94	–7.2	–2.6	7	8
WOOLWORTH F W CO	0.98	–1.5	5.6	9	9
JOHNS MANVILLE CORP	1.06	2.6	11.5		10
DU PONT E I DE NEMOURS & CO	1.02	4.0	11.2	10	
INTERNATIONAL BUSINESS MACHS COR	1.09	5.4	11.3		
ALUMINUM COMPANY AMER	0.94	8.7	14.3	6	
ALLIED CHEMICAL CORP	1.04	8.9	13.3		
INTERNATIONAL PAPER CO	1.09	13.5	20.5		
AMERICAN BRANDS INC	1.02	14.2	23.7		
MERCK & CO INC	1.14	17.3	21.2		
MINNESOTA MINING & MFG CO	1.06	17.4	23.5		
UNION CARBIDE CORP	1.13	19.6	28.6		
GENERAL ELECTRIC CO	1.16	21.0	27.9		
GOODYEAR TIRE & RUBR CO	1.09	24.3	36.1		
BETHLEHEM STEEL CORP	1.10	24.9	33.4		
OWENS ILLINOIS INC	1.04	25.9	33.0		
UNITED STATES STEEL CORP	1.18	41.4	52.8		
UNITED TECHNOLOGIES CORP	1.26	41.9	48.3		
EASTMAN KODAK CO	1.15	44.9	53.0		
EXXON CORP	1.15	46.3	57.7		
WESTINGHOUSE ELECTRIC CORP	1.16	47.2	55.6		
TEXACO INC	1.25	66.2	77.8		
STANDARD OIL CO CALIFORNIA	1.24	76.5	84.8		
Average	1.06	15.2	22.7		

Worst-to-First Performance

Price Change	1981 (%)	Close Ratio		1981 (%)
1-stock portfolio	–72.2	1-stock portfolio		–72.2
3-stock portfolio	–11.6	3-stock portfolio		–28.5
5-stock portfolio	–10.0	5-stock portfolio		–12.1
10-stock portfolio	–5.7	10-stock portfolio		–5.0
Dow	–3.4			

1981

Company Name	Close Ratio	Price Chg (%)	Total Return (%)	Rank Close Ratio	Rank Price Chg
INTERNATIONAL HARVESTER CO	0.55	–72.2	–72.2	1	1
MANVILLE CORP	0.80	–39.9	–33.4	3	2
UNITED TECHNOLOGIES CORP	0.84	–31.6	–28.2	6	3
TEXACO INC	0.94	–31.3	–25.7		4
INCO LTD	0.79	–30.1	–27.8	2	5
WOOLWORTH F W CO	0.82	–27.3	–21.1	5	6
EXXON CORP	0.95	–22.5	–15.3		7
ALLIED CORP	0.88	–18.0	–14.1	8	8
INTERNATIONAL BUSINESS MACHS COR	1.01	–16.2	–11.1		9
GENERAL MOTORS CORP	0.81	–14.4	–9.9	4	10
ALUMINUM COMPANY AMER	0.89	–14.0	–8.5	10	
WESTINGHOUSE ELECTRIC CORP	0.89	–13.9	–8.3		
STANDARD OIL CO CALIFORNIA	1.05	–13.8	–9.2		
BETHLEHEM STEEL CORP	0.96	–11.8	–5.9		
DU PONT E I DE NEMOURS & CO	0.84	–11.3	–5.6	7	
MINNESOTA MINING & MFG CO	0.99	–7.6	–2.6		
INTERNATIONAL PAPER CO	0.09	–6.8	–1.7	9	
GENERAL ELECTRIC CO	0.95	–6.3	–1.3		
AMERICAN BRANDS INC	0.94	–5.2	3.1		
MERCK & CO INC	0.96	0.0	3.1		
EASTMAN KODAK CO	0.99	2.0	7.0		
UNION CARBIDE CORP	0.95	2.2	8.6		
GENERAL FOODS CORP	1.01	5.0	12.5		
SEARS ROEBUCK & CO	0.90	5.7	14.6		
AMERICAN CAN CO	0.94	13.7	22.7		
OWENS ILLINOIS INC	1.00	16.2	22.4		
PROCTER & GAMBLE CO	1.09	16.7	23.1		
GOODYEAR TIRE & RUBR CO	1.03	18.0	77.1		
UNITED STATES STEEL CORP	1.00	20.7	29.2		
AMERICAN TELEPHONE & TELEG CO	1.03	22.7	35.0		
Average	0.92	–9.0	–3.1		

Worst-to-First Performance

Price Change	1982 (%)		Close Ratio	1982 (%)
1-stock portfolio	–40.4		1-stock portfolio	–40.4
3-stock portfolio	–8.1		3-stock portfolio	–27.9
5-stock portfolio	–7.2		5-stock portfolio	8.9
10-stock portfolio	15.5		10-stock portfolio	13.0
Dow	23.8			

1982

Company Name	Close Ratio	Price Chg (%)	Total Return (%)	Rank Close Ratio	Rank Price Chg
INTERNATIONAL HARVESTER CO	1.02	–40.4	–40.4	4	1
UNITED STATES STEEL CORP	1.04	–29.7	–23.7	5	2
ALLIED CORP	0.97	–26.2	–21.1	1	3
STANDARD OIL CO CALIFORNIA	1.05	–25.4	–19.3	8	4
INCO LTD	1.20	–17.5	–16.0		5
BETHLEHEM STEEL CORP	1.06	–17.2	–11.4		6
AMERICAN CAN CO	1.05	–10.2	–1.0	7	7
TEXACO INC	1.05	–5.7	4.4	6	8
EXXON CORP	1.05	–4.8	5.7	9	9
OWENS ILLINOIS INC	1.13	–4.6	1.8		10
MERCK & CO INC	1.11	–0.1	3.7		
DU PONT E I DE NEMOURS & CO	1.02	–3.7	3.0	2	
AMERICAN TELEPHONE & TELEG CO	1.06	1.1	11.2	10	
UNION CARBIDE CORP	1.10	2.9	10.4		
EASTMAN KODAK CO	1.07	20.9	26.3		
ALUMINUM COMPANY AMER	1.18	21.0	29.0		
INTERNATIONAL PAPER CO	1.21	23.6	31.4		
GENERAL FOODS CORP	1.02	24.8	32.5	3	
AMERICAN BRANDS INC	1.06	24.8	35.8		
UNITED TECHNOLOGIES CORP	1.26	35.6	43.4		
MINNESOTA MINING & MFG CO	1.22	37.6	45.2		
WOOLWORTH F W CO	1.23	43.8	57.4		
AMERICAN EXPRESS CO	1.29	46.0	53.1		
PROCTER & GAMBLE CO	1.24	47.1	54.1		
WESTINGHOUSE ELECTRIC CORP	1.28	52.5	62.4		
GENERAL MOTORS CORP	1.29	62.0	70.7		
GENERAL ELECTRIC CO	1.29	65.4	73.2		
INTERNATIONAL BUSINESS MACHS COR	1.35	69.2	77.9		
GOODYEAR TIRE & RUBR CO	1.35	84.2	94.9		
SEARS ROEBUCK & CO	1.32	86.8	99.1		
Average	1.15	18.8	26.5		

Worst-to-First Performance

Price Change	1983 (%)		Close Ratio	1983 (%)
1-stock portfolio	170.6		1-stock portfolio	81.0
3-stock portfolio	100.7		3-stock portfolio	56.8
5-stock portfolio	68.8		5-stock portfolio	78.3
10-stock portfolio	56.2		10-stock portfolio	54.7
Dow	25.7			

1983

Company Name	Close Ratio	Price Chg (%)	Total Return (%)	Rank Close Ratio	Rank Price Chg
GOODYEAR TIRE & RUBR CO	0.98	-13.2	-9.3	7	1
EASTMAN KODAK CO	1.04	-11.5	-7.2		2
PROCTER & GAMBLE CO	1.01	-3.8	0.4		3
AMERICAN EXPRESS CO	0.80	1.6	6.0	1	4
AMERICAN TELEPHONE & TELEG CO	0.95	3.6	13.4	5	5
MERCK & CO INC	0.98	6.8	10.2	8	6
STANDARD OIL CO CALIFORNIA	0.95	8.2	15.6	2	7
MINNESOTA MINING & MFG CO	0.99	10.0	14.5	9	8
TEXACO INC	1.01	15.3	25.6		9
UNION CARBIDE CORP	0.95	18.7	24.8	4	10
GENERAL MOTORS CORP	1.05	19.2	24.2		
INTERNATIONAL PAPER CO	1.09	22.0	27.2		
SEARS ROEBUCK & CO	0.95	23.2	28.4	3	
GENERAL ELECTRIC CO	1.10	23.6	27.9		
INCO LTD	0.98	24.5	26.2	6	
EXXON CORP	1.04	25.6	37.3		
INTERNATIONAL BUSINESS MACHS COR	1.02	26.8	31.0		
UNITED TECHNOLOGIES CORP	1.04	28.0	32.8		
AMERICAN BRANDS INC	1.12	29.2	38.5		
GENERAL FOODS CORP	1.11	29.7	36.9		
OWENS ILLINOIS INC	1.10	32.3	39.5		
WOOLWORTH F W CO	0.99	35.7	43.6	10	
WESTINGHOUSE ELECTRIC CORP	1.14	40.8	46.3		
UNITED STATES STEEL CORP	1.15	44.6	50.5		
ALUMINUM COMPANY AMER	1.12	44.8	49.2		
DU PONT E I DE NEMOURS & CO	1.06	44.9	52.6		
BETHLEHEM STEEL CORP	1.21	48.1	51.8		
AMERICAN CAN CO	1.10	51.8	63.8		
ALLIED CORP	1.08	72.2	81.0		
INTERNATIONAL HARVESTER CO	1.13	170.6	170.6		
Average	1.04	29.1	35.1		

Worst-to-First Performance

Price Change	1984 (%)	Close Ratio	1984 (%)
1-stock portfolio	-9.2	1-stock portfolio	19.9
3-stock portfolio	-1.6	3-stock portfolio	2.2
5-stock portfolio	8.9	5-stock portfolio	-0.3
10-stock portfolio	1.4	10-stock portfolio	-0.6
Dow	1.1		

1984

Company Name	Close Ratio	Price Chg (%)	Total Return (%)	Rank Close Ratio	Rank Price Chg
UNION CARBIDE CORP	0.72	-41.4	-37.5	1	1
BETHLEHEM STEEL CORP	0.89	-38.6	-36.7	2	2
INTERNATIONAL HARVESTER CO	1.12	-29.3	-29.3		3
ALUMINUM COMPANY AMER	1.05	-17.5	-14.7		4
INCO LTD	1.09	-15.4	-13.9		5
SEARS ROEBUCK & CO	0.98	-14.5	-9.8	5	6
GOODYEAR TIRE & RUBR CO	1.01	-14.4	-9.2	6	7
UNITED STATES STEEL CORP	1.02	-14.0	-10.7	8	8
CHEVRON CORP	0.89	-9.7	-3.5	3	9
INTERNATIONAL PAPER CO	1.05	-8.7	-4.3		10
ALLIED CORP	1.02	-7.2	-2.2	9	
EASTMAN KODAK CO	1.03	-5.6	-0.6		
TEXACO INC	0.95	-4.9	3.0	4	
DU PONT E I DE NEMOURS & CO	1.04	-4.8	1.1		
MINNESOTA MINING & MFG CO	1.01	-4.7	-0.5	7	
WESTINGHOUSE ELECTRIC CORP	1.08	-4.6	-0.6		
GENERAL ELECTRIC CO	1.03	-3.4	0.3		
UNITED TECHNOLOGIES CORP	1.03	0.0	4.1		
PROCTER & GAMBLE CO	1.07	0.2	5.1		
INTERNATIONAL BUSINESS MACHS COR	1.06	0.9	4.5		
MERCK & CO INC	1.07	4.0	7.6		
WOOLWORTH F W CO	1.05	5.3	11.0		
OWENS ILLINOIS INC	1.06	7.7	12.7		
AMERICAN CAN CO	1.08	7.7	14.6		
GENERAL MOTORS CORP	1.13	7.9	15.4		
AMERICAN BRANDS INC	1.09	8.4	15.5		
GENERAL FOODS CORP	1.02	8.8	14.0	10	
AMERICAN EXPRESS CO	1.18	15.3	19.9		
EXXON CORP	1.07	20.4	30.5		
AMERICAN TELEPHONE & TELEG CO	1.10	21.3	29.6		
Average	1.03	-4.4	0.5		

Worst-to-First Performance

Price Change	1985 (%)	Close Ratio	1985 (%)
1-stock portfolio	106.9	1-stock portfolio	106.9
3-stock portfolio	34.1	3-stock portfolio	42.6
5-stock portfolio	23.8	5-stock portfolio	30.4
10-stock portfolio	21.0	10-stock portfolio	26.1
Dow	32.8		

1985

Company Name	Close Ratio	Price Chg (%)	Total Return (%)	Rank Close Ratio	Rank Price Chg
TEXACO INC	0.83	−12.1	−4.7	1	1
BETHLEHEM STEEL CORP	0.95	−10.7	−9.2	3	2
GENERAL MOTORS CORP	1.03	−7.8	−1.2	6	3
INTERNATIONAL PAPER CO	1.04	−5.8	−1.2	8	4
UNITED STATES STEEL CORP	0.94	1.9	6.0	2	5
ALUMINUM COMPANY AMER	1.13	4.1	7.8		6
INTERNATIONAL HARVESTER CO	1.01	4.6	4.6	5	7
EASTMAN KODAK CO	1.12	5.7	11.3		8
INCO LTD	1.00	7.1	8.7	4	9
PHILIP MORRIS COS INC	1.06	9.6	14.9		10
MINNESOTA MINING & MFG CO	1.13	14.1	19.3		
AMERICAN CAN CO	1.05	18.8	25.3	9	
GOODYEAR TIRE & RUBR CO	1.11	20.2	27.0		
UNITED TECHNOLOGIES CORP	1.07	20.7	24.8		
CHEVRON CORP	1.04	22.0	30.2	7	
PROCTER & GAMBLE CO	1.20	22.4	28.0		
EXXON CORP	1.06	22.5	30.9	10	
SEARS ROEBUCK & CO	1.09	22.8	28.9		
INTERNATIONAL BUSINESS MACHS COR	1.19	26.3	30.6		
AMERICAN TELEPHONE & TELEG CO	1.13	28.2	35.1		
GENERAL ELECTRIC CO	1.18	28.5	33.1		
OWENS ILLINOIS INC	1.10	31.1	36.0		
ALLIED SIGNAL INC	1.08	35.5	41.4		
DU PONT E I DE NEMOURS & CO	1.16	37.1	44.3		
AMERICAN EXPRESS CO	1.18	40.9	45.0		
MERCK & CO INC	1.21	45.7	50.0		
MCDONALDS CORP	1.21	56.7	58.8		
WOOLWORTH F W CO	1.24	62.2	69.3		
WESTINGHOUSE ELECTRIC CORP	1.22	70.3	75.9		
UNION CARBIDE CORP	1.41	92.9	106.9		
Average	1.11	23.0	29.3		

Worst-to-First Performance

Price Change	1986 (%)	Close Ratio	1986 (%)
1-stock portfolio	31.7	1-stock portfolio	31.7
3-stock portfolio	−9.4	3-stock portfolio	−14.3
5-stock portfolio	2.2	5-stock portfolio	−19.4
10-stock portfolio	5.7	10-stock portfolio	6.3
Dow	26.9		

1986

Company Name	Close Ratio	Price Chg (%)	Total Return (%)	Rank Close Ratio	Rank Price Chg
BETHLEHEM STEEL CORP	0.56	−60.0	−60.0	1	1
NAVISTAR INTERNATIONAL CORP	0.60	−44.1	−44.1	2	2
INTERNATIONAL BUSINESS MACHS COR	0.87	−22.8	−20.4	3	3
U S X CORP	1.01	−19.2	−14.6		4
ALUMINUM COMPANY AMER	0.90	−12.0	−9.2	7	5
INCO LTD	0.90	−11.3	−10.0	5	6
GENERAL MOTORS CORP	0.89	−6.2	0.2	4	7
ALLIED SIGNAL INC	0.94	−4.2	−0.3		8
AMERICAN TELEPHONE & TELEG CO	1.02	0.0	5.2		9
SEARS ROEBUCK & CO	0.90	1.9	5.9	6	10
UNITED TECHNOLOGIES CORP	0.99	5.1	8.2		
AMERICAN EXPRESS CO	0.94	6.8	9.3	9	
PROCTER & GAMBLE CO	1.01	9.5	13.6		
MCDONALDS CORP	0.94	12.9	14.1	10	
GENERAL ELECTRIC CO	1.10	18.2	21.8		
CHEVRON CORP	1.09	19.0	26.0		
TEXACO INC	1.09	19.6	31.7		
DU PONT E I DE NEMOURS & CO	1.03	23.8	28.4		
WESTINGHOUSE ELECTRIC CORP	1.01	25.3	28.4		
EXXON CORP	1.10	27.2	34.8		
WOOLWORTH F W CO	0.92	28.8	32.4	8	
MINNESOTA MINING & MFG CO	1.08	29.9	34.4		
GOODYEAR TIRE & RUBR CO	1.18	34.0	40.1		
EASTMAN KODAK CO	1.16	35.6	41.1		
AMERICAN CAN CO	1.04	40.2	45.7		
UNION CARBIDE CORP	1.01	41.8	61.8		
INTERNATIONAL PAPER CO	1.13	48.0	53.5		
PHILIP MORRIS COS INC	1.04	62.7	68.7		
MERCK & CO INC	1.22	80.8	84.5		
OWENS ILLINOIS INC	1.33	100.9	105.9		
Average	1.00	16.4	21.2		

Worst-to-First Performance

Price Change	1987 (%)	Close Ratio	1987 (%)
1-stock portfolio	168.0	1-stock portfolio	168.0
3-stock portfolio	52.3	3-stock portfolio	52.3
5-stock portfolio	48.5	5-stock portfolio	49.1
10-stock portfolio	30.6	10-stock portfolio	25.9
Dow	6.0		

1987

Company Name	Close Ratio	Price Chg (%)	Total Return (%)	Rank Close Ratio	Rank Price Chg
PRIMERICA CORP	0.61	−42.6	−40.3	1	1
ALLIED SIGNAL INC	0.69	−29.6	−26.3	3	2
BOEING CO	0.81	−27.6	−25.4		3
UNITED TECHNOLOGIES CORP	0.72	−26.4	−24.0	6	4
AMERICAN EXPRESS CO	0.71	−19.2	−17.7	5	5
SEARS ROEBUCK & CO	0.70	−15.7	−12.0	4	6
CHEVRON CORP	0.75	−12.7	−8.3	8	7
WESTINGHOUSE ELECTRIC CORP	0.82	−10.8	−8.2		8
WOOLWORTH F W CO	0.73	−10.7	−8.1	7	9
NAVISTAR INTERNATIONAL CORP	0.64	−10.5	−10.5	2	10
GENERAL MOTORS CORP	0.78	−7.0	−0.6	10	
INTERNATIONAL BUSINESS MACHS COR	0.78	−3.8	−0.7	9	
UNION CARBIDE CORP	0.81	−3.3	2.5		
COCA COLA CO	0.87	1.0	3.6		
GENERAL ELECTRIC CO	0.83	2.6	5.2		
TEXACO INC	0.99	3.8	6.1		
DU PONT E I DE NEMOURS & CO	0.80	4.0	7.5		
EASTMAN KODAK CO	0.87	7.1	10.6		
AMERICAN TELEPHONE & TELEG CO	0.94	8.0	12.8		
MCDONALDS CORP	0.86	8.4	9.5		
EXXON CORP	0.86	8.7	13.8		
MINNESOTA MINING & MFG CO	0.94	10.4	13.6		
PROCTER & GAMBLE CO	0.93	11.8	15.2		
INTERNATIONAL PAPER CO	0.90	12.5	15.6		
PHILIP MORRIS COS INC	0.90	18.8	22.9		
MERCK & CO INC	0.91	28.0	30.0		
ALUMINUM COMPANY AMER	0.91	38.0	41.6		
U S X CORP	0.93	38.4	44.2		
GOODYEAR TIRE & RUBR CO	0.95	43.3	47.3		
BETHLEHEM STEEL CORP	1.11	168.0	168.0		
Average	0.83	6.4	9.6		

Worst-to-First Performance

Price Change	1988 (%)	Close Ratio	1988 (%)
1-stock portfolio	26.0	1-stock portfolio	26.0
3-stock portfolio	38.6	3-stock portfolio	24.6
5-stock portfolio	32.6	5-stock portfolio	24.7
10-stock portfolio	30.5	10-stock portfolio	28.1
Dow	14.9		

1988

Company Name	Close Ratio	Price Chg (%)	Total Return (%)	Rank Close Ratio	Rank Price Chg
GOODYEAR TIRE & RUBR CO	0.88	−14.8	−12.2	1	1
EASTMAN KODAK CO	1.02	−7.9	−3.8		2
MINNESOTA MINING & MFG CO	1.01	−3.7	−0.3	10	3
U S X CORP	0.99	−1.7	2.5	6	4
DU PONT E I DE NEMOURS & CO	1.05	1.0	5.6		5
GENERAL ELECTRIC CO	1.05	1.4	4.9		6
PROCTER & GAMBLE CO	1.11	1.9	5.5		7
INTERNATIONAL BUSINESS MACHS COR	1.04	5.5	9.6		8
WESTINGHOUSE ELECTRIC CORP	1.00	5.8	9.7	9	9
AMERICAN TELEPHONE & TELEG CO	1.06	6.5	11.3		10
MERCK & CO INC	1.04	9.3	12.0		
MCDONALDS CORP	1.06	9.4	10.8		
INTERNATIONAL PAPER CO	1.04	9.8	13.0		
ALLIED SIGNAL INC	0.97	15.0	21.4	3	
EXXON CORP	0.98	15.4	21.1	4	
CHEVRON CORP	0.98	15.5	22.0	5	
PRIMERICA CORP	1.02	16.0	26.0		
AMERICAN EXPRESS CO	0.99	16.4	20.7	7	
UNION CARBIDE CORP	1.09	17.8	24.0		
COCA COLA CO	1.11	19.3	22.8		
PHILIP MORRIS COS INC	1.11	19.3	24.6		
ALUMINUM COMPANY AMER	1.11	19.8	22.9		
UNITED TECHNOLOGIES CORP	1.06	21.4	26.3		
SEARS ROEBUCK & CO	1.09	22.0	28.8		
NAVISTAR INTERNATIONAL CORP	0.92	26.5	26.5	2	
GENERAL MOTORS CORP	1.08	36.0	45.2		
TEXACO INC	1.08	37.2	43.8		
BETHLEHEM STEEL CORP	1.09	38.8	38.8		
WOOLWORTH F W CO	1.00	50.0	54.7	8	
BOEING CO	1.05	63.9	68.5		
Average	1.04	15.8	20.2		

Worst-to-First Performance

Price Change	1989 (%)	Close Ratio	1989 (%)
1-stock portfolio	−11.8	1-stock portfolio	−11.8
3-stock portfolio	5.5	3-stock portfolio	−9.0
5-stock portfolio	17.8	5-stock portfolio	9.6
10-stock portfolio	29.4	10-stock portfolio	21.6
Dow	31.7		

1989

Company Name	Close Ratio	Price Chg (%)	Total Return (%)	Rank Close Ratio	Rank Price Chg
NAVISTAR INTERNATIONAL CORP	0.81	−27.9	−27.9	1	1
INTERNATIONAL BUSINESS MACHS COR	0.87	−22.8	−19.4	4	2
BETHLEHEM STEEL CORP	0.88	−20.4	−19.6	6	3
GOODYEAR TIRE & RUBR CO	0.86	−14.9	−11.8	3	4
UNION CARBIDE CORP HOLDING CO	0.85	−9.3	−6.0	2	5
EASTMAN KODAK CO	0.89	−8.9	−4.8	7	6
SEARS ROEBUCK & CO	0.88	−6.7	−2.3	5	7
GENERAL MOTORS CORP	0.97	1.2	8.3	8	8
ALLIED SIGNAL INC	0.98	7.3	12.8	9	9
EXXON CORP	1.11	13.6	19.6		10
TEXACO INC	1.13	17.5	41.9		
INTERNATIONAL PAPER CO	1.11	21.8	25.5		
U S X CORP	1.03	22.2	27.3		
WOOLWORTH CORP	1.10	23.4	27.5		
MINNESOTA MINING & MFG CO	1.08	28.4	33.1		
AMERICAN EXPRESS CO	1.00	31.0	34.3	10	
PRIMERICA CORP NEW	1.12	31.0	32.5		
UNITED TECHNOLOGIES CORP	1.04	31.9	36.2		
ALUMINUM COMPANY AMER	1.09	33.9	39.5		
MERCK & CO INC	1.07	34.2	37.5		
DU PONT E I DE NEMOURS & CO	1.08	39.4	45.0		
WESTINGHOUSE ELECTRIC CORP	1.14	40.6	45.8		
MCDONALDS CORP	1.16	43.4	44.9		
GENERAL ELECTRIC CO	1.18	44.1	48.8		
BOEING CO	1.11	46.9	50.2		
CHEVRON CORP	1.16	48.1	55.6		
AMERICAN TELEPHONE & TELEG CO	1.17	58.3	63.3		
PROCTER & GAMBLE CO	1.21	61.5	66.5		
PHILIP MORRIS COS INC	1.11	69.4	89.1		
COCA COLA CO	1.21	73.1	77.0		
Average	1.05	23.5	28.3		

Worst-to-First Performance

Price Change	1990 (%)	Close Ratio		1990 (%)
1-stock portfolio	−41.9	1-stock portfolio		−41.9
3-stock portfolio	−11.5	3-stock portfolio		−40.3
5-stock portfolio	−22.7	5-stock portfolio		−24.9
10-stock portfolio	−15.8	10-stock portfolio		−20.6
Dow	−0.6			

1990

Company Name	Close Ratio	Price Chg (%)	Total Return (%)	Rank Close Ratio	Rank Price Chg
GOODYEAR TIRE & RUBR CO	0.74	−56.6	−53.3	2	1
NAVISTAR INTERNATIONAL CORP	0.70	−41.9	−41.9	1	2
AMERICAN EXPRESS CO	0.81	−40.9	−38.5	5	3
AMERICAN TELEPHONE & TELEG CO	0.83	−33.8	−31.2	6	4
SEARS ROEBUCK & CO	0.81	−33.4	−29.2	3	5
UNION CARBIDE CORP HOLDING CO	0.91	−29.6	−25.7	10	6
ALUMINUM COMPANY AMER	0.93	−23.2	−19.3		7
WESTINGHOUSE ELECTRIC CORP	0.87	−23.0	−19.7	9	8
ALLIED SIGNAL INC	0.85	−22.6	−18.2	8	9
BETHLEHEM STEEL CORP	1.01	−20.3	−18.0		10
PRIMERICA CORP NEW	0.84	−19.7	−18.6	7	
GENERAL MOTORS CORP	0.81	−18.6	−12.7	4	
MCDONALDS CORP	0.95	−15.6	−14.6		
U S X CORP	0.93	−14.7	−11.0		
UNITED TECHNOLOGIES CORP	0.92	−11.8	−8.6		
GENERAL ELECTRIC CO	0.92	−11.0	−8.2		
DU PONT E I DE NEMOURS & CO	0.99	−10.4	−6.5		
INTERNATIONAL PAPER CO	1.06	−5.3	−2.1		
WOOLWORTH CORP	1.02	−5.3	−1.9		
EASTMAN KODAK CO	1.04	1.2	6.4		
TEXACO INC	1.01	2.8	8.1		
EXXON CORP	1.06	3.5	8.8		
CHEVRON CORP	1.02	7.2	11.7		
MINNESOTA MINING & MFG CO	1.04	7.7	11.6		
BOEING CO	0.91	14.6	16.9		
MERCK & CO INC	1.11	16.0	18.9		
INTERNATIONAL BUSINESS MACHS COR	1.02	20.1	25.5		
COCA COLA CO	1.08	20.4	22.7		
PROCTER & GAMBLE CO	1.10	23.3	26.4		
PHILIP MORRIS COS INC	1.13	24.3	28.6		
Average	0.95	−9.9	−6.5		

Worst-to-First Performance

Price Change	1991 (%)	Close Ratio		1991 (%)
1-stock portfolio	187.2	1-stock portfolio		16.7
3-stock portfolio	69.2	3-stock portfolio		87.2
5-stock portfolio	59.9	5-stock portfolio		50.5
10-stock portfolio	38.0	10-stock portfolio		43.0
Dow	23.9			

1991

Company Name	Close Ratio	Price Chg (%)	Total Return (%)	Rank Close Ratio	Rank Price Chg
WESTINGHOUSE ELECTRIC CORP	0.77	−36.8	−32.8	1	1
INTERNATIONAL BUSINESS MACHS COR	0.89	−21.2	−17.5	4	2
GENERAL MOTORS CORP	0.78	−16.0	−12.3	2	3
WOOLWORTH CORP	0.90	−12.4	−9.2	5	4
CATERPILLAR INC	0.93	−6.7	−4.3	7	5
BETHLEHEM STEEL CORP	0.92	−5.1	−2.5	6	6
CHEVRON CORP	0.95	−5.0	−0.7	8	7
AMERICAN EXPRESS CO	0.87	−0.6	3.6	3	8
TEXACO INC	0.97	1.2	6.6	9	9
BOEING CO	1.01	5.2	7.5		10
PROCTER & GAMBLE CO	1.13	8.4	11.0		
MINNESOTA MINING & MFG CO	1.06	11.1	15.0		
ALUMINUM COMPANY AMER	0.98	11.7	14.8	10	
DISNEY WALT CO	0.99	12.8	13.5		
UNITED TECHNOLOGIES CORP	1.17	13.3	17.6		
EASTMAN KODAK CO	1.12	15.9	21.3		
EXXON CORP	1.03	17.6	23.2		
UNION CARBIDE CORP HOLDING CO	1.03	23.7	30.2		
DU PONT E I DE NEMOURS & CO	1.04	26.9	31.8		
AMERICAN TELEPHONE & TELEG CO	1.04	29.9	34.5		
MCDONALDS CORP	1.12	30.5	31.9		
INTERNATIONAL PAPER CO	1.04	32.2	35.6		
GENERAL ELECTRIC CO	1.07	33.3	37.2		
SEARS ROEBUCK & CO	1.00	49.3	57.6		
MORGAN J P & CO INC	1.22	54.7	60.3		
PHILIP MORRIS COS INC	1.16	55.1	59.3		
ALLIED SIGNAL INC	1.25	62.5	70.5		
COCA COLA CO	1.31	72.8	75.4		
MERCK & CO INC	1.32	85.3	88.8		
GOODYEAR TIRE & RUBR CO	1.45	183.4	187.2		
Average	1.05	24.4	28.5		

Worst-to-First Performance

Price Change	1992 (%)	Close Ratio	1992 (%)
1-stock portfolio	−22.3	1-stock portfolio	−22.3
3-stock portfolio	−15.5	3-stock portfolio	6.3
5-stock portfolio	0.2	5-stock portfolio	0.6
10-stock portfolio	3.5	10-stock portfolio	6.3
Dow	7.4		

1992

Company Name	Close Ratio	Price Chg (%)	Total Return (%)	Rank Close Ratio	Rank Price Chg
INTERNATIONAL BUSINESS MACHS COR	0.61	−43.4	−40.0	1	1
WESTINGHOUSE ELECTRIC CORP	0.84	−25.7	−22.3	2	2
MERCK & CO INC	0.91	−21.8	−20.2	4	3
EASTMAN KODAK CO	0.97	−16.1	−12.0	8	4
BOEING CO	1.01	−16.0	−13.9		5
UNITED TECHNOLOGIES CORP	0.95	−11.3	−7.9	5	6
INTERNATIONAL PAPER CO	1.00	−5.8	−3.5		7
MORGAN J P & CO INC	1.11	−4.2	−0.6		8
PHILIP MORRIS COS INC	0.98	−3.9	−1.0	9	9
TEXACO INC	0.96	−2.4	2.7	7	10
EXXON CORP	1.00	0.4	5.2		
CHEVRON CORP	1.00	0.7	5.7	10	
DU PONT E I DE NEMOURS & CO	0.95	1.1	4.7	6	
COCA COLA CO	1.01	4.4	5.8		
MINNESOTA MINING & MFG CO	1.03	5.6	9.2		
ALUMINUM COMPANY AMER	1.01	11.3	13.8		
GENERAL MOTORS CORP	0.88	11.7	15.9	3	
GENERAL ELECTRIC CO	1.10	11.8	15.1		
PROCTER & GAMBLE CO	1.06	14.2	16.6		
BETHLEHEM STEEL CORP	1.16	14.3	14.3		
WOOLWORTH CORP	1.05	19.3	23.9		
SEARS ROEBUCK & CO	1.07	20.1	25.8		
AMERICAN EXPRESS CO	1.10	21.3	25.4		
CATERPILLAR INC	1.01	22.2	23.6		
GOODYEAR TIRE & RUBR CO	1.01	27.8	28.8		
MCDONALDS CORP	1.09	28.3	29.4		
AMERICAN TELEPHONE & TELEG CO	1.16	30.4	34.3		
ALLIED SIGNAL INC	1.09	37.9	40.5		
DISNEY WALT CO	1.14	50.2	51.0		
UNION CARBIDE CORP HOLDING CO	1.26	92.5	101.2		
Average	1.02	9.2	12.4		

Worst-to-First Performance

Price Change	1993 (%)	Close Ratio	1993 (%)
1-stock portfolio	15.6	1-stock portfolio	15.6
3-stock portfolio	2.0	3-stock portfolio	32.5
5-stock portfolio	12.1	5-stock portfolio	22.5
10-stock portfolio	9.7	10-stock portfolio	18.3
Dow	16.7		

1993

Company Name	Close Ratio	Price Chg (%)	Total Return (%)	Rank Close Ratio	Rank Price Chg
PHILIP MORRIS COS INC	1.09	-27.9	-24.2		1
MERCK & CO INC	1.01	-20.7	-18.2		2
WOOLWORTH CORP	0.96	-19.8	-16.2	3	3
ALUMINUM COMPANY AMER	1.01	-3.1	-0.9		4
DISNEY WALT CO	1.05	-0.9	-0.3		5
INTERNATIONAL PAPER CO	1.05	1.7	4.3		6
DU PONT E I DE NEMOURS & CO	0.99	2.4	6.1	7	7
AMERICAN TELEPHONE & TELEG CO	0.89	2.9	5.3	1	8
EXXON CORP	0.97	3.3	8.0	4	9
MORGAN J P & CO INC	0.98	5.5	9.3	5	10
WESTINGHOUSE ELECTRIC CORP	0.96	5.6	8.6	2	
PROCTER & GAMBLE CO	1.13	6.3	8.8		
COCA COLA CO	1.06	6.6	8.3		
BOEING CO	1.12	7.8	10.7		
MINNESOTA MINING & MFG CO	1.00	8.1	11.4	10	
TEXACO INC	1.00	8.4	13.9		
INTERNATIONAL BUSINESS MACHS COR	1.16	12.2	15.6		
MCDONALDS CORP	1.08	16.9	17.9		
GENERAL ELECTRIC CO	1.09	22.7	26.0		
AMERICAN EXPRESS CO	0.99	24.1	28.6	8	
CHEVRON CORP	0.99	25.4	30.5	6	
BETHLEHEM STEEL CORP	1.20	27.3	27.3		
UNITED TECHNOLOGIES CORP	1.11	28.8	33.2		
ALLIED SIGNAL INC	1.13	30.6	32.8		
GOODYEAR TIRE & RUBR CO	1.10	33.8	35.8		
UNION CARBIDE CORP HOLDING CO	1.16	34.6	40.1		
EASTMAN KODAK CO	1.00	38.9	43.9	9	
SEARS ROEBUCK & CO	1.00	56.6	60.8		
CATERPILLAR INC	1.15	66.0	67.4		
GENERAL MOTORS CORP	1.20	70.2	73.3		
Average	1.06	15.8	18.9		

Worst-to-First Performance

Price Change	1994 (%)	Close Ratio	1994 (%)
1-stock portfolio	9.2	1-stock portfolio	-1.9
3-stock portfolio	-4.7	3-stock portfolio	-17.3
5-stock portfolio	4.4	5-stock portfolio	-13.2
10-stock portfolio	4.0	10-stock portfolio	-1.6
Dow	5.0		

1994

Company Name	Close Ratio	Price Chg (%)	Total Return (%)	Rank Close Ratio	Rank Price Chg
WOOLWORTH CORP	0.94	-40.9	-38.0	5	1
GOODYEAR-TIRE & RUBR CO	0.93	-26.5	-25.0	4	2
GENERAL MOTORS CORP	0.86	-23.2	-22.0	1	3
MORGAN J P & CO INC	0.91	-19.1	-15.3	3	4
ALLIED SIGNAL INC	0.97	-13.9	-12.3	8	5
WESTINGHOUSE ELECTRIC CORP	0.97	-13.3	-12.0	10	6
SEARS ROEBUCK & CO	0.97	-13.0	-10.0	9	7
BETHLEHEM STEEL CORP	0.90	-11.7	-11.7	2	8
TEXACO INC	0.96	-7.5	-2.7	7	9
A T & T CORP	0.94	-4.3	-1.9	6	10
EXXON CORP	1.01	-3.8	0.9		
GENERAL ELECTRIC CO	1.05	-2.7	0.3		
MINNESOTA MINING & MFG CO	1.02	-1.8	1.5		
UNITED TECHNOLOGIES CORP	1.00	1.4	4.5		
CHEVRON CORP	1.03	2.4	6.9		
MCDONALDS CORP	1.03	2.6	3.5		
PHILIP MORRIS COS INC	1.04	3.4	9.2		
EASTMAN KODAK CO	1.01	5.8	9.5		
DISNEY WALT CO	1.09	7.9	8.6		
AMERICAN EXPRESS CO	1.05	8.0	12.3		
BOEING CO	1.03	8.7	11.1		
PROCTER & GAMBLE CO	1.07	8.8	11.2		
MERCK & CO INC	1.16	10.9	14.9		
INTERNATIONAL PAPER CO	1.05	11.3	13.9		
COCA COLA CO	1.14	15.4	17.4		
DU PONT E I DE NEMOURS & CO	0.97	16.3	20.1		
CATERPILLAR INC	1.01	23.9	24.9		
ALUMINUM COMPANY AMER	1.11	24.9	27.4		
INTERNATIONAL BUSINESS MACHS COR	1.13	30.1	32.2		
UNION CARBIDE CORP	1.01	31.3	34.8		
Average	1.01	1.0	3.8		

Worst-to-First Performance

Price Change	1995 (%)	Close Ratio	1995 (%)
1-stock portfolio	-12.5	1-stock portfolio	28.5
3-stock portfolio	18.0	3-stock portfolio	18.3
5-stock portfolio	29.1	5-stock portfolio	16.1
10-stock portfolio	29.6	10-stock portfolio	29.6
Dow	36.5		

1995

Company Name	Close Ratio	Price Chg (%)	Total Return (%)	Rank Close Ratio	Rank Price Chg
BETHLEHEM STEEL CORP	0.94	−22.9	−22.9	2	1
WOOLWORTH CORP	0.86	−13.3	−12.5	1	2
INTERNATIONAL PAPER CO	0.96	0.5	2.9	4	3
CATERPILLAR INC	0.97	6.6	8.8	5	4
CHEVRON CORP	1.08	17.4	22.1		5
ALUMINUM COMPANY AMER	1.04	22.1	24.0	7	6
INTERNATIONAL BUSINESS MACHS COR	0.95	24.3	25.7	3	7
MINNESOTA MINING & MFG CO	1.13	24.4	28.4		8
DU PONT E I DE NEMOURS & CO	1.05	24.5	28.5	8	9
GENERAL MOTORS CORP	1.13	25.5	28.5		10
UNION CARBIDE CORP	1.07	27.7	30.6	10	
DISNEY WALT CO	1.03	28.0	29.0	6	
A T & T CORP	1.14	28.9	31.8		
TEXACO INC	1.16	31.1	37.4		
EXXON CORP	1.12	33.5	39.4		
WESTINGHOUSE ELECTRIC CORP	1.11	33.7	35.5		
PROCTER & GAMBLE CO	1.12	33.9	36.7		
GOODYEAR TIRE & RUBR CO	1.12	34.9	38.1		
ALLIED SIGNAL INC	1.09	39.7	42.3		
AMERICAN EXPRESS CO	1.07	40.3	42.8	9	
EASTMAN KODAK CO	1.10	40.3	44.2		
GENERAL ELECTRIC CO	1.19	41.2	45.1		
MORGAN J P & CO INC	1.10	43.0	49.2		
COCA COLA CO	1.13	44.2	46.1		
UNITED TECHNOLOGIES CORP	1.16	50.9	54.9		
MCDONALDS CORP	1.16	54.3	55.3		
PHILIP MORRIS COS INC	1.17	57.0	64.5		
SEARS ROEBUCK & CO	1.18	64.3	69.0		
BOEING CO	1.22	66.8	69.6		
MERCK & CO INC	1.26	72.1	76.4		
Average	1.09	32.5	35.7		

Worst-to-First Performance

Price Change	1996 (%)	Close Ratio	1996 (%)
1-stock portfolio	−36.0	1-stock portfolio	69.2
3-stock portfolio	14.3	3-stock portfolio	33.6
5-stock portfolio	20.5	5-stock portfolio	28.3
10-stock portfolio	27.4	10-stock portfolio	27.3
Dow	28.6		

1996

Company Name	Close Ratio	Price Chg (%)	Total Return (%)	Rank Close Ratio	Rank Price Chg
BETHLEHEM STEEL CORP	0.82	−36.0	−36.0	1	1
A T & T CORP	1.05	−8.5	−6.2	8	2
MCDONALDS CORP	0.96	0.6	1.2	4	3
GENERAL MOTORS CORP	1.05	5.4	8.6	7	4
INTERNATIONAL PAPER CO	1.00	6.9	9.7	5	5
UNION CARBIDE CORP	0.93	9.0	10.9	2	6
GOODYEAR TIRE & RUBR CO	1.06	13.2	15.7		7
SEARS ROEBUCK & CO	0.96	17.9	20.3	3	8
DISNEY WALT CO	1.11	18.5	19.1		9
EASTMAN KODAK CO	1.05	19.8	22.4	9	10
ALUMINUM COMPANY AMER	1.04	20.6	23.3	· 6	
EXXON CORP	1.13	20.8	25.3		
MERCK & CO INC	1.16	21.3	24.0		
WESTINGHOUSE ELECTRIC CORP	1.10	21.4	22.8		
MORGAN J P & CO INC	1.12	21.7	26.2		
CHEVRON CORP	1.06	24.1	28.5		
TEXACO INC	1.08	25.0	29.8		
PHILIP MORRIS COS INC	1.16	25.2	30.9		
CATERPILLAR INC	1.07	28.1	31.0		
PROCTER & GAMBLE CO	1.16	29.7	32.2		
MINNESOTA MINING & MFG CO	1.19	29.7	33.3		
DU PONT E I DE NEMOURS & CO	1.10	34.7	38.4		
BOEING CO	1.18	35.9	37.6		
AMERICAN EXPRESS CO	1.20	36.6	39.8		
GENERAL ELECTRIC CO	1.12	37.3	40.3		
UNITED TECHNOLOGIES CORP	1.12	39.7	42.3		
ALLIED SIGNAL INC	1.08	41.1	43.2		
COCA COLA CO	1.10	41.8	43.2		
INTERNATIONAL BUSINESS MACHS COR	1.27	65.8	67.6		
WOOLWORTH CORP	1.06	69.2	69.2	10	
Average	1.08	23.9	26.5		

Worst-to-First Performance

Price Change	1997 (%)	Close Ratio	1997 (%)
1-stock portfolio	−2.1	1-stock portfolio	−2.1
3-stock portfolio	19.0	3-stock portfolio	1.6
5-stock portfolio	23.2	5-stock portfolio	10.0
10-stock portfolio	16.9	10-stock portfolio	10.5
Dow	24.8		

1997

Company Name	Close Ratio	Price Chg (%)	Total Return (%)	Rank Close Ratio	Rank Price Chg
EASTMAN KODAK CO	0.87	−24.5	−22.7	1	1
BOEING CO	0.93	−8.1	−7.1	7	2
SEARS ROEBUCK & CO	0.87	−1.6	0.2	3	3
MINNESOTA MINING & MFG CO	0.89	−1.1	1.2	4	4
UNION CARBIDE CORP	0.89	5.0	6.8	5	5
MCDONALDS CORP	0.98	5.2	6.0		6
INTERNATIONAL PAPER CO	0.87	6.5	8.8	2	7
UNITED TECHNOLOGIES CORP	0.93	9.9	11.7	6	8
ALUMINUM COMPANY AMER	0.93	10.4	11.9	8	9
MORGAN J P & CO INC	1.03	15.6	19.5		10
GENERAL MOTORS CORP	1.06	15.6	19.6		
ALLIED SIGNAL INC	0.97	15.9	17.4	10	
CHEVRON CORP	1.00	18.5	22.2		
PHILIP MORRIS COS INC	1.07	20.1	24.8		
GOODYEAR TIRE & RUBR CO	1.04	23.8	26.3		
HEWLETT PACKARD CO	1.03	24.1	25.3		
EXXON CORP	1.01	24.9	28.4		
COCA COLA CO	1.06	26.7	27.9		
DU PONT E I DE NEMOURS & CO	1.01	27.6	30.4		
CATERPILLAR INC	0.94	28.9	31.4	9	
JOHNSON & JOHNSON	1.09	32.0	34.3		
MERCK & CO INC	1.11	33.1	35.5		
INTERNATIONAL BUSINESS MACHS COR	1.11	38.1	39.3		
DISNEY WALT CO	1.20	41.9	42.8		
PROCTER & GAMBLE CO	1.14	48.3	50.0		
GENERAL ELECTRIC CO	1.13	48.4	50.9		
AT & T CORP	1.46	48.5	53.2		
AMERICAN EXPRESS CO	1.17	58.0	59.8		
WAL MART STORES INC	1.14	73.4	74.7		
TRAVELERS	1.23	78.1	79.7		
Average	1.04	24.8	27.0		

Worst-to-First Performance

Price Change	1998 (%)	Close Ratio	1998 (%)
1-stock portfolio	21.8	1-stock portfolio	21.8
3-stock portfolio	−5.0	3-stock portfolio	7.9
5-stock portfolio	−5.0	5-stock portfolio	2.8
10-stock portfolio	9.9	10-stock portfolio	5.4
Dow	18.0		

1998

Company Name	Close Ratio	Price Chg (%)	Total Return (%)	Rank Close Ratio	Rank Price Chg
BOEING CO	0.78	−33.3	−32.4	1	1
GOODYEAR TIRE & RUBR CO	0.84	−20.7	−19.1	4	2
MINNESOTA MINING & MFG CO	0.86	−13.3	−10.9	5	3
DU PONT E I DE NEMOURS & CO	0.81	−11.7	−9.7	2	4
DISNEY WALT CO	0.90	−9.1	−8.5	6	5
CITIGROUP	0.91	−7.8	−6.8	7	6
MORGAN J P & CO INC	0.92	−6.9	−3.5		7
SEARS ROEBUCK & CO	0.82	−6.1	−4.4	3	8
CATERPILLAR INC	0.91	−5.2	−3.0	8	9
UNION CARBIDE CORP	0.92	−1.0	1.0	10	10
COCA COLA CO	0.91	0.5	1.3	9	
INTERNATIONAL PAPER CO	0.98	3.9	6.4		
ALUMINUM COMPANY AMER	1.05	6.0	7.9		
CHEVRON CORP	1.01	7.7	11.1		
HEWLETT PACKARD CO	1.13	9.5	10.6		
ALLIED SIGNAL INC	1.07	14.2	15.9		
PROCTER & GAMBLE CO	1.10	14.4	15.9		
AMERICAN EXPRESS CO	1.05	14.8	15.6		
GENERAL MOTORS CORP	1.07	17.8	21.4		
PHILIP MORRIS COS INC	1.20	18.2	22.7		
EASTMAN KODAK CO	1.03	18.9	21.8		
EXXON CORP	0.97	19.5	22.4		
AT & T CORP	1.24	23.5	26.1		
JOHNSON & JOHNSON	1.10	27.3	29.0		
GENERAL ELECTRIC CO	1.18	39.0	41.0		
MERCK & CO INC	1.12	39.2	41.2		
UNITED TECHNOLOGIES CORP	1.18	49.4	51.7		
MCDONALDS CORP	1.18	60.9	61.8		
INTERNATIONAL BUSINESS MACHS COR	1.41	76.2	77.5		
WAL MART STORES INC	1.31	106.5	107.6		
Average	1.03	15.1	17.0		

Worst-to-First Performance

Price Change	1999 (%)	Close Ratio	1999 (%)
1-stock portfolio	28.8	1-stock portfolio	28.8
3-stock portfolio	9.0	3-stock portfolio	9.7
5-stock portfolio	10.5	5-stock portfolio	5.5
10-stock portfolio	18.4	10-stock portfolio	14.8
Dow	27.1		

1999

Company Name	Close Ratio	Price Chg (%)	Total Return (%)	Rank Close Ratio	Rank Price Chg
PHILIP MORRIS COS INC	0.67	–57.0	–54.4	1	1
COCA COLA CO	0.95	–13.1	–12.1	7	2
S B C COMMUNICATIONS INC	0.93	–9.1	–7.5	4	3
MERCK & CO INC	0.93	–8.9	–7.4	3	4
EASTMAN KODAK CO	0.95	–8.0	–5.5	5	5
DISNEY WALT CO	1.02	–2.5	–1.8		6
A T & T CORP	0.98	0.6	2.4		7
CATERPILLAR INC	0.84	2.3	4.7	2	8
MCDONALDS CORP	0.95	5.0	5.4	6	9
EXXON MOBIL CORP	1.03	10.2	12.6		10
JOHNSON & JOHNSON	0.97	11.2	12.4	10	
INTERNATIONAL BUSINESS MACHS COR	0.96	17.0	17.5	8	
UNITED TECHNOLOGIES CORP	1.02	19.5	21.0		
PROCTER & GAMBLE CO	1.12	20.0	21.5		
MORGAN J P & CO INC	0.97	20.5	24.4		
GENERAL MOTORS CORP	1.06	21.8	24.4		
DU PONT E I DE NEMOURS & CO	1.00	24.1	27.1		
INTERNATIONAL PAPER CO	1.09	25.9	28.6		
BOEING CO	0.98	27.0	28.8		
HONEYWELL INTERNATIONAL INC	0.96	30.2	31.8	9	
MINNESOTA MINING & MFG CO	1.08	37.6	41.2		
INTEL CORP	1.18	39.0	39.1		
CITIGROUP INC	1.17	42.2	69.9		
GENERAL ELECTRIC CO	1.30	51.7	53.5		
AMERICAN EXPRESS CO	1.21	62.2	63.4		
HEWLETT PACKARD CO	1.23	66.5	67.7		
MICROSOFT CORP	1.30	68.4	68.4		
HOME DEPOT INC	1.51	68.5	69.0		
WAL MART STORES INC	1.38	69.8	70.4		
ALCOA INC	1.34	122.6	126.0		
Average	1.07	25.5	28.1		

Worst-to-First Performance

Price Change	2000 (%)	Close Ratio	2000 (%)
1-stock portfolio	105.2	1-stock portfolio	105.2
3-stock portfolio	37.1	3-stock portfolio	50.4
5-stock portfolio	22.9	5-stock portfolio	22.5
10-stock portfolio	4.8	10-stock portfolio	8.0
Dow	–4.7		

2000

Company Name	Close Ratio	Price Chg (%)	Total Return (%)	Rank Close Ratio	Rank Price Chg
A T & T CORP	0.53	–66.1	–65.3	1	1
MICROSOFT CORP	0.62	–62.8	–62.8	4	2
EASTMAN KODAK CO	0.74	–40.6	–38.6	5	3
HOME DEPOT INC	0.90	–33.5	–33.3	10	4
HEWLETT PACKARD CO	0.62	–30.9	–30.5	3	5
GENERAL MOTORS CORP	0.76	–29.9	–27.7	6	6
PROCTER & GAMBLE CO	1.21	–28.4	–27.0		7
INTERNATIONAL PAPER CO	1.17	–27.7	–25.5		8
INTEL CORP	0.53	–27.0	–26.9	2	9
DU PONT E I DE NEMOURS & CO	1.03	–26.7	–24.4		10
WAL MART STORES INC	1.00	–23.1	–22.8		
INTERNATIONAL BUSINESS MACHS COR	0.77	–21.2	–20.8	8	
ALCOA INC	1.09	–19.3	–18.0		
HONEYWELL INTERNATIONAL INC	1.05	–18.0	–16.7		
MCDONALDS CORP	1.04	–15.7	–15.1		
GENERAL ELECTRIC CO	0.90	–7.1	–6.0	9	
S B C COMMUNICATIONS INC	1.01	–2.1	0.1		
DISNEY WALT CO	0.77	–1.1	–0.4	7	
AMERICAN EXPRESS CO	1.00	–0.9	–0.4		
CATERPILLAR INC	1.25	0.5	4.2		
COCA COLA CO	1.10	4.6	5.9		
EXXON MOBIL CORP	1.04	7.9	10.3		
JOHNSON & JOHNSON	1.15	12.7	14.3		
UNITED TECHNOLOGIES CORP	1.23	21.0	22.6		
CITIGROUP INC	1.02	22.3	23.6		
MINNESOTA MINING & MFG CO	1.30	23.1	26.3		
MORGAN J P & CO INC	1.17	30.7	33.7		
MERCK & CO INC	1.24	39.3	41.7		
BOEING CO	1.30	59.3	61.2		
PHILIP MORRIS COS INC	1.50	91.3	105.2		
Average	1.00	–5.6	–3.8		

Worst-to-First Performance

Price Change	2001 (%)	Close Ratio	2001 (%)
1-stock portfolio	37.2	1-stock portfolio	37.2
3-stock portfolio	22.7	3-stock portfolio	2.7
5-stock portfolio	9.2	5-stock portfolio	7.8
10-stock portfolio	4.5	10-stock portfolio	5.0
Dow	–5.4		

2001

Company Name	Close Ratio	Price Chg (%)	Total Return (%)	Rank Close Ratio	Rank Price Chg
BOEING CO	0.78	–41.2	–40.4	2	1
MERCK & CO INC	0.85	–37.2	–35.9	5	2
AMERICAN EXPRESS CO	0.97	–35.0	–34.5		3
HEWLETT PACKARD CO	0.85	–34.9	–34.0	4	4
HONEYWELL INTERNATIONAL INC	0.91	–28.5	–27.1	7	5
DISNEY WALT CO	0.82	–28.4	–27.7	3	6
EASTMAN KODAK CO	0.74	–25.3	–21.9	1	7
COCA COLA CO	1.01	–22.6	–21.4		8
MCDONALDS CORP	0.95	–22.1	–21.5		9
J P MORGAN CHASE & CO	0.88	–20.0	–16.5	6	10
S B C COMMUNICATIONS INC	0.94	–18.0	–16.0	10	
UNITED TECHNOLOGIES CORP	0.95	–17.8	–16.8		
GENERAL ELECTRIC CO	0.94	–16.4	–15.0	9	
DU PONT E I DE NEMOURS & CO	0.98	–12.0	–9.2		
EXXON MOBIL CORP	0.95	–9.6	–7.5		
GENERAL MOTORS CORP	0.91	–4.6	–1.0	8	
MINNESOTA MINING & MFG CO	1.06	–1.9	0.2		
CITIGROUP INC	1.05	–1.1	0.1		
INTERNATIONAL PAPER CO	1.06	–1.1	1.4		
PROCTER & GAMBLE CO	1.14	0.9	3.0		
PHILIP MORRIS COS INC	0.96	4.2	9.1		
INTEL CORP	1.11	4.6	4.9		
ALCOA INC	0.95	6.1	7.8		
WAL MART STORES INC	1.11	8.3	8.9		
CATERPILLAR INC	1.05	10.4	13.4		
HOME DEPOT INC	1.11	11.6	12.1		
JOHNSON & JOHNSON	1.12	12.5	14.0		
A T & T CORP	1.02	36.2	37.2		
INTERNATIONAL BUSINESS MACHS COR	1.12	42.5	43.0		
MICROSOFT CORP	1.04	52.7	52.7		
Average	0.98	–6.3	–4.6		

Worst-to-First Performance

Price Change	2002 (%)		Close Ratio	2002 (%)
1-stock portfolio	–13.5		1-stock portfolio	25.6
3-stock portfolio	–4.8		3-stock portfolio	–2.7
5-stock portfolio	–11.1		5-stock portfolio	–4.6
10-stock portfolio	–12.5		10-stock portfolio	–16.8
Dow	14.9			

2002

Company Name	Close Ratio	Price Chg (%)	Total Return (%)	Rank Close Ratio	Rank Price Chg
HOME DEPOT INC	0.70	–52.9	–52.6	2	1
INTEL CORP	0.75	–50.5	–50.3	3	2
MCDONALDS CORP	0.68	–39.3	–38.5	1	3
GENERAL ELECTRIC CO	0.83	–39.2	–37.7	7	4
INTERNATIONAL BUSINESS MACHS COR	1.00	–35.9	–35.5		5
ALCOA INC	0.81	–35.9	–34.6	6	6
J P MORGAN CHASE & CO	0.87	–34.0	–30.6		7
S B C COMMUNICATIONS INC	0.94	–30.8	–28.3		8
HONEYWELL INTERNATIONAL INC	0.78	–29.0	–27.4	5	9
A T & T CORP	1.05	–28.4	–27.2		10
CITIGROUP INC	0.96	–25.7	–24.4		
GENERAL MOTORS CORP	0.76	–24.2	–21.0	4	
MICROSOFT CORP	0.99	–22.0	–22.0		
DISNEY WALT CO	0.86	–21.3	–20.3	9	
HEWLETT PACKARD CO	1.08	–15.5	–13.7		
BOEING CO	0.85	–14.9	–13.5	8	
INTERNATIONAL PAPER CO	0.90	–13.3	–11.2		
CATERPILLAR INC	0.98	–12.5	–9.9		
WAL MART STORES INC	0.93	–12.2	–11.7		
PHILIP MORRIS COS INC	0.86	–11.6	–6.5	10	
EXXON MOBIL CORP	0.94	–11.1	–8.9		
JOHNSON & JOHNSON	0.94	–9.1	–7.9		
COCA COLA CO	0.86	–7.0	–5.5		
UNITED TECHNOLOGIES CORP	0.96	–4.2	–2.7		
MERCK & CO INC	1.08	–3.7	–1.1		
AMERICAN EXPRESS CO	0.96	–1.0	0.1		
DU PONT E I DE NEMOURS & CO	0.99	–0.3	2.9		
3M CO	1.00	4.3	6.4		
PROCTER & GAMBLE CO	0.97	9.5	11.5		
EASTMAN KODAK CO	1.10	19.1	25.6		
Average	0.91	–18.4	–16.5		

Worst-to-First Performance

Price Change	2003 (%)		Close Ratio	2003 (%)
1-stock portfolio	49.0		1-stock portfolio	56.8
3-stock portfolio	70.8		3-stock portfolio	70.8
5-stock portfolio	52.7		5-stock portfolio	61.7
10-stock portfolio	42.1		10-stock portfolio	52.8
Dow	28.3			

2003

Company Name	Close Ratio	Price Chg (%)	Total Return (%)	Rank Close Ratio	Rank Price Chg
EASTMAN KODAK CO	0.95	−26.7	−23.8	2	1
A T & T CORP	1.04	−22.3	−18.8	6	2
MERCK & CO INC	0.87	−18.4	−11.3	1	3
S B C COMMUNICATIONS INC	1.10	−3.8	1.8		4
JOHNSON & JOHNSON	0.99	−3.8	−2.1	4	5
WAL MART STORES INC	0.95	5.0	5.7	3	6
MICROSOFT CORP	1.04	5.9	6.9	5	7
DU PONT E I DE NEMOURS & CO	1.09	8.2	12.0	10	8
COCA COLA CO	1.13	15.8	18.1		9
PROCTER & GAMBLE CO	1.08	16.2	18.5	9	10
EXXON MOBIL CORP	1.12	17.3	20.6		
INTERNATIONAL BUSINESS MACHS COR	1.07	19.6	20.5	8	
INTERNATIONAL PAPER CO	1.13	23.3	26.6		
GENERAL ELECTRIC CO	1.06	27.2	30.7	7	
BOEING CO	1.23	27.7	30.4		
HEWLETT PACKARD CO	1.13	32.3	34.5		
PHILIP MORRIS COS INC	1.28	34.3	43.0		
AMERICAN EXPRESS CO	1.11	36.4	37.6		
3M CO	1.21	37.9	40.6		
CITIGROUP INC	1.10	37.9	41.5		
HONEYWELL INTERNATIONAL INC	1.21	39.3	43.3		
DISNEY WALT CO	1.12	43.0	44.3		
GENERAL MOTORS CORP	1.35	44.9	52.7		
HOME DEPOT INC	1.09	47.8	49.0		
UNITED TECHNOLOGIES CORP	1.24	53.0	55.4		
J P MORGAN CHASE & CO	1.10	53.0	60.1		
MCDONALDS CORP	1.13	54.4	56.8		
ALCOA INC	1.38	66.8	70.8		
CATERPILLAR INC	1.27	81.6	86.1		
INTEL CORP	1.25	105.8	106.5		
Average	1.13	28.7	31.9		

References

BOOKS

Beating the Dow (Harper Perennial, 1990, 2000), by Michael O'Higgins with John Downes

The Dow Jones Averages: 1885–1995 (Irwin, 1996), edited by Phyllis S. Pierce

The Smart Investor's Survival Guide (Doubleday, 2002), by Charles Carlson, CFA

NEWSPAPERS

Barron's Financial Weekly (options column by Kopin Tan), December 2, 2002

The Wall Street Journal, March 4, 1996

The Wall Street Journal, December 28, 2000

The Wall Street Journal, November 29, 2002

The Wall Street Journal, July 1, 2003

MAGAZINES/JOURNALS/PAPERS

Journal of Economic Perspectives, A Mean-Reverting Walk Down Wall Street, by Werner F. M. De Bondt and Richard Thaler, Winter 1989

Journal of Empirical Finance, The Power and Size of Mean Reversion Tests, by Kent Daniel, Kellogg School of Management, Northwestern University, 2001

Journal of Finance, Seasonality in Stock Price Mean Reversion: Evidence from the U.S. and the U.K., by Narasimhan Jegadeesh, September 1991

Journal of Financial Research, The Biggest Mistakes We Teach, by Jay R. Ritter, Summer 2002

Smart Money, A Salute to the Irrational, by Roger Lowenstein, January 2003

Temporary Movements in Stock Prices, by Jonathan Lewellen, MIT Sloan School of Management, March 2001

WEB SITES

www.dogsofthedow.com
www.dowjones.com
www.fool.com (History of the Dow)
www.efficientfrontier.com (Mean Reversion and You, William Bernstein)
www.thestreet.com (Introduction to Volatility, Dave Landry)

NEWSLETTERS (FOR SUBSCRIPTION INFORMATION, CALL [800] 233-5922)

Dow Theory Forecasts
DRIP Investor
Upside

RESEARCH TOOLS

Compustat
CRSP/Center for Research in Security Prices, The University of Chicago, Graduate
    School of Business. Used with permission. All rights reserved.
Dow Jones & Co.
S&P Stock Reports
Value Line Investment Survey

Index

Page numbers in **bold italics** refer to tables and charts

Eight Weeks Stock Advice —FREE

Enjoy the respected weekly *DOW THEORY FORECASTS* for two full months. You will receive eight weeks of unbiased, objective investment advice at **NO COST OR OBLIGATION**.

Here are some of the features subscribers see in any 60-day period:

◆ **Weekly Stock Market Forecast** – Know where the market's headed and what you can do to maximize and protect your investments.

◆ **Market Commentary Hotline** – Keep informed between issues, so you'll never go more than a few days without specific guidance.

◆ **Clear, Straightforward Recommendations** – We'll tell you what to buy when to buy, and, most importantly, when to sell.

◆ *Dow Theory Forecasts'* **Monitored List of Stocks** – Aggressive capital-gains selections, conservative buy and hold stocks, or something in-between, our Monitored List will serve you well with many recommendations for every type of portfolio.

◆ **Extensive Follow-up of Previous Recommendations** – Keep informed of any news, updates, or changes. And, we'll tell you when to lock up profits.

You'll have access to the Subscriber area of the *Dow Theory Forecasts'* Web site where you'll get detailed research reports, ratings on over 4,500 stocks and 9,000 mutual funds, Industry Group Studies, and much, much more. Take advantage of this FREE offer today. Simply complete the coupon below and send to:

Dow Theory Forecasts, **7412 Calumet Ave., Hammond, IN 46324**
1.800.233.5922 ext 254

- -

EIGHT WEEKS STOCK ADVICE– FREE

❏ **YES**, I want to get objective, unbiased stock advice every week for eight weeks FREE! Start my subscription at once! *(One offer per household, please.)*

Name: _____

Address: _____

City: _____ State: _____ Zip: _____

Phone: _____ Email: _____

DOW THEORY
FORECASTS
7412 Calumet Ave. ◆ **Hammond, IN 46324** ◆ **1.800.233.5922 ext 254**

The publisher does not guarantee that Dow Theory Forecasts *will improve any individual investor's results.*